A Movement of Movements

First published by Verso 2004
Collection © Verso 2004
All rights reserved

The moral rights of the authors have been asserted

1 3 5 7 9 10 8 6 4 2

Verso
UK: 6 Meard Street, London W1F 0EG
USA: 180 Varick Street, New York, NY 10014–4606
www.versobooks.com

Verso is the imprint of New Left Books

ISBN 1–85984–504–5
ISBN 1–85984–468–5 (pbk)

British Library Cataloguing in Publication Data
A movement of movements
1. Social movements 2. Globalization
I. Mertes, Tom II. Bello, Walden
322.4'4
ISBN 1859844685 (pbk)
ISBN 1859845045 (hbk)

Library of Congress Cataloging-in-Publication Data
A movement of movements / edited by Tom Mertes; with contributions by Walden
Bello . . . [et al.].
    p. cm.
Includes bibliographical references and index.
ISBN 1-85984-468-5 (pbk. : alk. paper) – ISBN 1-85984-504-5 (hardback : alk. paper)
1. Indigenous peoples—Politics and government. 2. Anti-globalization movement.
I. Mertes, Tom. II. Bello, Walden F.
GN380.M68 2004
303.48'4–dc22

2003023110

Typeset in 10/12pt Scala by New Left Review
Printed and bound in the USA by R. R. Donnelley

CONTENTS

TOM MERTES

INTRODUCTION

The young opposition movements that have discovered each other over the last five years—amid the tear-gas of Seattle, the global university at Porto Alegre, the mass marches against the war on Iraq—find themselves in a strange place today. The protests against neoliberal globalization, born with the late 1990s bubble, have had to confront the reassertion of a US militarism that some had thought a thing of the past. Indigenous voices, raised against political and environmental oppression, have faced repression by state and commercial forces. The popular revolts against Washington Consensus policies that have shaken the Latin American continent since 1977—from Buenos Aires to Caracas, Porto Alegre to La Paz—must now come to terms with the record in power of Lula's Workers Party in Brazil, hitherto closely connected to the movement's World Social Forum. The activist energies that flared up, North and South, against G8 and IMF summits, water and electricity privatization, motorways and mega-dams, need to be renewed. It is a good moment to look back over the development of what Naomi Klein here describes as a new 'movement of movements'; to consider the elements of rupture and continuity that exist with the now lost worlds of the revolutionary communist, anarchist and socialist traditions of the nineteenth and twentieth centuries; and to take stock of the tasks that lie ahead.

It is worth recalling the desolate landscape that confronted radical oppositionists at the beginning of the 1990s. Politically, the end of the Cold War brought not just the collapse of the Soviet Union and the communist parties of Europe and much of Asia but the dissolution of social democracy, as centre-left governments set about completing the agenda of neoliberal deregulation and marketization, under the banner of the Third Way. Economically, the free-trade measures enforced first through GATT, then the WTO, threatened ruin for Third World subsistence farmers deluged by the subsidized products of American and EU agribusiness. Organized labour was thrown onto the defensive, as trade unions with shrinking memberships struggled to combat deindustrialization and 'flexible' work patterns in the North, and the spread of Export Processing Zones [EPZs] in the South. Culturally, the global dominance of US capitalism saturated the media with the homogenized products of corporate America.

The first flickerings of a new anti-systemic dissent flared not in the old heartlands but on the periphery. Its symbolic founding moment might be 1 January 1994, the day the North American Free Trade Agreement came into force—obliterating, among other things, any right of economic sovereignty for small-scale maize farmers in Mexico, who faced swamping by subsidized US corn. In protest, a new model-guerrilla force, the Zapatista Army of National Liberation or EZLN, occupied six towns in the state of Chiapas. The roots of popular resistance already ran deep in the region, articulated through liberation theology and by the left groups of the 1960s. The Zapatistas, informed by this background, were trying something new—using the World Wide Web as their artillery and, in the very act of paying homage to the national-liberation guerrilla struggles of the 1960s and '70s, establishing their distance from them. From their base in the Mexican rainforest, whose natural wealth stands in stark contrast to the poverty of its inhabitants, the Zapatistas—as their leader, not Comandante but, teasingly, Sub-Comandante Marcos, explains here—sought not to overthrow the terminally corrupt PRI regime in Mexico City but simply to win recognition for the indigenous minority that they represented. The Zapatistas' 1996 call for an international *encuentro* of 'all the rebels around the world', for humanity and against neoliberalism, touched a chord among the dispossessed and disenchanted. *Ya Basta!* groups, in sympathy with the Zapatistas' motto, 'Enough!', were set up in over half a dozen cities across continental Europe in the aftermath of the *encuentro*. It was they who, in 1998, established the People's Global Action network that would put out one of the first calls for a protest against the 1999 WTO meeting in Seattle, along with the US-based Ruckus Society and Direct Action Network. They were one of the few groups that took a lead in opposing Clinton's Yugoslav war.

Another trail running from South to North through the 1990s lay in the resistance of the world's subsistence farmers to the GM seeds and dumping plans of US and European agribusiness. In 1993, half a million farmers in Bangalore marched in protest against the free-trade prescriptions of the Uruguay Round. In 1996 Sebastião Salgado's haunting, silvery photographs of Brazil's landless farmers on the march brought the long-term struggle of the Sem Terra movement to international attention. Small farmers' unions in Europe linked up with those in Latin America, India, Malaysia, the Philippines and South Africa to form Via Campesina, uniting a growing network of local campaigns against the food multinationals, whose programme for regulating world agriculture on neoliberal lines took a massive step forward as GATT morphed into the WTO in 1994. It was in the South, too, that struggles against water and electricity privatization, a key element of the neoliberal agenda, have had the most impact: the Soweto Electricity Crisis Committee and Anti-Privatization Forum in South Africa, *La Coordinara* in Bolivia, the Narmada Dam protests in India.

Yet another strand, this time North-based and on the right wing of the emerging coalition against the IMF, World Bank and WTO, consisted of the anti-poverty NGOs, Oxfam and its more radical sisters, which faced a sharp aggravation of their tasks in Africa and Latin America due to the debt burdens and structural adjustment programmes imposed by the world financial institutions. American trade unions were also under some pressure from their members to campaign against industrial relocation from North to South, while 'Students against Sweatshops' were mobilized by US garment-workers' unions to protest against the ultra-exploitation of GAP and Nike workers in South-East Asian EPZs.

French internationalists addressed the untrammelled power of finance capital itself. In December 1997, as financial meltdown and economic crisis swept Korea and South-East Asia, Ignacio Ramonet called in the pages of *Le Monde diplomatique* for an action campaign around a 'Tobin tax' on financial transactions—a symbolic first step to 'disarm the market'. By the following summer, as the rouble plummeted and Russia defaulted on its vast international debt, ATTAC branches were springing up across provincial France, and then beyond. As its organizer Bernard Cassen recounts here, the ATTAC network, with the Workers Party in Brazil, was a moving spirit behind the establishment of the World Social Forums at Porto Alegre that, for three consecutive years, provided the 'movement of movements' with an annual meeting place. Tens of thousands from Latin America, Europe and, to a lesser extent, North America, Africa and the Indian subcontinent, braved the heat of Brazil's deep south to debate, in crowded workshops and seminars, the ethics, politics and economics of neoliberal globalization and its alternatives. Meanwhile, mass protests continued against the Free Trade Area of the Americas meeting in Quebec City in April 2001, and the G8 summit in Genoa three months later.

It was with unconcealed delight that the financial press announced the death of what it called the anti-globalization movement, following September 11. If the celebrations proved premature—attendance at the WSF in January 2002 was five times that of the year before; in November, 40,000 delegates packed the European Social Forum meeting in Florence, which concluded with a demonstration against war in Iraq that Italian police estimated at 450,000 strong—nevertheless, the acceleration of US militarism since 2001 has posed a new set of problems for the radical opposition. The Northern movements' most widely read theorists—Toni Negri and Michael Hardt in *Empire*; Naomi Klein in *No Logo*—had focused on the multinational corporations and global financial institutions, ignoring or, in the case of Hardt and Negri, repudiating the role of the United States as the sole capitalist superpower. Only a minority had opposed the US bombing of Yugoslavia. With the bombardment of Afghanistan—and, even more so, with the Anglo-American occupation of Iraq—the 'movement of movements', if it is to go forward, needs to generate an understanding of how US military and political power operates not just in Iraq but across the Middle East, Asia, Africa and Latin America; to discern the superpower at work behind the multilateral screens of the UN Security Council, just as much as those of the IMF, World Bank or WTO; to build a global opposition capable of inflicting defeats on Washington's neo-imperialist ambitions as well as its neoliberal goals.

*

The imaginative direct-action tactics and communications skills of the new protest movements have generated vast amounts of media coverage, itself helpful as further publicity and propaganda, spreading in widening rings. A large and colourful literature now exists to applaud the global span and diversity of the new activism. Though in sympathy with these rebel instincts, the interviews and essays published here—most of which first appeared in the London-based journal *New Left Review*—have a different aim. Namely, to take the measure of the new movements—their actual membership and implantation, funding and internal structure, analysis and goals—without losing sight of the scale of the enemy they confront: the entrenched political and economic power of neoliberalism across the globe, backed by the unparalleled military might of the US.

Here, leading figures from a variety of different struggles, North and South, discuss their own radicalization, the history and development of their campaigns, the problems they face and the allies they have sought. Though the ages of the contributors range from 26 to 73, many were children in the 1960s and touched by the departing wing of those earlier protests; thirty-somethings form the second largest cohort, growing up in the transformed global context of the 1980s and 1990s. The selection is, inevitably, far from complete. Within Europe, the effervescent Italian scene is not represented, nor is the NoBorders campaign that has held open summer camps on the Polish–German and Ukrainian frontiers for the past three years, a direct-action breach in the curtain walls of Fortress Europe. In other respects, these voices reflect the geographical limitations of the 'movement of movements' itself: Canada, the US, Mexico and Brazil are represented, as are France, India, South Africa, Kenya, Indonesia and the Philippines; but the Middle East is absent, as is East Asia, including Korea and Japan—regions now in the frontline of neo-imperialist aggression. The final section, 'Analytics', raises some of the broader theoretical questions that confront those aiming to build a global opposition to neoliberalism today.

SOUTHERN VOICES

THE HOURGLASS
OF THE ZAPATISTAS

Interviewed by Gabriel García Márquez and Roberto Pombo

Seven years after the Zapatista Army of National Liberation (EZLN) declared that one day it would enter Mexico City in triumph, you are in the capital and the Zócalo is completely full. What did you feel when you climbed the dais and saw that spectacle?

In keeping with the Zapatista tradition of anti-climax, the worst place to see a demonstration in the Zócalo is from the platform. The sun was fierce, there was a lot of smog, we all had a headache, and got very worried as we counted the people passing out in front of us. I commented to my comrade, Commander Tacho, that we should get on with it, or by the time we began to speak no one would be left in the square. We couldn't see all the way across it. The distance we had to keep from the crowd for security reasons was also an emotional one, and we didn't find out what had happened in the Zócalo until we read the newspaper reports and saw the photos the next day. But yes, in our view and in the assessment of others, we do think that the meeting was the culmination of a phase, that our words on that day were appropriate and our message the right one, that we disconcerted those who expected us to seize the Palace or call for general insurrection. But also those who thought that we would be merely poetic or lyrical. I think an effective balance was struck and that, one way or another, on 11 March the EZLN could be heard speaking in the Zócalo, not so much about 2001, but about something that is yet to be completed: a conviction that the definitive defeat of racism will be turned into a state policy, an educational policy, into a feeling shared by the whole of Mexican society. As if this has already been settled, yet it still remains a short way off. As we soldiers say, the battle has been won, but a few skirmishes still remain to be fought. Finally I believe that the meeting in the Zócalo made it clear that it had been the right decision to put our weapons aside, that it was not our arms which brought us into dialogue with society, that the gamble on a peaceful mobilization was sensible and fruitful. The Mexican State has still to understand this, the government in particular.

You've used the expression 'as we soldiers say'. To a Colombian, accustomed to the way our guerrillas talk, your language doesn't sound very soldierly. How military is your movement, and how would you describe the war in which you have been fighting?

We were formed in an army, the EZLN. It has a military structure. Subcomandante Marcos is the military chief of an army. But our army is very different from others, because its proposal is to cease being an army. A soldier is an absurd person who has to resort to arms in order to convince others, and in that sense the movement has no future if its future is military. If the EZLN perpetuates itself as an armed military structure, it is headed for failure. Failure as an alternative set of ideas, an alternative attitude to the world. The worst that could happen to it, apart from that, would be to come to power and install itself there as a revolutionary army. For us it would be a failure. What would be a success for the politico-military organizations of the sixties or seventies which emerged with the national liberation movements would be a fiasco for us. We have seen that such victories proved in the end to be failures, or defeats, hidden behind the mask of success. That what always remained unresolved was the role of people, of civil society, in what became ultimately a dispute between two hegemonies. There is an oppressor power which decides on behalf of society from above, and a group of visionaries which decides to lead the country on the correct path and ousts the other group from power, seizes power and then also decides on behalf of society. For us that is a struggle between hegemonies, in which the winners are good and the losers bad, but for the rest of society things don't basically change. The EZLN has reached a point where it has been overtaken by Zapatismo. The 'E' in the acronym has shrunk, its hands have been tied, so that for us it is no handicap to mobilize unarmed, but rather in a certain sense a relief. The gun-belt weighs less than before and the military paraphernalia an armed group necessarily wears when it enters dialogue with people also feels less heavy. You cannot reconstruct the world or society, or rebuild national states now in ruins, on the basis of a quarrel over who will impose their hegemony on society. The world in general, and Mexican society in particular, is composed of different kinds of people, and the relations between them have to be founded on respect and tolerance, things which appear in none of the discourses of the politico-military organizations of the sixties and seventies. Reality, as always, presented a bill to the armed national liberation movements of those days, and the cost of settling it has been very high.

You also seem to differ from the traditional Left in the social sectors that you represent. Is that so?

Broadly speaking, there were two major gaps in the movement of the revolutionary Left in Latin America. One of them was the indigenous peoples, from whose ranks we come, and the other was the supposed minorities. Even if we all removed our balaclavas, we would not be a minority in the same way that homosexuals, lesbians, transsexuals are. These sectors were not simply excluded by the discourses of the Latin American Left of those decades—and still current today—but the theoretical framework of what was then Marxism–Leninism disregarded them, indeed took them to be part of the front to be eliminated.

Homosexuals, for example, were suspect as potential traitors, elements harmful to the socialist movement and state. While the indigenous peoples were viewed as a backward sector preventing the forces of production . . . blah, blah, blah. So what was required was to clean out these elements, imprisoning or re-educating some, and assimilating others into the process of production, to transform them into skilled labour—proletarians, to put it in those terms.

Guerrillas normally speak in the name of majorities. It seems surprising that you speak in the name of minorities, when you could do so in the name of the poor or exploited of Mexico as a whole. Why do you do this?

Every vanguard imagines itself to be representative of the majority. We not only think that is false in our case, but that even in the best of cases it is little more than wishful thinking, and in the worst cases an outright usurpation. The moment social forces come into play, it becomes clear that the vanguard is not such a vanguard and that those it represents do not recognize themselves in it. The EZLN, in renouncing any claim to be a vanguard, is recognizing its real horizon. To believe that we can speak on behalf of those beyond ourselves is political masturbation. In some cases it is not even that, because there is no pleasure in this onanism—at most, that of pamphlets read only by those who produce them. We are trying to be honest with ourselves and some might say that this is a matter of human decency. No. We could even be cynical and say that the honest admission that we only represent the indigenous Zapatista communities of one region of the Mexican South-East has paid off. But our discourse has reached the ears of many more people than those we represent. This is the point we have reached. That's all. In the speeches we made in the course of our march to the capital, we told people—and ourselves—that we could not and should not try to lead the struggles we encountered on our journey, or fly the flag for them. We had imagined that those below would not be slow to show themselves, with so many injustices, so many complaints, so many wounds . . . In our minds we had formed the image that our march would be a kind of plough, turning the soil so that all this could rise from the ground. We had to be honest and tell people that we had not come to lead anything of what might emerge. We came to release a demand, that could unleash others. But that's another story.

Were the speeches you gave along the route improvised from town to town until the address in Mexico City, or did you design them from the outset as a sequence, such that the last was not necessarily the strongest?

Look, there is an official version and a real version. The official story is that we saw at each stop what we had to do. The real story is that we wove this discourse together over the course of the last seven years. A moment arrived when the Zapatismo of the EZLN was overtaken by many developments. Today we are not expressing what we were before 1994, or in the first days of 1994 when we were fighting; we are acting on a series of moral commitments we made in the last seven years. In the end we didn't manage to plough the land, as we had hoped. But the mere act of our walking on it was enough to bring all these buried feelings to the surface. In every town square, we told people: 'We have not come to lead you, we have not come to tell you what to do, but to ask for your help'. Even so, we received during our march dockets of complaints going back to the time before the Mexican Revolution, given to us in the hope that finally someone might resolve the problem. If we could sum up the discourse of the Zapatista march to date, it would be: 'No one is going to do it for us.' The forms of organization, and the tasks of politics, need to be changed for that transformation to be possible. When we say 'no' to leaders, we are also saying 'no' to ourselves.

You and the Zapatistas are at the peak of your prestige. The PRI has just fallen in Mexico, there is a bill before Congress to create an Indigenous Statute, and the negotiations you have demanded can begin. How do you view this scene?

As a struggle between a clock operated by a punch card, which is Fox's time, and an hourglass, which is ours. The dispute is over whether we bend to the discipline of the factory clock or Fox bends to the slipping of the sand. It will be neither the one nor the other. Both of us need to understand, we and he, that we have to assemble another clock by common agreement, that will time the rhythm of dialogue and finally of peace. We are on their terrain, the arena of power, where the political class is in its element. We are there with an organization that is perfectly ineffectual when it comes to playing politics, at least that kind of politics. We are gauche, stammering, well-intentioned. Opposite us are skilled players of a game they know well. This too will be a dispute, over whether the agenda will be dictated by the political class or shaped by our requirements. Once again, I think it will be neither one nor the other. When we waged war we had to challenge the government, and now in order to build peace we have to challenge not only the government but the entire Mexican State. There is no table at which to sit in dialogue with the government. We have to construct it. The challenge now is to convince the government that we need to make that table, that it should enter into dialogue and that it stands to gain by doing so. And that if it doesn't, it will lose.

Who should be at that table?

The government on one side and ourselves on the other.

Hasn't Fox in practice accepted that table when he says he wants to talk to you, and will receive you in the Presidential Palace or wherever you please?

What Fox is saying is that he wants his slice of the media cake, in what has become a popularity contest, rather than a dialogue or negotiation. Fox is looking for a photo opportunity, to maintain his grip on the media. But a peace process is not to be constructed by a spectacle, but by serious signals, sitting down at a table and dedicating yourself to a real dialogue. We are ready to talk to Fox, if he takes personal responsibility for that dialogue and sees the negotiation with us through to the end. But we would ask him: who is going to run the country while you are meeting with us, which will be an arduous business? I don't have to explain this to anyone from Colombia, where you know from your own experience that the processes of dialogue and negotiation in an armed conflict are extremely tricky, and impossible for the head of the Executive to dedicate himself to full-time. Let Fox designate a representative of his government with whom we can construct a dialogue. There's no hurry. A handshake with Vicente Fox is not among our wet dreams

During that lengthy process, will you carry on as you are, dressed as a guerrilla, on a university campus? What's your average day like just now?

I get up, I give interviews and then it's time to go to bed [laughter]. We hold discussions with various of the groups I have mentioned: a large number of worlds or sub-worlds—the difference depends on how they are persecuted or marginalized—that have been affected by our message. We are sitting at two tables, swivelling between them on one of those chairs on wheels I remember from my youth. At the moment we are at one table with Congress and at another with the communities of Mexico City. But it worries us that Congress is treating us as it would anyone who asks to be seen, and is told to wait because it is attending to other matters. If that's the case, it will cause a lot of damage, because it's not only the recognition of indigenous rights that is at issue now. The knock-on effect would hit many people. People will not accept being looked in the eye only on election day. Besides which, it would send a signal to other, more radical politico-military groups, which have grown up under a banner that proclaims any political negotiation a form of surrender.

In parentheses, you said there were swivel chairs when you were young. How old are you?

I'm 518 . . . [laughter]

Does the dialogue you propose aim to create new mechanisms of popular participation in decision-making, or do you support government decisions you consider necessary for the country?

Dialogue means simply agreeing rules for the dispute between us to shift to another terrain. The economic system is not on the table for discussion. It's the way we're going to discuss it that is at issue. This is something Vicente Fox needs to understand. We are not going to become 'Foxistas' at that table. What the table has to achieve is to allow us to emerge with dignity, so that neither I nor anyone else has to go back and don all that military paraphernalia again. The challenge before us is to construct not only the table, but also our interlocutor. We need to make a statesman, not a marketing product designed by image consultants, out of him. It won't be easy. War was easier. But in war much more becomes irremediable. In politics, remedies can always be found.

Your attire is a little strange: a threadbare scarf tied at the neck and a cap that's falling apart. But you are also carrying a torch, which you don't need here, a communications device which looks very sophisticated, and a watch on each wrist. Are they symbols? What does all this mean?

The torch is because we have been put into a lightless pit and the radio is for my image consultants to dictate my answers to questions from journalists. No. More seriously: this is a walkie-talkie which allows me to communicate with security and with our people in the jungle in case there is a problem. We have received several death threats. The scarf was red and was new when we took San Cristóbal de las Casas seven years ago. And the cap is the one I had when I arrived in the Lacandón jungle eighteen years ago. I arrived in that jungle with one watch and the other dates from when the ceasefire began. When the two times coincide it will mean that Zapatismo is finished as an army and that another stage, another watch and another time has started.

How do you see the Colombian guerrillas and the armed conflict of our country?

From here I see very little. Just what the media filter through: the current process of dialogue and negotiation, and its difficulties. So far as I can tell, it's a very traditional kind of dialogue—it's not innovative. Both sides are simultaneously sitting at the table and bringing their military forces into play to gain an advantage at the table. Or vice versa, because we don't know what each of them has in mind. Perhaps the table offers advantages for military confrontations. We don't pay much attention to the accusations of links to drug-trafficking because it wouldn't be the first time such charges are made and then they turn out not to be true. We give the Colombians the benefit of the doubt. We don't label them good or bad, but we do keep our distance from them, as we do with other armed groups in Mexico, in so far as we consider it unethical to approve of *any* measures to secure the victory of the revolution. Including, for example, kidnapping civilians. The seizure of power does not justify a revolutionary organization in taking any action that it pleases. We do not believe that the end justifies the means. Ultimately, we believe that the means are the end. We define our goal by the way we choose the means of struggling for it. In that sense, the value we give to our word, to honesty and sincerity, is great, although we occasionally sin out of naïveté. For example, on 1 January 1994, before attacking the Army, we announced that we were going to attack. They didn't believe us. Sometimes this yields results and sometimes it doesn't. But it satisfies us that, as an organization, we are creating an identity as we go along.

Do you think it's possible to negotiate a peace in the middle of a war, as in Colombia?

It's very easy, and very irresponsible, to offer opinions from here on what is happening there. A process of dialogue and negotiation is unlikely to be successful if each party remains intent on winning. If one side uses negotiations as a test of force to see if it can defeat the other, sooner or later the dialogue will fail. In that event, the field of military confrontation is simply being transferred to the negotiating table. For dialogue and negotiation to succeed, both parties have to proceed from the assumption that they cannot defeat their opponent. They need to find a way out that means a victory for both—or, in the worst of cases, a defeat for both. But that brings the confrontation as it is to an end. Of course, this is difficult—above all for movements which have been active for many years, like the Colombian guerrillas. Much harm has been done on both sides and many debts have yet to be settled, but I believe it is never too late to try.

Do you still find time to read, in the midst of all these distractions?

Yes, because if not . . . what would we do? In previous armies, soldiers used their time to clean their weapons and stock up ammunition. Our weapons are words, and we may need our arsenal at any moment.

Everything you say, in form and content, suggests a considerable literary education of a traditional kind. Where does it come from?

From childhood. In our family, words had a very special value. Our way of approaching the world was through language. We learnt to read, not so much in school, as in the columns of newspapers. Early on, my mother and father gave us books that disclosed other things. One way or another, we became conscious of language—not as a way of communicating, but of constructing something. As if it were a pleasure more than a duty. In the underground, unlike the world of bourgeois intellectuals, the word is not what is most valued. It is relegated to a secondary position. It was when we got to the indigenous communities that language hit us, like a catapult. Then you realize that you lack the words to express many things, and that obliges you to work on language. To return time and again to words, to put them together and take them apart.

Could it not be the other way round—that a command of words was what made possible a new phase of struggle?

It's as if it all goes through a blender. You don't know what you tossed in first, and what you end up with is a cocktail.

Can we ask about your family?

It was middle class. My father, the head of the family, taught in a rural school in the time of Cárdenas when, as he used to say, teachers had their ears cut off for being communists. My mother also taught in a school in the countryside, then moved and entered the middle class: it was a family without financial difficulties. All of this was in the provinces, where the society pages of the local newspaper are the cultural horizon. The outside world was Mexico City and its bookshops—the great attraction of coming here. Occasionally there would be provincial book fairs, where we could get hold of something interesting. My parents introduced us to García Márquez, Carlos Fuentes, Monsiváis, Vargas Llosa (regardless of his ideas), to mention only a few. They set us to reading them. *A Hundred Years of Solitude* to explain what the provinces were like at the time. *The Death of Artemio Cruz* to show what had happened to the Mexican Revolution. *Días de guardar* to describe what was happening in the middle classes. As for *La ciudad y los perros*, it was in a way a portrait of us, but in the nude. All these things were there. We went out into the world in the same way that we went out into literature. I think this marked us. We didn't look out at the world through a news-wire but through a novel, an essay or a poem. That made us very different. That was the prism through which my parents wanted me to view the world, as others might choose the prism of the media, or a dark prism to stop you seeing what's happening.

Where does Don Quixote *come in all that reading?*

I was given a book when I turned 12, a beautiful cloth edition. It was *Don Quixote*. I had read it before, but in those children's editions. It was an expensive book, a special present which must still be out there somewhere. Next came Shakespeare. But the Latin American boom came first, then Cervantes, then García Lorca, and then came a phase of poetry. So in a way you [looking at GGM] are an accessory to all this.

Did the existentialists and Sartre come into this?

No. We arrived late at all that. Strictly speaking, we were already, as the orthodox would say, very corrupted by the time we got to existential literature and, before that, to revolutionary literature. So that when we got into Marx and Engels we were thoroughly spoilt by literature; its irony and humour.

Didn't you read any political theory?

Not to begin with. We went straight from the alphabet to literature, and from there to theoretical and political texts, until we got to high school.

Did your classmates believe that you were or might be a communist?

No, I don't think so. Perhaps the most they called me was a little radish: red outside and white inside.

What are you reading at the moment?

Don Quixote is always at my side, and as a rule I carry García Lorca's *Romancero Gitano* with me. *Don Quixote* is the best book of political theory, followed by *Hamlet* and *Macbeth*. There is no better way to understand the Mexican political system, in its tragic and comic aspects: *Hamlet*, *Macbeth* and *Don Quixote*. Better than any political columnist.

Do you write by hand or on a computer?

On a computer. Except on this march, when I had to write a lot by hand because there was no time to work. I write a rough draft, and then another and another and another. It sounds silly, but by the time I finish I'm on about the seventh version.

What book are you writing?

I was trying to produce a folly, which was to try to explain ourselves to ourselves from the standpoint of ourselves—which is virtually impossible. What we have to relate is the paradox that we are. Why a revolutionary army is not aiming to seize power, why an army doesn't fight, if that's its job. All the paradoxes we faced: the way we grew and became strong in a community so far removed from the established culture.

If everyone knows who you are, why the mask?

A touch of coquetry. They don't know who I am, but it doesn't matter to them anyway. At stake is what Subcomandante Marcos is, not who he was.

VENEZUELA

COLOMBIA

GUYANA

SURINAM

FRENCH GUIANA

RORAIMA

AMAPÁ

NORTH ATLANTIC OCEAN

Belém

Amazon River

PARÁ

MARANHÃO

CEARÁ

RIO GRANDE DO NORTE

AMAZONAS

Carajás

BRAZIL

PIAUÍ

PARAÍBA

PERNAMBUCO

ACRE

TOCANTINS

ALAGOAS

SERGIPE

RONDÔNIA

MATO GROSSO

BAHIA

PERU

GOIÁS

Brasília

DISTRITO FEDERAL

BOLIVIA

Paraná River

MINAS GERAIS

ESPÍRITO SANTO

MATO GROSSO DO SUL

SÃO PAULO

RIO DE JANEIRO

PARAGUAY

São Paulo

Rio de Janeiro

CHILE

PARANÁ

SOUTH PACIFIC OCEAN

SANTA CATARINA

SOUTH ATLANTIC OCEAN

RIO GRANDE DO SUL

Porto Alegre

ARGENTINA

URUGUAY

0 ———— 400 km

JOÃO PEDRO STEDILE

BRAZIL'S LANDLESS BATTALIONS

The Sem Terra Movement

Which region of Brazil do you come from, and what was your family background and education?

I was born in 1953 in Rio Grande do Sul, and grew up on my parents' farm there until I was about 18. There was a community of small farmers of Italian extraction in the region—it had been colonized in the nineteenth century by peasants from those parts of what was then the Austro-Hungarian Empire. My mother's family was originally from the Veneto, and my father's from what is today the Italian Tyrol. My grandfather came to Brazil in 1899. He was a farmer, too. My grandparents were almost certainly illiterate, but my father and mother had three years of primary school. But this was the period of industrialization, in the sixties, and my brothers and sisters already had wider horizons—they wanted to study. One of them became a metalworker. Some of the others went to the city, too.

The greatest influence on me at that stage was the Catholic Church— the Capuchin friars, in particular. In all the colonized regions of Rio Grande do Sul—Colônia, Caxias do Sul, Bento Gonçalves and the surrounding areas—the Church had a very strong presence, and the Capuchins were doing interesting work, preaching against injustice and taking up social issues. I owe my education to my uncle, a Capuchin, who helped me get a place at the Catholic grammar school where they taught the entire curriculum. I loved studying, and in the final year I applied for the advanced course. I was living at the house of an uncle by then, because my father had died. I worked on the land by day and studied by night, walking the ten kilometres to school. I knew I wanted to carry on learning, so I moved to Porto Alegre. I worked in various places, still earning my living by day, reading economics by night.

I had a stroke of luck in my second year at Porto Alegre. There was a competition for posts in Rio Grande do Sul's State Agriculture Department. I was from a farming family and I understood agriculture: I decided this was the route I should take. With the Agriculture Department, I'd travel a lot in the interior of the state and my work would still be linked to the farmers' lives. I got the posting, and from there I became involved with the local Sindicato dos Trabalhadores Rurais [Rural Workers Union], especially the grape-farmers. My first experience as a social activist was working with the Union's members to calculate the price of grapes. Every year there was a battle with the buyers over this—the big vintners would name a sum and none of the growers could contest it, since they had no idea how to calculate what the harvest was really worth. We went round to the communities, sat down with the farmers and worked out how much it actually cost to produce a kilo of grapes, from trellising the vines to the manual labour of the harvest— since I was reading economics, I was able to help. In the process, the farmers became increasingly conscious, they got together and began to confront the wine producers. This coincided with the multinationals' entry into the market, and we won some important victories—there was a leap in the average price the farmers got for their grapes. At the same time, I'd maintained my links with the Church, and when the Commissão Pastoral da Terra [Pastoral Commission on Land] was set up in 1975, I met with them to discuss how to organize the farmers.

In 1976, I won a bursary from the Agriculture Department to go and study in Mexico for two years. It was there that I met Francisco Julião, from whom I learned a tremendous amount.[1] I only ever had two

---

[1] Francisco Julião (1915–99): leader of the Farmers' Leagues in the North-East of Brazil, federal deputy for the Brazilian Socialist Party; exiled after the military coup in 1964.

questions for him: 'What did you get wrong?' and 'What did you get right?'. It was a great privilege to be at UNAM at the same time as some of the major exiled intellectuals of the Brazilian Left such as Rui Mauro Marini, who gave courses on *Das Kapital*; Teotônio dos Santos himself, in sociology; Vânia Bambirra, who taught us dependency theory. I concentrated mainly on agrarian questions, but I took a few courses in economics and other disciplines. There were scholars from other Latin American countries who were also in exile in Mexico—Pedro Vuskovic, Allende's economics minister; Jacques Chonchol, Allende's minister for agrarian reform. I was very young, but I learnt a phenomenal amount from them. It was probably the best period of my life.

What were the origins of the Sem Terra Movement?

The MST was the result of the conjunction of three basic factors. First, the economic crisis of the late seventies put an end to the industrialization cycle in Brazil, begun by Kubitschek in 1956. Young people had been leaving the farms for the city, and getting jobs quite easily. Now they had to stay in the countryside and find a living there. The second factor was the work the friars were doing. In the sixties, the Catholic Church had largely supported the military dictatorship, but with the growing ferment of liberation theology there was a change of orientation, the emergence of the CPT and a layer of progressive bishops. Before, the line had been: 'No need to worry, you'll have your land in heaven'. Now it was: 'Since you've already got land in heaven, let's struggle for it here as well'. The friars played a good role in stirring up the farmers and getting them organized. And the third factor was the growing climate of struggle against the military dictatorship in the late seventies, which automatically transformed even local labour conflicts into political battles against the government.

It was against this background that land occupations began to spread throughout the South, the North and the North-East. None of them was spontaneous—all were clearly planned and organized by local activists—but there were no connexions between them. From 1978 onwards, the first great strikes began to take place in the cities: they served as a good example of how to lose your fear. In the five years from 1978 to 1983—what you could call the genesis of the movement—there was an outbreak of large-scale land occupations, and people really did begin to lose their fear of struggling against the dictatorship. The role of the CPT was of crucial importance here—the Church was the only body that had what you might call a capillary organization, across the whole country. They soon realized that these occupations were happening in different areas, and started setting up meetings between the local leaders. I'd already been involved in helping organize various actions in Rio Grande do Sul, the first one in September 1979. The CPT contacted me and other comrades and we began to hold national meetings, along the lines Julião and I had discussed. The farmers talked things over, in their own way: 'How do you do it in the North-East?', 'How do you do it in the North?'. Slowly, we realized we were facing the same problems, and attempting similar solutions. Throughout 1983 and 1984 we held big debates about how to build an organization that would spread the struggle for land—and, above all, one that could transform these localized conflicts into a major battle for agrarian reform. We knew it changed nothing just to bring a few families together, move onto unused land and think that was the end. We were well aware from the agrarian struggles of the past that if farmers don't organize themselves, don't fight for more than just a piece of land, they'll never reach a wider class consciousness and be able to grapple with the underlying problems— because land in itself does not free the farmer from exploitation.

In January 1984, we held an Encontro Nacional in Cascavel, Paraná, where we analyzed all these questions and resolved to set up an organization. The name was of no great importance, but the press already had a nickname for us. Every time we occupied some land the newspapers would say, 'There go the Sem Terra again'. Fine, since they called us that, we'd be the 'Movimento dos Sem Terra'. We were ideologically more inclined to call ourselves the 'Movement of Workers for Agrarian Reform', because the idea was to build a social force that would go beyond the struggle just for land itself. But history never depends entirely on people's intentions. We got our reputation as the 'Sem Terra', so the name stuck; the most we did was to invent the abbreviation—MST.

Another important decision we took at the Encontro Nacional was to organize ourselves as an autonomous movement, independent of the political parties. Our analysis of the farmers' movements of Latin America and Brazil taught us that whenever a mass movement was subordinated to a party, it was weakened by the effects of inner-party splits and factional battles. It was not that we didn't value parties, or thought it was wrong to join them. But the movement had to be free from external political direction. It also had to be independent of the Catholic Church. Many of the farmers were strongly influenced by the Church and argued that since it had helped us so much we should form a movement of Christians for agrarian reform. Fortunately, some of the most politically aware comrades were from the Church. They had had previous experience with Ação Católica or in the JOCs, and they themselves warned us against it—the moment a bishop comes to a different decision from the mass organization, the organization is finished. We also decided then on the general tactics we would use. We were convinced that the fight for agrarian reform could only move forward if it were a mass struggle, so we had to try to involve as many people as possible. When we set out on a land occupation, we would try to take everyone along—fathers, mothers, sons, daughters, old people, children, the lot. We listed the ten or twelve objectives our movement would serve—the struggle for agrarian reform, for a different Brazil, for a society without exploiters. That was the initial framework.

So the movement didn't start out from Rio Grande do Sul?

No—that's the usual story, but it's not completely true. It's been characterized like that for various reasons. Firstly, because it was in Rio

Grande do Sul, north-east of Porto Alegre, that we built the Encruzilhada Natalino encampment, and the press turned that into a historic event. It was based at the junction of three counties, Sarandi, Ronda Alta and Passo Fundo—hence the name, *encruzilhada* [crossroads]. The president, General Figueiredo, sent the Army to destroy the settlement, under the command of Major Curió. It was the dictatorship that politicized our struggle. All we wanted was land, but overnight the encampment was encircled by the Federal police, the Army and even the Air Force, to airlift the farmers to the Mato Grosso—they took over a hundred families, in the end. Curió was such a symbol of the military repression that all those who opposed the dictatorship began to sympathize with us, and Encruzilhada Natalino became a counter-symbol, like the strike at the Scania truck factory, or Lula's imprisonment. There's a commemorative monument there now. The encampment grew into a historic nexus for the Sem Terra—we took over several unproductive *fazendas*—large properties, or ranches—in the area and eventually a new municipality was set up there. It's called Pontão, because 80 per cent of the population are squatters, including the mayor. It's a mini-free territory, the result of agrarian reform.

That was one experience that gave the movement a southern imprint, although as I said, there were land occupations going on in the North-East, the North, the Bico do Papagaio, and here in São Paulo, in the Andradina region, between 1979 and 1983—though only a few of these became well known. The other factor that's contributed to the impression of a southern bent to the Sem Terra Movement is that this is where many of our activists have come from—for the simple reason that, south of the Paraná, farmers' children had a better chance of an education: a fundamental requirement if you're going to help to articulate struggles, to get in contact with people, to establish relations with them. Dozens of militants from the South could then be sent to other regions—not because there was an ideology of wanting to teach northerners, but because of the different educational level. We adopted a method others have used before: the Brazilian Army posts officers from the South across the whole country, the Federal Savings Bank transfers its employees—so does the Catholic Church.

Could you describe a typical land occupation?

For two or three months, our activists visit the villages and communities in an area where there are lots of landless farmers, and start work on raising awareness—proselytizing, if you like. They explain to people that they have a right to land, that the constitution has a clause on agrarian reform but that the government doesn't apply it. Next, we ask the farmers if there is a big, underused land-holding in the region, because the law is clear: where there is a large unproductive property, the government is obliged to expropriate it. They get involved in the discussion, and start to become more conscious. Then comes the decision: 'You have a right to land. There are unused properties in the region. There is only one way to force the government to expropriate them. You think they'll do it if we write them a letter? Asking the mayor is a waste of time, especially if he's a landowner. You could talk to the priest, but if he's not interested, what's the point? We have to organize and take over that land ourselves'.

When that decision is reached, we can bring to bear all the historical experience we've accumulated—which, from a political point of view, is simply what the Sem Terra Movement does: our role is to pass on what we've learnt, as a class. As far as land occupations are concerned, we know our business—not everything, but a lot. Everyone has to go, all the families together. It has to be done during the night to avoid the police. Those who want to join in have to organize themselves into committees of 15 or 20 people. Then, each committee—there may be 20 or so of them—has to hire a truck, and set up a kitty to buy canvas and stock up on provisions. It takes three or four months to get ready. One day there's a meeting of representatives from each of the 15-person committees to decide when the occupation will take place. The decision has to be kept secret. On the night, the hired trucks arrive, well before daybreak, and go round the communities, pick up all they can carry and then set off for the property. The families have one night to take possession of the area and build their shelters, so that early the next morning, when the proprietor realizes what's happened, the encampment is already set up. The committee chooses a family to reconnoitre the place, to find where there are sources of water, where there are trees for shade. There are a lot of factors involved in setting up an open-air encampment. It's better if you're near a road, because then you don't have to carry so much on your back. This sort of logistical experience has a big influence on how an occupation works out. But success really depends on the number of families involved—the more there are, the less favourable the balance of forces for the proprietor and the police; the fewer the families, the easier it is to evict them, and the more limited the political repercussions will be.

By morning, the settlement is established—and the basis for conflict is sprung. It will be covered in the press, and the proprietor will apply to the authorities, asking for the squatters to be evicted. Our lawyers will arrive on the scene, arguing that the property is large and unproductive, and therefore in breach of the constitution. From the Sem Terra point of view, if we win it's because the INCRA makes an inspection of the property and decides to expropriate.[2] If we lose, it's because the proprietor has enough force at his disposal to carry out the eviction. If the police come to evict the squatters, we always try to avoid there being violence. The encampment gets shifted—to the edge of the road, for example— and we go on from there, to occupy another unused property. But the main thing for a group, once it's gathered in an encampment, is to stay united, to keep putting pressure on the government.

The biggest occupation of all was in 1996, on Fazenda Giacometti, in Paraná. The property took up 80,000 hectares—nearly 200,000 acres—of good, fertile land, covering three municipalities. It was an insult to society that that land was lying unused—all the farmers in the region were enraged about it; everybody was. We started work in the

[2] INCRA: Instituto Nacional de Colonização e Reforma Agrária.

region, discussing with the farmers, and decided to set up an encampment by the side of the road where people could gather if they wanted to join the occupation, rather than going to the Fazenda Giacometti straightaway. We kept the encampment there open for a week, and more and more people turned up. When the leaders decided on the date for the occupation, we assumed it would be the traditional method—they'd hire trucks, pile everyone into them and drive to the site. But on the night, there were so many families involved that we decided not to use the lorries. We walked the 21 kilometres—13 miles—all through the night. When we reached the Fazenda day was breaking, and the police were called out immediately. But there were so many people—10,000 squatters, with their bundles of belongings on their heads—that all the police could do was to help the procession down the road, and make sure there were no car accidents. The sheer scale of numbers transformed the balance of forces. That was our biggest victory, and since we knew it would be a historic event, we invited Sebastião Salgado to take photographs of the march. It was an epic, the greatest of all the land occupations we've carried out to this day.

What is the structure of the MST—how many are involved? How are decisions taken, at local and national level?

We are a mass social movement, whose principal objective is to gather people for the struggle. How do you join the Sem Terra Movement? There is no membership, no cards, and it's not enough just to declare that one wants to be in the MST. The only way to join is to take part in one of the land occupations, to be active on the ground. That's how we get members. It's very hard to pin down statistically. We wanted to get away from party or union-style bureaucracy—filling in forms, and subscription fees. When your base is poor, illiterate farmers, you have to develop ways of going about things that are as open as possible, drawing people in rather than putting up barriers or bureaucratic hiccups.

To describe the MST's structure: our base is the mass of those who would benefit from agrarian reform—according to the last IBGE census, around four million landless families.[3] This is the layer we're working with. Many of them will come along on some sort of action—protest marches, for example—but not all will dare to occupy land. That's a very radical form of struggle, and you need to have been through several previous stages first. Recently, the government tried out a little test on us. They started putting out propaganda saying that it wasn't true that there are so many landless farmers in Brazil, that the MST had invented it. Raul Jungman, Cardoso's Minister for Agrarian Development, went on TV to launch a programme calling for the landless to register by post with the INCRA, promising the government would allocate them land. He thought there would be a tiny response, and we'd be demoralized. We took up the challenge. We went to our base and campaigned for postal registration. We said: 'You see this government propaganda saying, whoever wants land should write in for it? Come on, let's reply en masse. Let's organize and do it collectively, instead of on our own'. During 2001, 857,000 families registered, and the government found themselves in a pickle—they couldn't give land to any of them, because that would have meant allocating it to all. It was a simple, effective way of proving the existence of the millions of landless in Brazil.

Many of these people have been mobilized during the eighteen years of the Sem Terra Movement. Some 350,000 families have taken over land. In February 2002, we had 80,000 families camped on roadsides or on unused properties, their problems unresolved—they're in the front line in the battle against the government. There have been about 20,000 activists involved in this—the comrades with the greatest ideological clarity, who've helped to organize the rest. The activists come on courses, they take part in the regional and state-level meetings, where our leading bodies are elected—these consist of between 15 and 21 comrades. Every two years we hold national meetings, where a national commission is elected, with representatives from each state. Every five years we hold a

---

[3] IBGE: Instituto Brasileiro de Geografia e Estatística.

nationwide congress, which is always massive—a moment of real political debate. At the last congress—the fourth at national level—in August
2000, in Brasília, we spent five days in a sports hall with 11,750 delegates. From what I know of farmers' movements, this was the largest
farmers' congress in Latin America, and maybe in the world. Though
we could be beaten by the Indians and the Chinese. You can get 10,000
people there easily—click your fingers and you get more. But it was certainly the biggest in Latin America.

I also want to stress how much we've learnt from earlier farmers'
movements in Brazil and throughout Latin America. It was this that
taught us we should organize in collective bodies, that we should have
committees to govern political decision-making and the allocation of
tasks—that we shouldn't have a president. Even the encampments
run themselves and resolve their problems through committees—an
encampment doesn't have a president. It's the same at regional, state
and national levels—I'm one of 21 national directors, but decisions are
taken by the whole committee, and tasks divided between us. Some are
better known than others, because the press always go for the chatter-
boxes. But the best known aren't the most vital for the organization. The
most important are those who stay quiet but take decisive actions for the
movement to grow and spread.

How many Brazilian states do these delegates come from?

Of the 27 states, our movement has a presence in 23. We're strongest
where there are most farmers, in the South and North-East—or, in
order of importance: the North-East and the South. The South-East
is highly urbanized, there aren't many poor people left on the land—
they're either rural wage-earners, who dream of going to the big city,
or else the *lumpens*, who live on the city outskirts. In the North and
West-Central areas, there aren't many landless farmers. It's the agricultural frontier—even if there was a big settler movement in these parts,
there'd still be a good deal of land available. The most common form

of action there is individual initiatives. A tenant moves onto a patch, and for a few years he can delude himself he has land of his own, until someone takes it away from him. In Amazonas, Acre, Roraima and Amapá, the MST doesn't exist, because there is no mass base of farmers. Sometimes sectors of the Catholic Church and the rural unions try to tempt us to work there. The PT runs Acre now, and every time we meet the governor he asks when we're going to come there and organize.[4] The answer is: when you have some farmers. There's no point in us going there, putting up banners and opening an office—our problem is not lack of branch offices. If there aren't large numbers who will organize to occupy land, there is not going to be a farmers' movement. That's why we prefer to concentrate our work in regions where there is a real base of landless farmers—hence the priority of the South and North-East.

How is the MST financed, and by whom? Does the greater part of your funding come from your own activities, or are there other sources?

In terms of the land occupations themselves, we have a principle: all the costs have to be borne by those who participate. Otherwise things get confused: 'I don't know who' buys the tents, 'I don't know who' pays for the transport; the farmers end up depending on 'I don't know who'. At the first sign of trouble they'd say, 'No, I didn't come here on my own, so-and-so brought me' and they'd leave, because they wouldn't see the struggle as a personal sacrifice. We could carry out much larger actions if we asked for money from outside—but it would have a disastrous ideological effect. Instead, every family taking part in an occupation spends months working, to get materials for shelter, to get food—they know that they'll be surrounded by police, that they'll have no food, that they'll have to hold out for weeks until there are political repercussions, and solidarity begins to bring in resources. On a lot of occupations we've had to reduce the number of families taking part because some were so poor,

---

[4] PT: Partido dos Trabalhadores.

we would have had to pay for their transport and shelter. We've been faced with this dilemma many times.

Secondly, there is a great deal of solidarity at a local level. Trade unions and churches help us with training courses and funds, which we use to develop the movement. But another of our principles is that everything must be decentralized—we don't have a national treasury, or any centralized state-level ones. Thirdly, when we occupy land, every farmer—if he wants to be in the MST—agrees to give two per cent of the encampment's production to the movement. This doesn't go to some far-off authority, but to help the people camped in the region, to organize the movement and train activists. Sometimes a settlement produces very little, and the comrades say: 'We can't give you two per cent, we're working like dogs just to feed ourselves. But we can release two of our people, and we'll support their families, so that those two can go to train other landless farmers.' This is a very important contribution, although money doesn't enter into it.

Fourthly, when we help set up an encampment we provide for the community's basic needs: housing, electricity, school, teacher-training, and so on. But these should be the responsibility of the State, so we try to force the government to make the local authorities pay for these. We get further where the state governments are more progressive; where they are more conservative, it's harder for us. For example, we have agreements with the universities for training seven hundred MST teachers a year. The government bears the cost, but we decide on the curriculum and the orientation. It's the same when we need an agronomist—the State should supply one, it's their responsibility. To those who say 'Ah, the government's paying to train your teachers, you've been co-opted', we reply: 'No, we want to train seven thousand, but they won't give us the money'.

These are our usual sources of funds, although we also get some help from organizations in Europe and the States. Incredible as it seems, there's a group of US businessmen who send us funds every so often, without us even asking. In general, the money from Europe goes

for training activists. We're building a school—the National Florestan
Fernandes School, here on the Via Dutra—as a joint project with the
EU. We wanted it to be near São Paulo, where there's a concentration of
well-qualified leftist teachers and intellectuals—it's much easier to get
them to come 50 kilometres out of São Paulo than to resettle them in
the Normandia encampment in the interior of Pernambuco. It will be
a school for training cadres, true to the spirit of Florestan Fernandes.[5]
We see no contradiction in going to the EU with a construction project,
because the European countries have already stolen so much from
Brazil—it's high time some of it was paid back. There are other projects,
too—for instance, one with a European human-rights organization, to
help us get legal representation.

*How would you characterize the MST's social base—not only in terms of
class, but also of gender and 'race'? Does it have specific sectors for work with
indigenous peoples?*

The indigenous peoples are a minority in Brazil and here, unlike in
Andean or Aztec America, they were traditionally hunters and gather-
ers, not farmers as they are in Ecuador, Peru or Mexico, where they work
inside the farmers' organizations. Our relations with the indigenous
peoples start from the recognition that they are the original inhabitants
of Brazil. There is no discussion about that—all the land they claim as
theirs is theirs, and they should do with it as they wish.

In terms of ethnic composition, it depends on the situation of the
farmers in each state. There are very few blacks in the MST, and very
few Sem Terra farmers in the areas where they mainly live—Bahia,
Pernambuco, Maranhão. Pedro II's Law 601 of 1850 was designed to
prevent freed black slaves from becoming landowners; as soon as they
got their formal freedom, they had to migrate to the ports, and work
in the docks. Blacks were excluded from the formation of the Brazilian

---

[5] Florestan Fernandes (1920–95): doyen of radical sociology in Brazil. Via Dutra:
motorway connecting São Paulo and Rio de Janeiro.

farming classes, and that's had a lasting influence. To this day, the farming layers are composed mainly of *mestizos* in the North-East, and European immigrants in the South. This is clearly reflected in the composition of the MST.

As far as gender goes, because our form of struggle involves whole families, there's been a break with the traditional model of men-only farmers' movements. This is not to say there's not still a strong macho culture among the men in the countryside—on the contrary. But the way our movement is organized means the women are bound to play a role. In an encampment there are as many women as men—and even more children. In general, the women are very active in the committees set up to solve everyday problems, but they're much less represented at higher levels—which is where the influence of machismo comes in. A male comrade will often object to his partner travelling so much, or going to meetings in the capital. Family life imposes restrictions that impede women's broader participation at state and national level. All the same, even though we haven't adopted a quota system, 40 per cent of the 21 comrades on the national executive committee are women—and they got there by contesting elections against men, and not just because we'd saved places for them.

In terms of class, the rural population has been classified in many ways—structuralists say one thing, ECLA-types another, Marxists a third. In our movement, we try to use terminologies that take account of the fact that there are a great many *lumpens* in the country areas—the numbers living in misery there have risen with the economic crisis. The agrarian proletariat constitutes around a third of the rural population, but their numbers are dropping sharply with mechanization. They're still a strong force in sugar-cane production, in São Paulo and Pernambuco, but in cacao farming the organized workforce has virtually been destroyed. There are a lot of wage-workers in cattle-rearing, but they're widely scattered, which makes it difficult for them to organize. The same goes for large-scale agribusiness—soya or orange production, for instance: a ranch of 10,000 hectares, or 25,000 acres, with ten tractors, will produce a lot; but there will only be ten employees, who will never be able to provide a solid basis for a union. Then there is the classically defined layer of small farmers, the *campesinato*—those who work with their families on a little bit of land, whether it belongs to them or not. Of this fraction, a third are landless—our base of four million families. They work as share-croppers, or tenants; or they could be farmers' children, who need to earn a wage. Another third—again, around four million families—are small farmer-proprietors, owning up to 50 hectares, about 125 acres. There is also an agrarian petty bourgeoisie, whose properties can vary from 50 hectares in some regions to 500, or 1,250 acres. Over that—the big ranchers and landowners—we'd consider as part of the agrarian bourgeoisie.

According to the Gini index, Brazil has the highest concentration of land ownership in the world. One per cent of the proprietors—around 40,000 of the biggest ranchers, or *latifundiários*—own 46 per cent of the land, some 360 million hectares, in *fazendas* of over 2,000 hectares, more than 5,000 acres each. In general, these are either occupied by livestock or entirely unproductive. Below them, the agrarian bourgeoisie own another 30 million hectares, roughly 75 million acres, on properties of between 500 and 2,000 hectares (1,200 to 5,000 acres); this is the most modernized sector, producing soya, oranges, coffee. The holdings of the small farmers—under 100 hectares, or around 250 acres—produce mainly for subsistence, selling a small surplus at markets.

In which areas has the Sem Terra Movement been involved most actively—Rio Grande, São Paulo, Nordeste, Mato Grosso, Goiás?

The regions where the social struggle is at its broadest are those where there's the greatest concentration of landless people—in the North-East and the South. For the press, though—and, sometimes, for Brazilian public opinion—it seems as if most of the confrontations take place in the North or the West-Central region. The reason is that 'Brazilian civilization' has yet to arrive in those parts—in Pará or Rondônia—and the ranchers and landowners exercise a lot more violence: assassinating union leaders, using the police to do their bidding. This ultra-brutality is more entrenched in those regions, but that doesn't mean the struggles there have the same breadth as those in the North-East and the South.

I wanted to ask you about something not generally raised by the press—the question of fear. Do you or the farmers ever get scared during land occupations?

Collective actions release energy—there's a physical surge of adrenaline, and who knows what else, medical experts say. The occupation itself is a festival. The fear comes with the evictions, especially when the balance of forces is all on their side. If there are 50 or 100 families facing several hundred shock troops it can be very frightening—they'll lash out at the squatters indiscriminately, women and children too. It's a terrible, fraught situation, with the children screaming and the women getting beaten about. Evictions of small groups of squatters are often tragedies—they impose such a degree of humiliation on the families involved. That's why we always try to stage large-scale actions—they have a much better chance of success. But with the growing social crisis, we're running into difficulties. In many regions, the poverty is so bad and, since the landless movement's gained a reputation, sometimes communities just organize themselves and squat on some land, thinking it'll work. They don't realize the movement has accumulated some vital experience, which it can pass on. The police turn up with their batons and they get evicted in the most brutal way.

What do you consider the greatest successes of the MST?

By the simple fact of existing for 18 years, a farmers' movement that contests the ruling class in this country can consider itself something of a triumph—it's longer than any previous one has lasted. We've won some economic victories: the lives of the 350,000 families that have occupied land are improving—they may still be poor, but things are getting better. But maybe the greatest success is the dignity the Sem Terra farmers have won for themselves. They can walk with their heads held high, with a sense of self-respect. They know what they're fighting for. They don't let questions go unanswered. That's the greatest victory. No one can take that class consciousness away.

There have been other actions that have made a big impact in folk-lore terms, so to speak, like the Giacometti occupation, or the march to Brasília in 1997, when nearly 1,500 comrades covered 1,500 kilome-tres—a thousand miles—in a few months. That was an epic, too. No mass movement had ever marched such a distance before—the Prestes Column, so important in our history, was on horseback, or in cars.[6] It was a heroic moment when we arrived in Brasília. There were over a hundred thousand people waiting for us there—not just the local people but trade-unionists and CUT and PT members who had come from all over the country. The march had a big impact in terms of winning over public opinion. A large part of this was due to Sebastião Salgado and his photographs. The 'Terra' exhibition was a worldwide success, and it gave the Sem Terra Movement a global visibility in the field of the arts, without the need for an ideological discourse. Salgado's images launched us internationally, and for that we're very grateful to him.

When did the MST decide to start organizing in the favelas, as well as in the countryside? What kinds of action are possible in urban areas?

Organizing in the favelas isn't our principal work—there hasn't been a shift of emphasis to the cities. But because the South-East is highly urbanized, a lot of the rural working class has been absorbed into

---

[6] Luís Carlos Prestes (1899–1990): army captain who led a column of insurgents several thousand miles across Brazil in the late 1920s; later leader of the Brazilian Communist Party (PCB) until his death.

the *lumpenproletariat*, living on the outskirts—our social base from the country transplanted to the city. We have an obligation to them still, so we have to go to the favelas, to try to organize them. It's for that reason that our work in the cities is mainly in the South-East—São Paulo, Rio de Janeiro, Minas.

From the realities of organizing there, our activists have come up with a new proposal: what they call 'rurban' settlements—*assentamentos rurbanos*. Instead of grabbing a guy who lives on the outskirts and dropping him into the depths of the countryside, we set up encampments closer to the city, on small lots. These are people who are used to a more urban way of life—as opposed to a farmer from the North-East, who wants 15 hectares (35 acres). Here in the South-East that's a vast amount of land. So we get them lots of one hectare, two or three acres, where they can do more labour-intensive sorts of farming, such as fruit-growing or chicken-rearing, combined with local agroindustrial work for the women and children, so they still have some connexion to agriculture. The kids can study computing and work in the administration of a milk or fruit concern, for example. We're discussing this with some of the regional governments, to see if it's viable. In São Paulo, we're working on an experimental settlement project with three hundred families, in partnership with the city Prefecture. There are already 'rurban' settlements like this in other states.

Will this still involve land occupations?

Yes, the struggle will be triggered by occupations, but maybe not in such a dramatic manner. For example, in São Paulo, there was a land occupation on the Anhanguera road out of the city—to a farmer's eyes, there were 10 or 15 hectares, nearly 40 acres, lying totally abandoned—but it's not necessarily the typical unproductive cattle-ranch. There are places close to the city that could be put to better social use, too, and in those sorts of cases there'll be a different focus to the occupations.

Will they follow a similar pattern to those in the country?

The form is similar—occupations have to have a mass character, they have to take place at night, they have to protect the squatters. It's the political work of raising consciousness that's different. Favela people have another sort of culture, with its own habits and vices and pleasures. Working with them is much faster. The farmer is more of a Doubting Thomas, he wants to take it slowly, to try things out. He needs to visit a settlement to see if it works. People on the city outskirts are more in touch with the mass media and the rest of the world, they're quicker to absorb new information and debate things—and also more readily distracted.

What has been the rate and rhythm of growth of the MST—continuous expansion, or sporadic? Has there been any regression in numbers since the early 1980s?

We've grown, but the rhythm has depended on the balance of forces— when the landowners or the government have had the upper hand, our rate of growth has dropped. For the last two years we've made very few gains, despite the fact that we now have a substantial presence as a movement, because the Cardoso government has been drawing us into one fight after another, trying to force us onto the defensive politically. We've resolved to assault their neoliberal programme, and they're deter- mined to defeat us.

How would you assess the record of the Cardoso presidency on the agrarian question, compared with the Sarney (1984–89), Collor (1990–92) or Itamar Franco (1992–94) periods?

The struggle for agrarian reform in Brazil—and the growth of the Sem Terra Movement itself—can't be measured solely in terms of numbers of families settled on land. Our struggle is a social and political one: some- times we win victories that can't be measured in terms of hectares, and sometimes we occupy a lot of land but the cumulative political effect is not so great. It's very complex, but we'd make the following analysis. The Sarney administration in 1984 was faced with the great social ferment that followed the fall of the dictatorship. These were highly favourable times for agrarian struggles. There were lots of land occupations. Brazil's ruling class was in crisis: industry had come to a halt and the old economic model had failed. They didn't know where to go next, which resulted in the elections of 1989. The enemy was weak in this period and we could move forward. The MST was born in 1984, but consolidated during the Sarney years.

Collor's victory in '89, and the implementation of the first neoliberal measures, put an end to any hopes for agrarian reform. Collor wanted to crush us. He set the federal police on us—for two years we had to eat whatever bread the devil kneaded, as we say. Many of our state-level headquarters were raided. There was even an attempt to kidnap me from outside our national office. A comrade from the CUT who looks a lot like me was seized, taken away and tortured. He was only released when they looked at his documents and realized they had the wrong person. The UDR had grown in strength, and there were a lot of assassinations between 1990 and 1992.[7] They were terrible years for us. There was little organic growth, it was more a question of keeping going. Instead of our slogan 'Occupy, Resist, Produce', it was more like 'Get beaten up and hold out'. Fortunately, Globo TV brought Collor down once they realized he was just a *lumpen*-bourgeois. Then came the period of transition, under Itamar Franco. He certainly had no plans for agrarian reform, but he did stop the repression—the boot was lifted, and we began to resurface. The two years under Itamar were a time of restoring our energies. We made few gains, and there were not many new settlements. It was a hybrid government, with no political will and no programme of its own.

The Cardoso administration underestimated the agrarian issue initially, in '94. Cardoso was being advised by Francisco Graziano da Silva,

---

[7] UDR: União Democrática Republicana, an organization of ranch-owners and agrarian capitalists, modelled on the Ku Klux Klan.

whose doctoral thesis 'The Tragedy of Land' set out to prove there were neither large land-holdings nor landless farmers in Brazil. Cardoso wrote a preface for the book when it was published—it had a strong influence on him. Then came the Rondônia and Carajás massacres and he got a fright—as did the ruling class—at the scale of the social problem they revealed.[8] They were as stunned as roaches, as the saying goes. It was a much better period for us in terms of morale—after the Carajás massacre, the government had to give in to the public outcry at the treatment of the Sem Terra. They had no way of repressing us. We had a stronger position in society and that helped us a great deal. There were lots of land occupations between '96 and '98, even though the neoliberal programme Cardoso was implementing didn't seem to offer much hope for land expropriations or agrarian reform.

When Cardoso won his second term in '98, he put his foot down. The transition to the new economic model had been consolidated. In agriculture, the entry of international capital was put on the fast track, together with what they call the application of the North American model to Brazilian farming, and the internationalization of our food production. The concentration of land and agro-industry in the hands of large-scale capital was speeded up. All agricultural trade is now under the control of the multinationals. The public sector has disappeared— going against the First World's actual practice of developing agriculture through strong state support. Instead, the Cardoso administration has put everything in the hands of the market. The INCRA budget was three billion reales in 1997; in 2001 it was down to 1 billion. There is no more technical assistance, no more state stockpiling, no more funding, no more government research; Embrapa has been scrapped.[9] Clearly, there is no room for land expropriation or popular agrarian reform.

Over the last three years we have been faced with a situation similar to the Collor period, only worse in that the neoliberal model is widely

---

[8] Rural workers were killed by the police in Corumbiara, Rondônia on 9 August 1995 and at Eldorado dos Carajás on 17 April 1996.
[9] Embrapa: Brazilian State Agricultural Research body.

accepted now. At the same time, the fight of the landless has been trans-formed into a much wider class question. It's this that has made us recognize that we, too, need to broaden our struggle, as we decided at our last Congress in 2000. We'll carry on squatting land, because that's the only way for families to resolve their immediate problems—to have a place where they can work. But if we are to move towards popular agrar-ian reform we have to confront the neoliberal programme itself, and that can't be done by land occupations alone. For that reason, the Sem Terra Movement has joined other farmers' organizations to combat the multinationals in milk production and, especially, GM seeds. They are the most extreme expression of the extension of the multinationals' con-trol under the new economic model. In five years' time, all the seeds Brazilian farmers need to plant could be owned by the big corporations. The country's food sovereignty is in jeopardy.

That's our assessment of the Cardoso Presidency—a government that has subordinated itself completely to the interests of international capital, and has imposed that surrender on Brazilian agriculture. The Sem Terra have only escaped because over the last 18 years we've man-aged to build a social movement with a coherent ideology and a layer of activists. If we had been the usual type of farmers' movement, they would have wiped us out. The avalanche of propaganda against the lan-dless farmers in the media, the economic offensives against us, the attempts to suffocate us, to flatten us along with our settlements—all this has been impressive. For three years not a single newspaper has spoken well of the MST—it's just attack, attack, attack. What's saved us has been the support of the social forces that don't believe their propa-ganda, and protect us. Otherwise they would have finished us long ago.

What specific measures has the state taken to repress the MST? Have assassi-nations and arbitrary imprisonments decreased under Cardoso, or gone up?

The number of brutal killings has gone down under Cardoso, partly because Brazilian society has been more vigilant and partly because we've given increasing priority to mass struggles. Under Collor and Sarney, most of the assassinations were of union presidents—it was easier for the ranch-owners or the police to pick off a figurehead. Some 1,600 people have been killed in agrarian conflicts since 1984, but only about a hundred of these were Sem Terra members—most of them at Carajás and Rondônia. The point to stress—and I don't say this to boast: on the contrary, we share the grief and solidarity for those comrades from other organizations who were killed—is that our form of mass organization protects our members and activists, our committee structure and collective leadership shelters our leaders, and deters assassinations. This has been an important factor for the drop in the number of killings during Cardoso's second term.

Instead, they've taken up cannier, more disguised forms of repression, linked to the intelligence services. Firstly, Cardoso has reorganized the federal police, setting up new departments specializing in agrarian conflict in each state, with inspectors who are experts on the Movement— they've read more of our literature than most of our activists, since it's their professional duty; they're Sem Terra PhDs. This is basically a reconstruction of the rual DOPS of the dictatorship years.[10] Their officials keep opening inquiries on us, so the MST's energies are constantly being wasted on protecting its activists from the federal police. They listen in on our phone lines and they've stepped up surveillance on our leadership. The ranch-owners are no longer at liberty just to have us bumped-off, but there are men following us like shadows. Our leaders have to be rock-solid in their beliefs, because it's a terrible drain on their energies.

The second form of repression we're facing is through the judiciary, where the PSDB government and the land-owners have a lot of influence. They use the courts as a way to grind us down. Last week I spent a day in the prison in Mãe do Rio, a small municipality in Pará, where fourteen of our comrades have been held for 31 days, without charge, in a cell measuring 4 by 6 metres, while the judge systematically denies

---

[11] DOPS: Department of Political and Social Order

them the right of habeus corpus. They were in a group of 300 families, occupying unused ranch-land belonging to Jader Barbalho.[11] It's clear the local judiciary is under Barbalho's influence, and he's openly told the newspapers that the MST should be taught a lesson: 'They'll see who they've got mixed up with'. So the 14 comrades have been held for a month, and the movement's energies have been spent on getting them freed rather than on the struggle for land.

The third form of repression I've already mentioned: the concerted use of the media against us, the attempt to stigmatize us among broad layers of society, and especially among the least politicized sectors of the urban lower-middle class—the readers of Veja, which is very heavily biased against us.[12] Fortunately, the impoverished working class don't read *Veja*. But the way the media are systematically ranged against us by the Palácio de Planalto, in order to conduct a permanent campaign against us, is no less a form of repression.

What is your opinion of Cardoso as a person, president and statesman?

As a person, I think he was betrayed by his enormous vanity—everyone who's had a long-term association with him testifies to that. It's led him to renege on whatever principles he may have had, as an intellectual—or at least, that his academic reputation suggested. As a president, he's been no more than a mouthpiece for a ruling class that's given up on national goals, and united around the programme of becoming the foreman for international capital on Brazilian territory. As a statesman? I've never heard anyone call him that—he's never had the dignity to represent the Brazilian people. At most, he represents a bourgeoisie that lives here, but has no national project—so he could never even constitute himself as a statesman in terms of his own class. History will be right to categorize him as the great traitor of the Brazilian people.

---

[11] A key Cardoso lieutenant in Congress, president of the Senate, forced to resign after corruption scandals.
[12] *Veja*: the largest circulation news weekly in Brazil.

Who do you, and the MST, feel closest to internationally, on agrarian questions? How would you compare the MST to the EZLN?

Our relations with the Zapatistas are simply those of solidarity. Their struggle is a just one, but its social base and its method are different to ours. Theirs is, at root, a struggle of indigenous peoples for autonomy—and if there's a criticism to be made of their experience, it would be that the slowness of their advance is due to their inability to broaden it into a class struggle, a national one. They have accepted the terms of fighting for a specific ethnicity, within a particular territory—whereas ours is a farmers' movement that has been transformed and politicized as a result of the advance of capitalism, of neoliberalism. If the fight we're carrying on today had been waged in the 1930s—if Brazilian farmers had been able to organize then as well as they can now—it would have just been a movement for agrarian reform, seeking only to meet the needs of its own sector.

On the international plane, the context is far broader, politically. The Sem Terra have made a modest, but proud, contribution to the international network of farmers' movements, Via Campesina, which has a presence in 87 countries. There have been several international meetings and congresses, the last in 2001 in India. It is very striking that it is only now that farmers are starting to achieve a degree of worldwide coordination, after five hundred years of capitalist development. Workers have had an international day for over a century, and women for not much less, but farmers have only just agreed to mark one—17 April, a source of pride to us: a tribute to Carajás. As long as capitalism meant only industrialization, those who worked on the land limited their struggle to the local level. But as the realities of neoliberal internationalization have been imposed on us, we've begun to hear stories from farmers in the Philippines, Malaysia, South Africa, Mexico, France, all facing the same problems—and the same exploiters. The Indians are up against Monsanto, just as we are in Brazil, and Mexico, and France. It's the same handful of companies—seven groups, in total, worldwide—that monopolize agricultural trade, and control research and biotechnology, and are tightening their ownership of the planet's seeds. The new phase of capitalism has itself created the conditions for farmers to unite against the neoliberal model.

In Via Campesina, we're building a platform independent of the particular tendencies of the farmers' movements within each country. One plank on which we agree, at the international level, is that there must be the sort of agrarian reform that would democratize the land—both as a basis for political democracy, and for building an agriculture of another kind. This has major implications. From the time of Zapata in Mexico, or of Julião in Brazil, the inspiration for agrarian reform was the idea that the land belonged to those who worked it. Today we need to go beyond this. It's not enough to argue that if you work the land, you have proprietary rights over it. The Vietnamese and Indian farmers have contributed a lot to our debates on this. They have a different view of agriculture, and of nature—one that we've tried to synthesize in Via Campesina. We want an agrarian practice that transforms farmers into guardians of the land, and a different way of farming, that ensures an ecological equilibrium and also guarantees that land is not seen as private property.

The second plank is the concept of food sovereignty. This brings us into head-on collision with international capital, which wants free markets. We maintain that every people, no matter how small, has the right to produce their own food. Agricultural trade should be subordinated to this greater right. Only the surplus should be traded, and that only bilaterally. We are against the WTO, and against the monopolization of world agricultural trade by the multinational corporations. As José Martí would say: a people that cannot produce its own food are slaves; they don't have the slightest freedom. If a society doesn't produce what it eats, it will always be dependent on someone else.

The third plank we are working on for the Via Campesina programme is the idea that seeds are the property of humankind—agricultural techniques cannot be patented. Biotechnology is a good thing. Scientists can develop things in the laboratory that would take nature millions of years to evolve. But it's only a good thing if these developments are democratized, if everyone has access to them, and if there are proper safeguards for the environment and for human health. This is not the case with GM technology. No scientist is prepared to give an absolute assurance as to what the effects of cloned animals and genetically modified seeds could be, so they should be restricted to experiments in laboratories, in limited areas, and their use shouldn't be extended until we're completely certain. The history of BSE should have taught us this.

Something that's not much known abroad is that, between 1998 and 1999, Cardoso pushed through a patent law granting the right to private ownership of living beings. The first draft was circulated to Congress in English, because the American Embassy that had imposed the programme on Brazil didn't even bother to translate it. Locally, it was the handiwork of Ney Suassana, the current Minister of National Integration and notorious for toadying to the US. Once the government had bent to their masters and the law was approved, the Institute of Biology here received 2,940 applications for patents, 97 per cent of which were from multinational corporations who wanted property rights over an Amazonian butterfly or some sort of shrub. It sounds absurd. But exactly the same thing is going on in India, Chile, the Philippines, South Africa—despite the illusion that the ANC would be a progressive government, it's a neoliberal administration, just like Brazil.

What has been the contribution to the Sem Terra movement of environmentalists and other democratic activists from outside the ranks of the landless?

There are many currents in the environmentalist movement, some very sectarian—sometimes a farmer cuts down a tree on an encampment, and there's a flurry of denunciations—but in general the majority of the groups here have helped us, including Greenpeace, which I find the liveliest. They've taken up the fight against GM technology, and they've been helping us raise people's consciousness on that. We've built a grand coalition on the issue with all the environmental movements in

Brazil. There's a division of labour: some of the groups involved work in the juridical sphere, others—such as Greenpeace—on propaganda, and we organize mass actions. Today we occupied a 1,200-hectare—3,000 acre—property in Rio Grande do Sul where all the soya was genetically modified. There were 1,500 young people there and it turned into an educational exercise for them. After an intensive, five-day course on GM plants, they had a practical lesson in destroying a genetically modified soya crop. I think our involvement has also managed to politicize the environmental movements a bit more. Two or three years ago, they were still only focusing on animals in danger of extinction, or defending the forest, when here in the Third World, humans are the living beings most at risk.

What is the position of the MST on the use of violence for social ends—including, specifically, agrarian reform?

We have a tradition of ideological pluralism within the movement, in the sense that we never claim to be the followers of any one thinker—we try to treat each one as synthesizing a particular historical experience, and to see how we can make use of them. As far as violence is concerned, we've learnt a lot from two Asians: Ho Chi Minh and Gandhi. Ho was the only one who's managed to defeat the USA. He systematically taught the Vietnamese peasants that their strength lay not in what they held in their hands, but in what they carried in their heads. The achievements of the Vietnamese soldier—a farmer, illiterate and poor—came from his being conscious of what he was fighting for, as a soldier and as a man. Everything he could lay hold of, he turned into a weapon. The other main lesson we've learned is to raise people's consciousness, so that they realize it's our vast numbers that constitute our strength. That was what Gandhi taught us—through the Indians' Salt March against the British, for instance. If we ever decided to use the same weapons as our enemies, we would be doomed to defeat.

What is the best help that direct-action groups and NGOs in North America and Europe can give to the MST and sister movements?

The first thing is to bring down your neoliberal governments. Second, help us to get rid of foreign debt. As long as we're still financially dependent—which is what the plunder of 'debt' represents—it won't be possible to construct economic models that meet the needs of our population. Third, fight—build mass struggles. Don't delude yourself that because you have a higher living standard than us, you can build a better world. It's impossible for you to maintain your current patterns of consumption without exploiting us, so you have to battle to change the type of consumerism that you're caught up in. Fourth, stop importing Brazilian agricultural products that represent nothing but exploitation: wood, mahogany—all that wooden furniture in England made with Amazonian timber. What's the point of campaigning to save the rain-forest if your governments and companies carry on boosting the saw-mills and timber-yards that are exporting its wood to you? Again, stop buying soya to feed your mad cows—let the people here have a chance to organize agricultural production to guarantee our own food needs first. Fifty-six million people in this country go hungry every day.

What is the relationship of the Sem Terra Movement to the Brazilian Left in general, and in particular to the Partido dos Trabalhadores?

The MST has historical connexions to the PT—both were born during the same time period. In the countryside there are many activists who helped to form the PT and work for the MST, and vice versa. There's been a natural overlap of giving mutual assistance, while always maintaining a certain autonomy. The majority of our activists, when they opt for a party, generally choose the PT, but there are Sem Terra farmers affiliated to the Partido Socialista Brasileiro, and to Lionel Brizola's Partido Democrático Trabalhista—though not to the PCdoB, because it's adopted the classic line of forming its own farmers' movement, the

Movimento de Luta de Terra. Those who came up through the struggle with us but sympathized with the PCdoB automatically preferred to join that.[13] Another reason for the predominance of the PT.

The MST is autonomous from the PT, but at election time we've traditionally supported their candidates, as they're the major left party. But we feel that the Brazilian Left in general is going through a period of crisis at the moment, presenting difficulties for organic left accumulation—irrespective of the electoral results of any one set of party initials, or of the diverse currents within the PT. The crisis is a complex one. Firstly, the Left has no clear project for Brazil—or it falls into the simplification of socialism versus capitalism, without managing to formulate clearly what first steps socialists should take. Secondly, the institutionalization of the parties and currents has distanced them from the mass movements. It seems that the Left has forgotten that the only force that can bring social change is the organized mass of the people, and that people organize themselves through struggle, not through the vote. A vote is an expression of citizenship, not a form of struggle. The Left has to regain the belief that we alone are going to alter the balance of forces, through mass struggles against the bourgeoisie. There is always a preference for negotiations, for accommodating to class pressures.

A third criticism—and this is also a form of self-criticism, because we consider ourselves as part of the Left: we need to recover our predecessors' tradition of grass-roots work, the microscopic business of organizing people—something the Church talks about a great deal. Activists no longer have the patience to conduct meetings with depoliticized people. I don't know how the mass political parties used to do this work historically in England and Europe. Often when we speak of propaganda, it's really only agitation, the sort carried out by the Trotskyists here in Brazil; but they don't raise consciousness, they don't organize—often they simply give up. One constantly hears criticism of this sort of thing: the trade-union leadership calls demonstrations for the 1st of May, which even the union president doesn't attend, let alone the members.

---

[13] PCdoB: founded in 1961, a Maoist split from the PCB.

The fourth point is the question of political education. It's very rare for movements of the Left to maintain a consistent education programme for their militants, in the broadest sense. Activists need to read the classics, so they can master the tools necessary for a correct interpretation of reality. The Left here has simply abandoned the classics and even, from a theoretical perspective, the study of Brazilian reality itself. It's lazy when it comes to analyzing its own situation, its contradictions, the class struggle, the living conditions of the working class. It falls back on generalizations which it doesn't understand, and is unable to explain. We need to recover the sense of a theoretical training for activism, without resorting to theoreticism. We need to marry theoretical education with political practice. It's pitiful to see where our young people end up, even those affiliated to the PT or the CUT—as if the only thing for young people to do today was hold music festivals or campaign for the legalization of cannabis. The Brazilian Left needs to overcome those challenges in order to reconstitute, in the not-too-distant future, a great mass movement with the consistent, revolutionary aim of an alternative project for our society.

THE GLOBAL SOUTH

Could you tell us about your education and family background?

I was born in Manila, in 1945. My father was in the movie business in the Philippines, and involved in advertising and entertainment. My mother was a singer and composer—both of them were interested in the arts. My father read widely. The story goes that he was immersed in Thoreau when I was born, and decided to name me Walden; though I have two or three Spanish names as well. My parents were both Spanish-speakers, but they didn't transmit it to us—English was more or less the first language in our household when I was growing up. I had two other Philippine languages, but just spoken ones, not written. I was taught by Jesuits, from first grade through to college graduation, and my initial radicalization was a reaction against that conservative educational system—the Jesuit schools in the Philippines essentially catered for the children of the elite. I wasn't from that background, and was instinctively opposed to their strict class bias, in a pre-political way.

This was prior to the development of liberation theology?

There were only a handful of people from the university who took up radical positions in the early part of the Marcos period. For the most part, the Jesuit system has been a fairly efficient producer of ruling-class minds. As in Latin America, a layer of Christians with a national-liberation perspective did emerge from some of the religious orders, especially the relatively newer ones, such as the Redemptorists. But that never predominated among the Jesuits. I knew them all, and very few of them—maybe eight or ten—ever embraced a progressive politics. The Jesuits always had a liberal façade; but in terms of their education and the people they produced, they were really quite conservative.

What did you do after graduation?

Upper-class education in the Philippines led automatically either to a corporate career with the multinationals, or into law and government. I didn't want to be trapped in either—at least, not so soon. So I went down to Sulu and taught in a college in Jolo for about a year. There I got involved in discussions with Muslim intellectuals—people who would go on to form the Mindanao National Liberation Front, in which a number of my students later became active too. I was in sympathy with their analysis of a systematic discrimination against Muslims in the Philippines, although I might not have supported outright secession.

After that I worked for a few years as publications director of the Institute of Philippine Culture, which had been set up by anthropologists from the University of Chicago. Their approach was highly empirical but their ideas about Filipino social structure and behavioural patterns still had a lot of influence. They were closely linked to the US Agency for International Development. At that time, a huge proportion of American funding for social-science research came from the military. People would go to the Philippines—to places like the IPC—on US naval-research grants. This was in the second half of the sixties, at the height of the war against Vietnam—but the social scientists there still claimed their research had no military application. It was a highly politicizing moment for me, in understanding how the system worked: that there was no distinction at all between this sort of funding and academic research.

Was this the time of Marcos's re-election?

I left for post-graduate studies at Princeton just before the elections in '69—it was a vicious campaign. These were momentous times. In 1970 there was the so-called First Quarter Storm in the Philippines, with the rise of the student movement. But it was the American student struggle against the war in Vietnam that really politicized me, in the United States itself. My next important experience was going down to Chile for my doctoral research in 1972. I was attracted by Allende's constitutional road to socialism, and wanted to study political mobilization in the shanty towns. I spent a couple of months working with Communists organizing in the local communities, but as soon as I arrived I realized that the correlation of forces had already shifted: it was now the counter-revolution that was in the ascendant. So I ended up re-focusing both my academic work and political interests on the emergence of the reaction in Chile. Coming from the Third World, this wasn't easy to do. If you weren't Chilean, and were brown-skinned, you tended to be marked down as a Cuban agent. That got me into trouble a number of times.

The dissertation developed into a comparative study of counter-revolution in Germany, Italy and Chile. It acknowledged the role of the CIA, but put equal, if not greater, weight on domestic class forces in explaining the consolidation of the anti-Allende bloc. The experience gave me a healthy scepticism—running clean against much standard American political science on developing countries—about the democratic role of the middle class. I could see that this was a very ambivalent layer.

By the time I got back to the US to defend my thesis in early '73, Marcos had declared martial law, and the Filipino community in the States was in uproar. It was then that I first became active in exile Filipino politics. Various groups were forming. There was a Movement for a Free Philippines, associated with Senator Raúl Manglapus, one of the stalwarts of the elite opposition to Marcos who had fled to the US straight after the declaration of martial law. A number of Americans, some of them specialists in the area, set up a group called the Friends of the Filipino People; among them was Daniel Schirmer from Boston, who had just written *Republic or Empire*. I gravitated towards the Union of Democratic Filipinos—the Katipunan ng Demokratikong Pilipino (KDP)—which was allied to the Communist Party of the Philippines and the New People's Army.

Given the direct relationship between the US and the martial-law regime, which you analyzed at the time in Logistics of Repression,[1] *how far did the broad Left in the Philippines see its fight as a national liberation movement, rather than simply opposition to military rule?*

Marcos, of course, claimed that the rising revolutionary movement was his central reason for declaring martial law, saying it demanded a tough centralized response. His other pretext was what he called the 'democratic stalemate'—a stand-off between the traditional elite and the Left, which he maintained hampered development. The Communist Party of the Philippines had been refounded in 1968—the 'old' CP was regarded as hopelessly compromised and pro-Soviet—and in March 1969 formed the New People's Army, based essentially in central and north-eastern Luzon. Its strategy was classically Maoist: create liberated areas in the countryside, treating the towns as a secondary front, mainly important for recruiting people to the NPA. So when Marcos imposed martial law, there was already a very active, revived Philippine Left.

Could you go back to the Philippines after '72?

No—when I tried to renew my passport in '74 or '75, it was confiscated without explanation. So I was effectively stateless for the next several years. The KDP was now the central focus of my life. I taught at the City College in San Francisco, the State University of New York, and at Berkeley for about four years—not in order to pursue an academic career, but to survive. I joined the CPP and ended up wherever they sent me: New York, San Francisco, Washington. But I was also developing

---

[1] *The Logistics of Repression: The Role of US Aid in Consolidating the Martial Law Regime in the Philippines*, Washington, DC 1977.

an area of analysis and writing that didn't automatically reflect the party's priorities, but that I felt was important for understanding what was
really going on. Most of the Left weren't very interested in the World
Bank at the time, but I had a sense that, for a variety of strategic reasons, it was absolutely critical. One of the biggest development projects
in the Philippines was a nuclear-power plant; that got me interested in
energy issues more generally. In 1979 Peter Hayes, an Australian, Lyuba
Zarskey and I set up the Nautilus Institute, to research the intersections
between energy and politics. It still exists today, but I was mainly associated with it in the eighties, when we produced documentation on the
nuclear plant in the Philippines, and then went on to look at US deployments and military structure in the Pacific.[2]

It was when we were researching the question of US bilateral aid to
Marcos that we realized how much of it was being channelled through
the World Bank. The role of multilateral institutions—and the Bank in
particular—in the Philippines dwarfed direct American support. That's
where my own interest began. I had no formal background in economics;
it was all on-the-job training. Figuring out the contours of this comprehensive development strategy became a passionate, all-consuming task, that
eventually led to a book, *Development Debacle*. I began to realize that the
process had a dynamic of its own, powered by a very specific ideology.

In the Philippines, the years from 1980 to 1986 were marked by a
combination of economic crisis and dwindling regime legitimacy. The
South was badly hit by the world recession of '82. Marcos lost a lot of
his local power base, and became increasingly reliant on the multilaterals and US support. At the turn of the decade, the World Bank forced
Marcos to appoint a cabinet of technocrats to protect its more open-
market model of export-oriented production from the depredations of his
cronies. Before '83, the Americans' great fear had been that the opposition to Marcos might fall under the sway of the NPA, since the oligarchic

---

[2] See 'Marcos and the World Bank', *Pacific Research*, vol. 7, no. 6, 1976; *Development
Debacle: The World Bank in the Philippines*, San Francisco 1982; *American Lake:
Perils of the Nuclear Pacific*, London 1987.

alternative was weak and fragmented—its main leader, Benigno Aquino, was out of the country—and the Left appeared to be largely hegemonic in the resistance to martial law. That changed in 1983, when Aquino returned and was assassinated. His martyrdom revived middle-class and elite opposition, which was gradually able to win the initiative away from the Left.

From then on, Marcos became a thorn in the side of the United States. He didn't want to open up the system, and wouldn't agree to the various suggestions from Washington that he should incorporate the illegal opposition into substantive political roles. The tensions between the two came to a head in early 1986, when the US pushed Marcos into holding elections, and he stole them. The result was to trigger middle-class and elite civil resistance, and an uprising with military backing took place. In Washington functionaries like Michael Armacost, the State Department official responsible for the area, took alarm when Marcos prepared to bombard the rebels, and the US stepped in. Marcos was flown out to Hawaii, and Corazon Aquino was installed in power, to popular acclaim. In effect, oligarchic democracy was restored in the Philippines. The CPP, which had boycotted the elections of 1986, arguing they were just a façade to let Marcos to stay in power, was a bystander as these events unfolded. This was one of the reasons for the eventual marginalization of the Left from the mainstream of political life in the country.

What did you do after the fall of Marcos?

When I went back to Manila, I joined the faculty at the University of the Philippines. By then I was more interested in working on broader issues—the role of multilaterals, the Asian development model, the newly industrializing countries—than in specifically national concerns. From the late eighties I was involved with a number of organizations—the Philippine Resource Centre, Food First, Oxfam and Greenpeace—in a personal capacity, rather than in connexion with the CPP. It was not that I was disillusioned at a general level, but I felt that the Left in the archipelago was out of touch with both local and world realities. The purge of the New People's Army in the mid-eighties, when it executed many of its own militants in a panic over infiltration by spies from the military—I wrote about this—made me question a number of the movement's philosophical assumptions, about class and the individual.[3] Its miscalculation over the elections of 1986 also had a big impact on me.

Was it at this stage that you founded Focus on the Global South?

We wanted to establish an institute that would look at Asian economic, political and ecological issues, linking them into the broader picture. We based it in Bangkok, partly for reasons of cost, and partly because of conditions for research and analysis there not to be found elsewhere in Asia. Also, Philippine NGOs have a way, naturally enough, of absorbing people into local issues, while we wanted to concentrate on regional and global work. Examining World Bank development models and other patterns of domination had made me increasingly aware that these couldn't simply be challenged at the national level. Whether it was a question of opposing the US military, or the World Bank or IMF or multinational corporations, it was crucial to begin creating cross-regional links. When the movement in the Philippines succeeded—helped by various contingent factors—in getting the American bases shut down in the early nineties, a number of us warned that, unless we changed the military equation in the region, the victory would not last very long. It didn't change, and today US troops are back in the Philippines with a vengeance. National movements, important as they are, have to combine with the creation of regional and global movements. Traditional paradigms of international solidarity are no longer appropriate in the current situation.

Who else did you draw into Focus on the Global South?

Kamal Malhotra, from India, was my co-director. The people who helped set us up in Bangkok were Thai scholars, like Suthy Prasartsert, who

---

[3] 'The Crisis of the Philippine Progressive Movement', *Kasarinlan*, vol. 5, no. 1 (1992).

made a very important intellectual contribution. We were also in touch with the Korean movement, and people like Muto Ichiyo in Japan. Quite a few of these have come onto the board of Focus, which we've tried to make as diverse as possible. So far as the name goes, although we started from Asian and Pacific issues, our horizons were always the global patterns of domination and resistance.

On the question of terminology: do you see problems in defining, or reclaiming, words like 'South' and 'North' or 'development' and 'globalization', which international institutions often deploy in a mystifying way?

I hope Focus hasn't contributed to this. We have always been sceptical about the word 'development': capitalist development would be a clearer phrase, and we usually speak of 'corporate-driven globalization', tying it to the dynamics of world capitalism. I resisted using 'globalization' at all at first; people were tossing it about in such a rhetorical fashion that it obscured the real class forces involved. In fact, all these terms tend to be used much too loosely. I was appalled when Oxfam branded some of its allies as 'globaphobes', distorting everything they were fighting for. So far as 'North' and 'South' are concerned, a distinction between the super-industrialized, advanced countries and the rest of the world—or between the centre of the global capitalist economy and its periphery—is clearly valid. At the same time, unequal relations of the North–South type are reproduced within the North itself, while there are Third World elites in the South whose economic interests and lifestyles are closely integrated with the North. So we've tried to inflect these terms in a more nuanced way.

Could you describe the activities of Focus?

Our work has been dictated by the priorities of the global struggle. Trade is a major axis. International trade relations, and organizations like the WTO, have become so central to the structuring of the global economy that they demand special attention. 'Security issues' are a second axis—that is, tracking the emergent patterns of US military and political hegemony, especially in the Asia–Pacific region, and helping to build resistance. We also look at the ways in which local elites—globally, as well as more specifically in South and East Asia—become integrated into the strategic system. A third area is civil society. We examine the different facets of the popular organizations it harbours, their tremendous potential contribution to democratization, but also their strong tendency to be co-opted and to impose their own agenda on broader movements. Finally, we look at the role of ideologies. Many of the ultra-simplistic conceptualizations of Islam broadcast by CNN and the like are being naïvely reproduced by people in the South. We wanted to adopt a more critical perspective on the various aspects of Islamic revivalism. Bearing in mind its many retrograde elements, we still need to ask: why has it been in the forefront of the struggle against the United States? But Muslim 'fundamentalism' is not the only sort we discuss—we look at Hindu and Christian versions too. Still, the two key institutions to which we always come back are the WTO and the Pentagon. One of our criticisms of the movement against corporate globalization is its tendency to de-link the economic logic of the multinationals and WTO from American military dominance. We need to understand how the two connect—which also means trying to bring together two different movements.

In concrete terms, much of our research and analysis comes out in Focus publications. Take a look at our website—www.focusweb.org—and you'll see the range of what we do. We organize conferences, particularly on financial, trade and military issues. We work to bring together the global movements—in particular, the peace movements and the anti-corporate globalization campaigns. We are also involved in what bureaucrats call a 'capacity-building' role. The Vietnamese government got in touch with us to discuss whether or not they should join the WTO. We gave them a great deal of technical information about the Organization that demonstrated how and why it would be a disaster if they did. One of our jobs is to keep grass-roots communities and national organizations, including some governments, informed about the workings of global institutions. In the process, we get to hear about a lot of interesting initiatives from the grass roots. For instance, there have been efforts in Thailand to bypass the national currency system; people have set up their own common currencies in some of the regions. In Argentina and Chile too, they are improvising barter systems giving local people more control over trade. There's a two-way process of learning in this sort of work.

How are you funded?

We have more than 20 funders, including European NGOs like NOVIB, Oxfam, Inter Pares and Development and Peace in Canada. We also get some money from the Ford Foundation and other outfits on a project-by-project basis. We have several principles about this. Firstly, we diversify our funding—no more than 20 per cent should come from any one source, to guarantee our independence, and to make sure we don't tie our financial survival to just one or two funders. Secondly, we need to make sure that there are no strings attached. Thirdly, no funding from the US state. Fourthly, with other governments and institutions, our board always considers proposals on a case-by-case basis. So far, it's worked quite well. For instance, although we receive a lot of funding from Oxfam, and respect many aspects of their work, our 20-per-cent and no-strings-attached rules have allowed us to be very open in our criticisms of their market-access campaign and recent Trade Report, which argues that it is the access of Southern countries to Northern markets which is the critical problem of the global trade regime.

What are your differences here?

We don't agree that market access is the key issue—to pose it as such effectively supports the paradigm of export-oriented growth, and presupposes a quid pro quo of open Southern markets. Moreover, Oxfam's campaign actively deflects the movement from far more important problems. The overriding priority right now is to oppose the WTO's push for a wider mandate. Its current agenda is to consolidate the concessions extracted from the developing countries at Doha in order to make the fifth round in Mexico next year a springboard for broadening the WTO's scope to include investment, government procurement and competition policy—an expansion whose scale would rival the Uruguay Round. This is what the opponents of neoliberalism should be concentrating on: increasing the domestic pressure on the real areas of conflict within the WTO, exacerbating the differences over steel tariffs and farming subsidies. Its formal requirement for consensus is a weakness we should try to exploit—it means that talks can founder. In that sense, the *Economist* is right: corporate-driven globalization is reversible.

How would you summarize your own critique of the WTO ?

The WTO is an opaque, unrepresentative and undemocratic organization driven by a free-trade ideology which, wherever its recipes—liberalization, privatization, deregulation—have been applied over the past twenty years to re-engineer Third World economies, has generated only greater poverty and inequality. That's the first point: implementation of neo-liberal dogmas leads to great suffering. Secondly, the WTO is not an independent body but a representative of American state and corporate interests. Its development has been closely linked to the changing needs of the United States, which has moved from supporting a weak GATT to promoting a muscular WTO as a nominally multilateral order with strong enforcement rules. Neither the EU nor Japan were particular partisans of the WTO when it was founded, at the behest of the Clinton administration. The American state is very flexible in how it pursues its ends—it can be multilateral when it wants to, and uni-lateral at the same time. The Achilles heel of the WTO is its secretive, undemocratic, oligarchic decision-making structure. This is where we should take aim.

What would you propose as a positive alternative to the WTO regime?

What we call for is deglobalization—hopefully, the term won't contribute to the confusion; I still think it's a useful one. If you have a centralized institution imposing a one-size-fits-all model across the globe, it eliminates the space for developing countries to determine their economic strategies themselves. The use of trade policy for industrialization is now banned by the WTO. Yet if you look at the experience of the newly industrializing countries—of Latin America in the sixties and the seventies, say—the reason they were able to achieve a modicum of capitalist development was precisely because they had that room for manoeuvre. We believe that the WTO and similar bodies need to be weakened, if not eliminated entirely. Other international institutions, such as UNCTAD—the UN Conference on Trade and Development, which was performing reasonably well until the rug was pulled out from under it by the WTO—should be strengthened, as should regional organizations like MERCOSUR, which has the potential for being an effective, locally directed import-substitution bloc. Regional financial institutions need to be created, too. If the Asian Monetary Fund had existed in 1997 and '98—when it was pushed by all the countries in the region—the course of the Asian financial crisis would have been different. Instead, the idea was killed off by Rubin and Summers, as a challenge to the hegemony of the IMF.

In world terms, then, we call for greater decentralization, greater pluralism, more checks and balances. In a less globalized order, grass-roots groups and popular movements would be in a stronger position to determine economic strategies. At the moment, local elites can always say, 'We have no choice but to follow this course—if we don't, the IMF or WTO will rule our policy protectionist'. Focus on the Global South is not against trade; well managed, an increase in imports and exports could be a good thing. But in the Third World the pendulum has swung so far in the direction of export-oriented production, that it does need to be corrected back towards the domestic market—the balance between the two has been lost in the drive to internationalize our economies. We can only do that if we structure trade not through WTO open-market rules but by practices that are negotiated among different parties, with varying interests. Deglobalization doesn't imply an uncritical acceptance of existing regional organizations. Some of them are merely outposts of the globalized economy, common markets controlled by local technocrats and industrial elites. Others could sustain a genuine regional development programme.

What would deglobalization mean for finance?

The deregulated character of global finance has been responsible for much of the instability that has rocked our economies since the late eighties. We definitely need capital controls, both at regional and local level. In different ways, the experiences of Malaysia, Chile and China have all shown their efficacy. What's required is an Asian monetary mechanism that would not only support countries whose currencies are under attack, but would also begin to furnish a basis for regional control. As to a world monetary authority, I am very sceptical of its viability as way of controlling global finance, since these centralized structures are now so permeable by the existing market powers, especially the big central banks. I don't think such an institution would provide an effective defence of the interests of Third World countries. I have never believed that access to foreign capital was the strategic factor in development, although it can be a supplementary one. In fact, our local elites—locked as they are into the existing international order—typically have tremendous reserves of capital. The problem is whether governments in the region have the ability to impose capital controls on them. The same goes for tax regimes, which in South-East Asia are very retrograde. Of course, the wealth of these elites should be subject to proper taxation.

Land reform?

The distribution of land remains a central issue. One reason why export-oriented production could be pushed so successfully by the World Bank in the seventies, and had such strong support from local establishments and technocrats, was that the markets in developing countries were so limited, precisely because of highly unequal asset and income distributions. A focus on exports was seen by the elites as a way out of the trap of shrunken local markets—attaching your industrialization to the big market outside. It was a way to dodge the massive land reform needed to create—in Keynesian terms—the local purchasing power that could drive an indigenous process of industrialization. So agrarian reform is a necessity throughout Asia, as well as Latin America, for both social and economic reasons.

From Seattle onwards it's been clear that a critical fault line within the movement runs between those, essentially Northern, activists and organizations who group themselves around a combination of environmental and labour-rights issues—the position you've described as Green protectionism—and those in the South who see development in a much wider sense as the main priority. It would clearly be an illusion to think that these two perspectives could fit together easily. Yet if the movement is to develop, this tension has somehow to be negotiated and resolved.

The fault line is real, though I would point out that there are large areas of agreement between Northern and Southern movements—a shared critique of multinationals and global capital, a common perception that citizens need to play a stronger role in curbing the rules of the market and of trade. The fact that people from both tendencies can come together in coalitions and work on a range of points is testimony to the strength of these overlapping interests. However, I think the labour question has to be worked out. We were very critical of the way that trade unions in the US—and, to a great extent, in Europe, through the ICFTU—argued that the WTO would be strengthened if it took up tariffs and labour rights.[4] In our view they should not be calling for a more powerful WTO. That's a very short-sighted response. Beneath the surface rhetoric about human rights in the South, this is essentially a protectionist movement, aimed at safeguarding Northern jobs. Whenever we raise this in a fraternal way, they get very defensive about it. We say, let's cut out the hypocrisy: of course we should fight for the jobs of workers in the North—but in a way that supports working-class movements everywhere; not so as to protect one section and leave the rest aside. We need to work out long-term strategies to respond to the way that capital is re-stratifying the working class throughout the world—a division in which hundreds of millions of rural workers get the short end of the stick. The dynamics of global capital are creating a vast underclass, with no support from Northern unions. This is where we need to focus our strategy, on a powerful, visionary effort to organize the world working class. So far, the response from the North—especially from the trade unions—has been a very defensive one, hiding behind the mask of human rights. It makes us deeply uneasy when people from our countries, who have been strongly supportive of workers' rights and have actively opposed ecologically damaging development policies, are cast in these polemics as anti-environmentalist and anti-labour.

Market access is not the central problem, but it is *a* problem. There is a tendency in the North—though not all Green organizations fall into this—to use environmental standards as a way of banning goods from developing countries, either on the grounds of the product itself or because of the production methods. The result is a form of discrimination. We need to find a more positive solution to this. We've called for a global Marshall Plan—one in which environmental groups would actively participate—to upgrade production methods in the South and

---

[4] ICFTU: International Confederation of Free Trade Unions.

accelerate the transfer of Green technology. The focus should be on supporting indigenous Green organizations in developing countries and
this sort of positive technological transfer, rather than on sanctions.
Sanctions are so easy—they appeal to defensive, protectionist interests,
which even some progressive organizations in the North have taken
up. It's very unfortunate that the US labour movement has adopted
this hypocritical stance, saying that it's really concerned about people
in China, whereas in fact its objectives are quite egotistical. If we can
get past this sort of pretence and establish a dialogue at the level of
principles, on the interests of the global working class as a whole, we'll
be moving forward.

*How far do you regard the World Social Forum in Brazil as a representative
arena in which these differences can be hammered out?*

When the idea of a global forum was first broached, Focus was one of the
organizations that immediately gave its full support. What the Brazilians
were proposing was a safe space where people in the movement could
come together to affirm their solidarity. This was a very important element of the first Social Forum in 2001. There was a strong sense of
the need to talk about alternatives, after Seattle. I think there were real
efforts to integrate people from Southern movements, both within the
organizing structure and on the panels, although this might not have
been successful everywhere. Vandana Shiva and others from the South
were brought in from the start, not in a paternalistic way but so they
could make genuine suggestions about who should be there. It's true
that *Le Monde Diplomatique* and ATTAC played an important part in
bringing it together, and the support of the PT state government was
fairly crucial. But while ATTAC and *Le Monde Diplomatique* were still
vital players in the second Forum, they had a much less central role.
If anything, it has been the Brazilian NGOs, civil-society groups and
the PT that have, not dominated, but been the moving force. One very
positive thing they've done since the first Social Forum is to create an

international committee, where regional-representation questions can be discussed. Most Third World participants are still Latin Americans, though, and there is a need to bring Africans and Asians into the process—which is why the Brazilians themselves have proposed that the next one could be held in India.

It's true that in many of the panels the main speakers, figures like Noam Chomsky and Immanuel Wallerstein, have come from the North. But I don't object to that because we have benefited so much from their work. Others like Rigoberta Menchú and Samir Amin also played a central role. We do need more people from the South—this is a developing process. But the real function is to have a space, every year or two, to be able to get together and exchange viewpoints, in a safe atmosphere—not just another protest demonstration. The main focus now should be on developing the battle of ideas at the WSF. It shouldn't be a love-fest where people with different positions all pretend to agree. We need to get beyond that, to sharpen our ideas about alternatives, not settle for peaceful coexistence.

Would you envisage a time over the next four or five years when the WSF might organize collective actions? So far we've seen very big, single protests in particular spots—Seattle, Prague, Washington. But there's another level beyond that, of synchronized global campaigns on specific issues. Or would that imply too great a degree of centralized coordination?

I don't think the WSF is structured for that sort of thing. What it has principally tried to do is to bring people together to discuss alternatives and affirm their sense of solidarity, and it would be very difficult to transform it into a fighting organization along the lines of, say, Our World is Not for Sale. It needs to be an all-inclusive forum, where people who might not be able to agree on medium-level strategic factors can nevertheless still come and have a good, clarifying debate. What I would hope is that all these different movements and coalitions feel that it's inclusive enough to provide a yearly or bi-yearly arena where strategies and tactics can be discussed, not just ideas about alternatives. It's in the coalitions, a step below the Social Forum, that these actual strategies will be hammered out. The Our World is Not For Sale coalition is now leading an effort to derail the next WTO ministerial. 50 Years is Enough, which has also played a key role in the WSF, is organizing against the IMF and the World Bank. The campaign around sweatshops and Nike is very dynamic—it could emerge as the principal anti-corporate network. The anti-war movement is being reborn. It's these coalitions, rather than the WSF, that could be the axis of a brains-trust on global strategies.

You speak of the World Social Forum being all-inclusive, but doesn't this run the risk that it might share the fate of the Non-Aligned Movement, where the noble original objectives of the Bandung conference eventually degenerated to the point where you had Suharto and his ilk hob-nobbing with leaders who were genuinely trying to better the world, making it a meaningless spectacle? The worst of these butchers always turned up, seizing the opportunity to burnish their Third World credentials. Mutatis mutandis, this last Social Forum was decorated by all kinds of centre-left politicians from Italy, France and elsewhere, who'd been ardently cheering on the war against terrorism, the attack on Afghanistan.

Yes, I would fully agree that this is a danger. A number of the people who showed up at Porto Alegre were there just to polish up their progressive credentials, even while playing a pernicious role at home. At the same time, I think the Forum will become more discriminating about whom it invites. With those who simply turn up, it's more difficult. But quite a few of those politicians were not asked to speak. Some World Bank officials came and *demanded* a platform, and were told, 'No. You can speak elsewhere in the world but this is not your space.' Then their spokesman went out and told the *Economist*, 'I was banned, this is a denial of free speech'. So, of course, the *Economist* took it up.

There is another challenge: how to remain independent of the established political parties. At present, the Forum's centre of gravity continues to lie in the social movements—despite the leading role of the PT, it hasn't attempted to bring in like-minded political parties. But now there is a danger that the old Centre-Left and socialist parties are looking at the WSF and wondering how they can harvest such a rich crop of grass-roots organizations. In a number of places, we're seeing efforts to establish social forums with political groups of a more traditional sort in charge.

What has been the effect of September 11 on the movement as a whole? The business press has triumphantly declared it a death-blow to the anti-globalization campaign, since it showed that anti-capitalist demagogy always leads to violent protests in the streets, which lead straight to terrorism; now 9.11 has fortunately had a sobering effect. Many activists were indeed very disorientated or dispirited, partly by the way in which the war on terrorism captured broad attention, but also by the fact that the movement itself was not well-equipped to respond to it. You alluded earlier to the disconnexion between the campaign against corporate-driven globalization, which targets multinationals as the enemy, and the pattern of military deployments and structures of the US state, felt by some to be a divisive issue that is best kept off the movement's agenda. So perhaps it didn't have the resources for an immediate response, when confronted with this reality. How serious a setback has all this been?

The initial impact of September 11 was extremely disorientating, especially when the World Bank and IMF cancelled their meeting that month in Washington, which they were delighted to do. Thanks to Al Qaeda, they then managed to override both grass-roots protests and the qualms of developing countries and ram through the WTO's declaration at Doha—when previously, there had been a 50–50 chance that we could have stopped it. There is no denying this was a defeat. At the same time, there have been some countervailing developments. Firstly, Enron erupted; one should not underestimate the delegitimizing role that played, in taking the wind out of the triumphalism and the ideological push that followed September 11. Secondly, there's been the ongoing crisis in Argentina, a social and economic catastrophe brought about by neoliberalism. Both have reignited a widespread scepticism about the corporate-globalization project. Thirdly, there has been the United States' own performance. The Pentagon still hasn't managed to get bin Laden, and is now becoming over-extended in areas from which it will be difficult for the US to extricate itself. Going into Iraq will create even greater problems.

Given the tensions in South Asia and the conflict in the Middle East, it's arguable that the strategic situation of the United States is probably worse now than it was prior to September 11, precisely because of this over-extension. The American response has served to strengthen Islamic-fundamentalist tendencies rather than reduce them. Mahathir and Musharraf are bending over backwards for the United States, but a big gulf is emerging between these leaders and their populations. Finally, I think there has been an evolution in the role of many of the anti-corporate globalization groups, who are now beginning to confront issues of warfare and militarism. In the recent conflict in Palestine we had quite a number of people trying to break through Israeli lines.

There were 50,000 people at the World Social Forum this year, as opposed to 15,000 in January 2001. At the EU summit this March in Barcelona, there were 300,000 protesters—much bigger than Genoa. There's a lot of work to be done before we get back to the situation we were in prior to September, but there are several indications that the movement is on its way back to a fighting stance. One example of this is that, when the US sent troops to the Philippines in January, we put out an appeal for people to participate in an international peace mission, and got so many volunteers that we were able to mount a full-scale investigation: to go to Basilan, study the situation, talk to people—including the Americans—and come back with a critical report that was lambasted by the Philippines government, and became an issue in the archipelago's politics. This was an instance of people who had simply been concerned with trade questions moving towards broader security-related issues.

The Euro-parliamentarian, Matti Wuori, who went to Basilan is a former head of Greenpeace; these are the sort of links and transformations that are being made.

You often allude to class politics, not all that common in the anti-globalization movement. Where do you see your intellectual tradition today coming from?

I would say I've been a pragmatist, working with whatever seemed useful to the task in hand. That obviously includes the theoretical arsenal of Marxism. But I wouldn't call myself a Leninist any longer, because I think the crisis that hit the Communist societies was related to the elitist character of Leninist vanguard organizations. One can understand the historical reasons why they emerged, in repressive situations, but when they become permanent and develop theoretical justifications for their lack of internal democracy, they can become a really negative force. I have been attracted to aspects of the new movement—its decentralized form, its strong anti-bureaucratic impulses and its working through of the ideas of direct democracy, in the spirit of Rousseau—whether one labels that anarchism or not. Still, at this stage I think the movement's most valuable contribution is its critique of corporate-driven globalization, rather than the model it offers for coming together and making decisions. But there is a global crisis of representative democracy throughout the West today, as well as in countries like the Philippines. The movement does represent an alternative to this. Can direct democracy work? It did in Seattle and Genoa; so we should ask how we can develop it further. How might we—I hate to use the word—institutionalize methods of direct democratic rule?

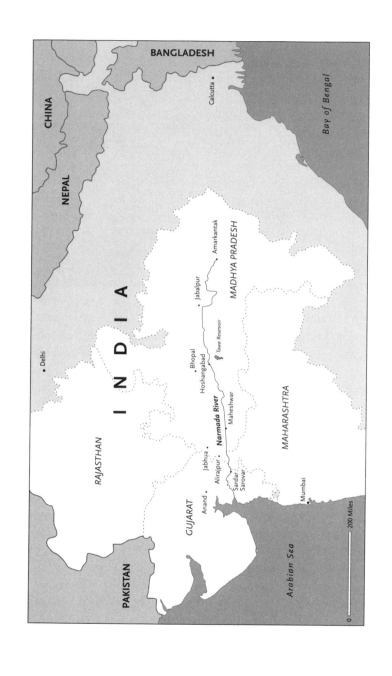

CHITTAROOPA PALIT

MONSOON RISINGS

Mega-Dam Resistance in the Narmada Valley

What were your family origins and early influences?

I was born in 1964, to a middle-class Bengali family. My father was an engineer in the Indian Railways and my mother was a college lecturer. My father's work took us all over India, so I learnt early on about the country's extraordinary ecological and geographical variety, and how different communities, tribals and poor farmers, lived and worked. As a child I developed a strong sense of identification with the underprivileged—with the people who worked in our house and the children I played with in the railway colonies. Growing up, I also began to chafe against the confines of the typical feminine role. Love of literature—prose and poetry—opened my mind and made me something of a romantic; a streak that eventually pushed me towards work in the villages. But at Delhi University—I studied at Indraprastha College, a women's college there, from 1981 to '84—I read economics.

At the time I was a strong China fan, full of admiration for the Long March and Mao's dictums of 'going to the countryside' and 'living with the people'. I wasn't attracted to any of the left-affiliated student organizations though, because of their insistence on following the party line, which seemed to me antithetical to the freedom to think things through for oneself. So I stayed away from the Students' Federation of India—the student wing of the CPI(M), the largest left party—although many of my friends were in it. But my incipient Maoism was undermined by 1989. I was deeply shocked at the Tiananmen Square massacre. It taught me to be a lot more cautious and reinforced my determination to work things through for myself. Mine was a rough-and-ready Marxism, more inspired by humanistic values and Marx's historical and early, idealistic writings than by his economic analysis, even though I was studying economics. Feminism had a more direct impact on me, partly because it is something you get involved in not individually but collectively, with other women. Groups like Saheli and the Boston Women's Collective, who held a workshop in Delhi, made me far more aware of my body and of sexual politics in general. It became an everyday question for me. Issues of human dignity—and the systems that deny it—seem even more important than questions of wages and material well-being. But it was the student environmentalist group, Kalpraviksh, which means the Tree of Imagination, that first exposed me to the Narmada Valley's concerns. In 1984, they produced a path-breaking report on the dam projects there.

After college I did a postgraduate course at the Institute of Rural Management in Anand, Gujarat, where there is a strong tradition of rural cooperatives. Then, with an NGO called Professional Assistance to Development Action, I worked for two years with women and children in the slums of Jabalpur, in Madhya Pradesh. I soon rejected the IRMA/ PRADAN approach, however. They believed the only reason development was not working was the lack of professional input: if we provided this, poverty would magically vanish. It was an analysis that utterly failed to address questions of social structure or history. In 1988, I left to join a group called Khedut Mazdoor Chetna Sangat, the Organization for Awareness among Peasants and Workers, operating in the Narmada Valley tribal district of Jhabua, in Madhya Pradesh. The KMCS had been set up in 1982 and was mainly composed of young activists—architects, engineers and so on—who had rejected professional careers and were trying, in some small way, to contribute to social transformation.

Could you tell us about the Narmada Valley Development Project, and how the opposition to it started?

The Narmada River itself flows westwards across Central India over a course of some 800 miles, rising in the Maikal hills, near Amarkantak, and cutting down between the Vindhya and Satpura ranges to reach the Arabian Sea at Baruch, 200 miles or so north of Mumbai. It is regarded as a goddess by many of those who live along its banks—the mere sight of its waters is supposed to wash one clean of sins. The Valley dwellers are adjured, once in their lifetime, to perform a *parikrama* along its course—walking up one side of the river to its source, and back down the other. The Narmada runs through three different states—Madhya Pradesh, Maharashtra, Gujarat—and its social and physical geography is incredibly diverse. From the eastern hills it broadens out over wide alluvial plains between Jabalpur and Harda, where the villages are quite highly stratified and occupied by farming communities and fishermen. Between Harda and Omkareshwar, and again between Badwani and Tanchala, steep, forested hills close in once more, mainly inhabited by tribal or *adivasi* peoples—the Kols, Gonds, Korkus, Bhils and Bhilalas. On the plains, there are Gujars, Patidars, Bharuds and Sirwis, as well as Dalits and boat people—the Kewats, Kahars, Dhimars and others.

Although over 3,300 big dams have been built in India since Independence, the Narmada Valley Development is one of the largest projects of all, involving two multipurpose mega-dams—Sardar Sarovar, in Gujarat, and the Narmada Sagar, in Madhya Pradesh—that combine irrigation, power and flood-control functions; plus another 30 big dams and 135 medium-sized ones. The four state governments involved—the non-riparian Rajasthan as well as the other three—have seen the Narmada's waters simply as loot, to be divided among themselves. In 1979, the Dispute Tribunal that had been adjudicating between them announced its Award—18.25 million acre feet to Madhya Pradesh, 9 to Gujarat, 0.5 to Rajasthan and 0.25 to Maharashtra—and prescribed how high the dams must be to ensure this distribution. There was no question of discussing the matter with the communities that had lived along the river for centuries, let alone respecting their riparian rights.

Even before this, in the seventies, a Save the Soil campaign—*Mitti Bachao Abhiyan*—had arisen in the Hoshangabad district of Madhya Pradesh, in response to the large-scale water-logging and salinization of the rich black earth around the Tawa dam, part of the NVDP. The protest was Gandhian and environmentalist in character but rooted in the farming communities of the area. In 1979, a huge though short-lived popular movement arose against the Narmada Award, led by mainstream politicians, many from the Madhya Pradesh Congress Party—including Shankar Dayal Sharma, a future president of India, who was jailed for protesting against the height of the dam. But when they got into office, these leaders compromised completely, which led to much bitterness among the Valley communities and made it harder to start organizing from scratch again.

Nevertheless, by the mid-eighties there were several groups working in the Valley. In 1985, Medha Patkar and others formed the Narmada Ghati Dharangrast Samiti in Maharashtra, working with some thirty-three tribal villages at risk from the Sardar Sarovar dam. They demanded proper rehabilitation and the right to be informed about which areas were to be submerged. It was natural for them to link up with us in the KMCS, on the north bank of the river. There was also a Gandhian group called the Narmada Ghati Nav Nirman Samiti that worked in the villages of the Nimad plains in Madhya Pradesh. Their leader was a former state finance minister, Kashinath Trivedi. They undertook numerous 'long treks', or *padyatras*, to inform the villagers about the impact of the Sardar Sarovar dam, advocating an alternative 'small is beautiful' approach. The Jesuit fathers had also been doing ongoing work in the Gujarat area. The NBA—the Save Narmada Movement, or *Narmada Bachao Andolan*—emerged from the confluence of all these protests, though the name was only officially adopted after 1989. Medha Patkar played a central role in uniting these initiatives, across the three different states.

But though the Narmada movement started with protests around rehabilitation for the villagers affected by the Sardar Sarovar project, within three years it had become plain that they were facing a much greater problem. The Narmada Tribunal Award had specified that those displaced by the dams should be recompensed with land of equal extent and quality, preferably in the newly irrigated area—the command zone—before any submergence took place. By 1988, the villagers had learnt from their own bitter experience that there was no such land available. As the mass mobilization spread eastwards from Maharashtra to the tribal and plains villages of Madhya Pradesh, it became clear that this was going to be an even worse problem further upstream. There was growing anger at the complete denial of the villagers' right to information by the state and central governments, combined with a deepening awareness of the environmental destruction that was being planned— and of the existence of viable alternatives. During the summer of 1988 there was a tremendous churning of resistance, with a series of meetings and mass consultations. In August 1988, the NBA called a series of simultaneous rallies in villages throughout the Valley, where the villagers proclaimed that they were no longer merely demanding proper rehabilitation—that they would fight the Sardar Sarovar dam itself.

Could you elaborate on the alternatives to the big-dam project, and the NBA's critique of the development paradigm?

We found that there were perfectly viable, decentralized methods of water-harvesting that could be used in the area. Tarun Bharat Sangh and Rajendra Singh of Rajasthan were able to revive long dried-up rivers in almost desert-like conditions by mobilizing local villagers' collective efforts to build tanks on a large scale. In Gujarat, remarkable pioneering work inspired by Prem Bhatia, Pandurang Athwale and Shyamji Antale has recharged thousands of wells and small water-harvesting structures using low-cost techniques. For a maximum cost of Rs. 10 million each—less than $220,000—the problems of Gujarat's 9,000 water-scarce villages could largely be solved, with a total outlay of Rs. 90 billion, or $1.9 billion. Whereas the official figure for the Sardar Sarovar dam alone—almost certainly an underestimate—is at least Rs. 200 billion, over $4 billion.

Contrary to the Gujarat government's promises that Sardar Sarovar would provide for the state's two most drought-prone regions, Kutch and Saurashtra, we found that only 1.5 per cent of Kutch's total cultivable area was slated for the water, and only 7 per cent in Saurashtra. Most of it would go to the politically influential, water-rich areas of central Gujarat. Yet sugar mills were already being constructed in anticipation of water-guzzling sugar-cane crops. Aqua parks and tourist resorts had also been planned; they and the urban centres would take the lion's share of the Narmada waters. The entire political economy of the dam project was beginning to unravel in front of us.

Huge multipurpose dams are full of contradictions. Their flood-control function demands that the reservoir be kept empty during the monsoon; yet irrigation requires stored water and, in turn, drains off the vast amounts required by hydroelectricity. Newly irrigated lands are often used to grow thirsty cash crops instead of traditional staples for direct consumption, leaving farming families at the mercy of the global market. There is also a huge ecological price to pay. In India, land irrigated by well water is twice as productive as that fed by canals—these raise the water table excessively, causing water-logging and salinization. Up to a fifth of the world's irrigated land is salt-affected. Dams have also eliminated or endangered a fifth of the world's freshwater fish. The Land Acquisition Act of 1894, originally passed by the British, allows for the confiscation of properties on grounds of 'public interest'. The NBA challenges the Narmada land expropriations on the basis that the public interest clearly isn't served.

If you look at the various Narmada projects it's obvious that these aren't based on any real assessment of needs, or even on an integrated view of the river valley. I doubt that the government has a consolidated map of all the command and submergence zones that have been planned. The entire approach has been fragmentary, based on a concept of impoundment. This is true not only of the Narmada dams but of many other such developments, including the Linking of Rivers Project that the BJP government is now pushing—an insane proposal, both socially and ecologically. It represents an intensification of the neoliberal programme of enclosing the commons: appropriating the rivers from the common people as a precursor to their takeover by global corporations for large-scale trade in water and energy markets. The NBA has opposed this destruction of forests and rivers, and the communities who have lived along their banks for centuries, in the name of 'development'. At village meetings sometimes 30,000 strong we've highlighted the role of the Indian state and private capital, domestic and foreign, in this process of commodifying public goods—asking who pays and who benefits. This won us new friends but also new enemies, since the elites who stood to gain from the dam began to target the NBA as 'anti-development'.

The NBA campaign famously forced the World Bank to withdraw from the Sardar Sarovar project. Can you describe how this momentum was built?

In 1985, when the central bureaucracy in Delhi began to raise questions about Sardar Sarovar, the World Bank stepped in with a $450 million loan for the dam. The intervention made a nonsense of the Bank's customary defence for its funding of environmentally dubious projects—that these were matters upon which national governments must decide. The truth is that the Bank itself pushes for such projects and, in this instance, merely proposed 'better' rehabilitation policies. Though some NGOs worked with them to develop such practices for the oustees in Gujarat, the NBA refused to collaborate. The people of the Valley suffered terribly under the terms of the World Bank loan. Before each instalment was disbursed, the Bank demanded that certain conditions be met—specific villages evacuated, surveys completed, data gathered—and the state governments of Madhya Pradesh, Maharashtra and Gujarat translated this timetable into a series of brutal assaults, with police opening fire on NBA protesters, making numerous arrests and even attacking pregnant women. Every time a World Bank deadline loomed, we knew repression in the Valley would intensify.

By the late eighties, the Bank was facing growing criticism over its support for dam construction—from the southern-based International Rivers Network, Brazilian protest groups and northern NGOs such as Friends of the Earth. Northern environmentalists lobbied their governments, questioning what the public money going to the World Bank was being used for. As the international movement developed, our resistance strengthened too. In 1990, a huge rally in Manibeli, Maharashtra—the first village due to be inundated by the Sardar Sarovar project—passed an 'international declaration' against the World Bank. The turning point came in 1991, when we launched a mass 'struggle trek', or *sangharsh yatra*, to Gujarat, to protest against the dam. Nearly 7,000 people walked in the bitter cold of winter. We were stopped at the state border, a place called Ferkuwa. The trekkers set up camp there and seven people, including Medha, went on an indefinite fast. It was at this point that the World Bank gave way, and agreed to an independent review on the Sardar Sarovar project—the first in its history.

The Review's research team—led by Bradford Morse, a former UN Development Project head—spent a year and a half in India, travelling through the Valley and meeting everyone from bureaucrats to NGOs and villagers. Sometimes we resented their pointed questions, their whiteness, the fact that a team from the West could pass judgement on what was happening here. But the Morse Report, when it came out, was excellent. It argued that, given the lack of available agricultural land and political will, proper rehabilitation would be impossible; and that to push the project through in these circumstances would lead to an unmitigated disaster. Plans for Sardar Sarovar were fundamentally flawed on environmental and hydrological grounds, and its benefits had been greatly exaggerated. The World Bank was indicted for its self-deluding incrementalist approach—presuming that things would improve if it simply exerted more pressure. The Report's level of scholarship was outstanding, on a par with some of the treatises that early British scholars in India had written on forestry, tribes and so on.

The World Bank management responded by bringing out a document called 'The Next Steps'. This gave the Indian state six months to 'normalize' the situation, after which the Bank would take a final decision. We all knew this meant the repression would intensify. We were at a meeting in the tribal village of Kakrana, in Madhya Pradesh, when the news came through. The villagers laughed—they said that if they had been able to withstand the last ten years of brutality, the government was not going to succeed in the next six months. Sure enough, the officials and police we were supposed to be meeting with arrived within fifteen minutes of this discussion. They beat up and arrested several key activists from the area, myself included, and for the next four days subjected many of us to third-degree torture, with threats of electrocution. Over the next few months the repression escalated. There were mass arrests. Entire tribal villages, such as Anjanwada, were demolished. Homes and basic utensils were destroyed, seeds confiscated and so on. Their strategy failed. The villagers refused to relent and there were international protests against the treatment being meted out to the people of the Valley—which put even more pressure on the World Bank. In 1993, they announced they were withdrawing from the Sardar Sarovar project. The Morse Report had broken the back of the NVDP's legitimacy, though this did not stop the domestic repression. In reaction to the scrapping of the loan, the Maharashtra police opened fire on the protesters, killing a sixteen-year-old tribal boy, Rehmal Puniya.

A new phase began, with the NBA now face to face with the Indian State. In December 1994, we held yet another fast and month-long sit-in at Bhopal, the capital of Madhya Pradesh. The government there at last agreed to stop construction and, since all three states had to operate consensually, work came to a halt in Gujarat and Maharashtra as well. We had also submitted a comprehensive petition on the Narmada issue to the Indian Supreme Court earlier that year. In May 1995, the Court called for an interim stay on any further construction at Sardar Sarovar, pending its final judgement. When that came, in 2000, it was a bad blow to the movement, but there is no doubt that the temporary respite offered much-needed relief to the Narmada Valley people, who were facing enormous repression at that time.

The NBA has also succeeded in forcing foreign capital to withdraw from another dam project, at Maheshwar. How did you achieve this? What general lessons would you draw?

When construction stopped on the Sardar Sarovar site, people came to seek the NBA's help against other dam projects in the Narmada Valley. By June 1997, we were organizing people against six or seven dams— people began to connect up and share their experiences, on a pan-Valley basis. One key battle was over the Maheshwar dam in Madhya Pradesh. In 1992, this had been the first hydro-power project to be privatized— handed over to S. Kumars, an Indian textile company with no record in energy production. In line with the neoliberal policies introduced by the Indian government in the early nineties, the company was guaranteed payment by Madhya Pradesh of Rs. 600 crores, or nearly $130 million, over the next thirty-five years, whether any power was generated or not. Estimates for the project had increased five-fold by 1999, and the electricity it was set to produce had become prohibitively expensive—at least three times the cost of existing power. Meanwhile, the dam was slated to submerge or adversely affect the livelihoods of over 50,000 people in sixty-one villages. Again, the NBA argued that the project was flatly against the public interest.

Construction on the dam began in earnest in November 1997. On 11 January 1998, 24,000 people took over the Maheshwar site; thousands squatted there for the next 21 days, demanding a comprehensive review of the project, and five people went on a fast. With state elections looming, the Madhya Pradesh government agreed to halt building work and set up a Task Force to report on the dam; but as soon as the elections were over, they restarted construction. Thousands of people then re-occupied the site on two consecutive days in April 1998. We were tear-gassed and badly beaten up. More than a thousand were jailed. As we got to know the terrain better, we managed to take over the dam and stop work there eleven times over the next three years. S. Kumars and the state government responded by drafting in some 2,000 police, including paramilitaries.

In May 1998, we started another form of agitation, setting up 24-hour human barricades on the roads leading to the dam site, to stop the trucks that were delivering construction materials. Of course, we let through those with food for the workers, mostly bonded labourers from Andhra Pradesh and Orissa and themselves brutally exploited. The government, initially non-plussed, responded by a cat-and-mouse strategy—every ten days they would send in a large police force to carry out mass arrests, often with a great deal of violence, and then push through a whole convoy of trucks while we were being held in custody. Though we could not stop all the material reaching the site, the barricades helped a lot to slow the pace of construction down. The protest also mobilized large numbers of people for months on end. The leading role of women in these actions—they braved hot summers and monsoons, kept vigil in the darkest of nights, suffered violent police beatings and brutal arrests—electrified the surrounding areas and put enormous pressure on the Madhya Pradesh government. But it was clear we were getting close to the limits of human endurance, so we shifted to another strategy: barricading the finances of the dam.

There were hugely lucrative opportunities for global capital when India's energy sector was thrown open for privatization in 1991. The initial plan for the Maheshwar dam project envisaged as much as 78 per cent of the finance coming from foreign sources. After failing to clinch deals with Bechtel and PacGen, S. Kumars found two German power utilities, VEW Energie and Bayernwerk, to take 49 per cent of the equity; they were supposed to bring in tied loans to purchase, among other things, $134.15 million's worth of electro-mechanical equipment from Siemens, with an export guarantee backed by the German government—underwritten, in other words, by public money. On the Indian side, again, this would be counter-guaranteed by more state funds. This is a weak point in the privatization strategies of global capital, the chink that leaves them open to popular intervention and interrogation—not only because the use of public money creates a potential space for democratic control, but because it exposes the contradictions of corporate globalization: the absence of the 'free-market competition' and 'risk-taking' that are supposed to be the virtues of private entrepreneurship.

In April 1999, the villagers affected by the Maheshwar dam set out on a month-long demonstration and indefinite fast at Bhopal. After twenty-one days of this, Bayernwerk and VEW withdrew from the project, with Bayernwerk citing the lack of land-based rehabilitation as a major concern. In March 2000, Ogden Energy—a US power company, part of the corporate entourage of President Clinton when he visited India that spring—agreed to take over the Germans' 49 per cent stake. Over the next few months, we mounted a struggle on all fronts, involving public actions in both Germany and the US. In Germany, the campaign was led by the NGO Urgewald, run by Heffa Schücking, who succeeded in making the export guarantee for Maheshwar a major issue for the SPD–Green government. In the US, protests were mounted by the Indian diaspora, particularly students, and by groups like the International Rivers Network. We also held big demonstrations outside the German and American embassies in New Delhi. The result was that, after carrying out their own field survey, the German government refused an export guarantee for Siemens, who subsequently withdrew. In a parallel move, the Portuguese government vetoed a guarantee for Alstom–ABB's power equipment. The Maharashtra government, meanwhile, had reneged on an earlier agreement with Enron and, in light of all this, in 2001 Ogden Energy pulled out of the Maheshwar project too.

After the foreign corporations withdrew, S. Kumars tried to carry on with funds from state institutions—even though privatization had been justified in the first place on the grounds that insufficient public money was available. So in May 2002, the NBA took the struggle to the glass-fronted banks and financial corporations in Mumbai, combining dialogue with coordinated mass protests. We compiled a list of serious financial irregularities in S. Kumars' use of public money. The company got an ex-parte gagging order against the NBA, preventing us from organizing mass protests or putting out 'defamatory' press releases. But the publicity stopped the dribble of public funding that was keeping the Maheshwar project alive. All construction work came to a halt and, on 20 December 2002, the project's 'movable and immovable' properties were impounded by one of the state financial institutions that had been backing it.

We learnt a lot about the structures and processes of globalization through these struggles—and about the need for global alliances from below, to confront it. But though international political factors—the character of the governments involved, the existence of able support groups in the North—play an important part, they cannot supplant the role of a mass movement struggling on the ground. Soon after the SPD government in Berlin refused a guarantee to Siemens for Maheshwar, it agreed to underwrite the company's involvement in the Tehri dam in the Himalayas and the catastrophic Three Gorges Dam in China—both just as destructive as the Narmada project; but in neither instance were there strong mass struggles on the ground. We never thought, when we began the struggle against the Maheshwar project, that it would become such a full-fledged battle against corporate globalization and privatization. One important outcome was that we found allies in other women's groups, trade unions and left parties, who had not participated as vigorously in our earlier protests.

What role have women played in the struggle?

On 8 March 1998, we set up a separate women's organization within the NBA—the Narmada Shakti Dal. Some two-thirds of those on the dam barricades and occupations at Maheshwar were peasant women, and they also played an important role in the core decision-making group. In fact, we found that the choices that had to be made in order to sustain such a relentless struggle, in the face of growing exhaustion and terrible odds, could only be made because of the participation of women. They proved far more radical and militant than the men, and capable of more imaginative protests.

Peasant women were to the Maheshwar struggle what tribals were to Sardar Sarovar. They could give a moral leadership, firstly because their distance from the market meant that they never saw the land and the river—which they worshipped as a mother—as commodities that could be sold for cash. S. Kumars and the central government offered high levels of compensation when critical reports went against them, and that naturally attracted some of the families. But the majority refused to accept the compensation, basically because the women did not want to swap their lands for money and were prepared to fight for that position in their communities, and often in their own households. Villages like Behgaon saw the emergence of a strong women's leadership, and stand-offs within families as women pitted themselves against the men's willingness to take the money. The women prevailed and the unity of the village was preserved, at some small cost.

Secondly, the women's relative exclusion from the political system meant that their minds had not been colonized by mainstream party ideologies—they hadn't been deluded into construing their own destruction as 'development'. Nor did the power of the state leave them cynical or demoralized. Their imaginative approach kept opening up unexpected forms of struggle. For example, in January 2000, several thousand of us once again occupied the dam site. We were arrested and taken to Maheshwar jail. The authorities wanted to release us immediately but the women spontaneously refused to leave the prison until our questions had been answered. How much would the electricity from the new dam cost, compared to existing power sources? Where was the alternative agricultural land for the affected people? How much water-logging would there be in the surrounding region? How could the state government justify its huge buy-back guarantees, which protected private promoters with public funds regardless of whether any power was produced? For the next three days we locked ourselves in, while the prison wardens fled. So although we had no illusions about negotiating with the Madhya Pradesh government, we were able to establish a much broader critical consciousness about the Maheshwar project through our repeated protests and pointed questions—even among those who were in favour of more electricity.

What lessons would you draw from the NBA's experience with the Indian Supreme Court? In retrospect, do you think it was a mistake to adopt a legal approach?

Firstly, the NBA never relied entirely on a legal strategy. We always kept up a process of direct action too. For example, every year since 1991 we've organized a monsoon *satyagraha*—'urging the truth', in the Gandhian sense—in which people bodily confront the rising waters of the reservoirs, standing waist deep. Secondly, in answer to your question: no, I don't believe we made a mistake in taking the issue to the courts in 1994. We can't completely dismiss the judiciary as a ruling-class institution—it represents a contested space and, like every other space in a democracy, people have to fight to retrieve it from the elites.

Nevertheless, when we submitted our petition on the Narmada Valley project in 1994, it was to a Supreme Court substantially different from the one that delivered the final verdict in 2000. Personnel apart, the shifting political climate of the nineties has been reflected in the higher echelons of the Indian legal system. The more activist judiciary of the previous decades—which allowed for a tradition of public-interest litigation that gave access to the poor and dispossessed—has reinvented itself, and produced a string of notorious judgements over the last two years. We have seriously underestimated the extent to which our democratic institutions—the judiciary included—have been reshaped, over the past two decades, by the processes of neoliberal globalization. If these have worked, at the micro-level, by a system of incentives and rewards, they have also succeeded in imposing a larger ideological framework in which any obstacle to capital's search for super-profits—whether popular movements, environmental considerations or concerns about people's livelihood—is seen as a constraint that has to be removed. What better way to do this than through the judiciary, whose verdicts are presumed to be just and impartial, and therefore beyond criticism?

Still, the final Supreme Court ruling on our petition in 2000 came as a shock. The majority judgement argued specifically that large dams served the public interest, at the expense of only a small minority; it completely dismissed the environmental issues. In a step back from the 1979 Narmada Award, it permitted construction to proceed before people had been rehabilitated. The judges made a few trivial recommendations for improvements to existing rehabilitation sites—more swings for the children, for instance—and then ruled that the height of the Sardar Sarovar dam wall could be raised first by two metres and then by five.

For the few of us who had stayed on in Delhi to hear the Supreme Court decision, those five metres were far more than an abstract figure. The reservoir would now engulf the *adivasi* area that had lain just above the submergence level for a number of years and whose people had not been rehabilitated. We were really shocked that the judiciary—that pillar of democracy—had betrayed us. The press called us repeatedly in the evening for our comments and all we could say was that the people of the Valley would meet to decide on what to do next. Then, almost immediately, there was a TV report saying that 4,000 people had already gathered in the Narmada Valley to condemn the judgement and to decide on its implications in a united manner, 'from Jalsindhi to Jalkothi'. We couldn't understand how they could have mobilized so quickly, but it turned out that the Maheshwar project villagers had occupied the dam site that afternoon anyway, in one of their many guerrilla actions. As soon as they heard about the Sardar Sarovar decision they sent out a press release, pledging their solidarity with the people there.

Two days later, we had a meeting at Anjanwada, where the tribals of Alirajpur had assembled, as they were gathering elsewhere in the Valley. I was in such a deep depression I could hardly speak—it was like announcing a death sentence. Someone broke the ice by saying what we all already knew: that the Supreme Court had permitted a five-metre increase, on the basis of claims by the Gujarat, Madhya Pradesh and Central governments that adequate alternative land was available. Everyone began talking at once and within a few minutes the meeting had made its decision, without any disagreement: firstly, we would show those in power that we weren't mice, to be flooded out; and secondly, that we would expose the governments' land claims as false. Late that night, one of the tribal activists woke me up, one who had shared our faith in democratic structures. What happened, he asked, how could they give such a judgement? Was the fact that there was no land for our rehabilitation not clear to them? But the *adivasis* were up early the next morning, as always, laughing their inexplicable early morning laughter, displaying their characteristic mixture of stoicism and balance.

How are decisions of this sort normally taken within the NBA? How would you describe the movement's internal structures?

In the Valley itself, there are two independent centres where decision-making takes place, one in the Sardar Sarovar region and another for the Maan and Maheshwar struggles; both bring together the organic village leaderships in those areas, plus a few urban activists. Also, because the NBA is spread across three different states, a loose network is necessary, coordinated by meetings at several levels. Resistance to the dams project is predicated as a matter of survival—of life or death—for the communities of the Narmada Valley. One of the first slogans was 'Nobody will move, the dam will not be built'—*koi nahi hatega, bandh nahi banega.* When the waters began to rise, the people came up with another chant, 'We will drown, but we will not move'—*doobenge, par hatenge nahi.* Such positions have to be based on mass support and participation, rather than minority activist structures.

The rhythm of activism is also dictated by the pattern of the seasons. Every monsoon, as the people of the Valley face the rising waters, we hold a mass meeting. People from the various villages affected will come together for a whole day, sometimes two, to discuss the situation. How much submergence will take place, and how might it best be confronted? If the dam wall has been increased over the last year, what are the implications? What forms of resistance are most appropriate for each *satyagraha*? How should the logistics of wood, water, grain and transport be managed, in the context of the rising reservoir? Most of the time, we are fighting with our backs against the wall and we often have only a certain number of options to choose from—state officials to confront, buildings to occupy, sympathetic supporters to call on, and so forth. So the range of disagreement is limited and, in practice, there is a great deal of consensus about these decisions.

After each set of meetings we hold a collective consultation, in which representatives from the different regions come together to work out broader strategies for calling attention to the distress and struggle of the Valley people. Further discussion takes place on the Coordination Committee, the *samanvaya samiti*, comprised of intellectuals and activists from outside the movement who contribute to forging wider links. Ground-level resistance needs to be supported by legal initiatives and media campaigns, and by alliances at national and international levels. The NBA's attempt to question the development paradigm, for example, has involved taking the debate to the Indian middle classes, who are among the strongest supporters of the Narmada Valley project. We currently have some 60 urban support centres, in cities all over India. There have been periods over the last decade when these structures have broken down or fallen into disuse; but it is clear to us that, without widespread consultation at many levels, both inside and outside the movement, sustained collective action would be impossible.

Often, as on the question of what general course to take after the Supreme Court judgement, decisions are swift, consensual and to the point—reactions in other tribal areas were very similar, in that instance. But sometimes we cannot reach a consensus. For example, one senior activist wanted to respond to that crushing final verdict by 'immersion', or *jal samarpan*—where one remains motionless in the face of the incoming waters, up to death. This was hotly debated and opposed among the Valley people and their supporters—a stance that has so far prevented such a tactic from being deployed. In good times, we don't require formal structures, elected representatives, articulated organizational principles. But in times of crisis or vacuum, when everything else has collapsed, we see the need for them.

Can you describe some of your methods of struggle? How central is non-violence to NBA philosophy—and how frustrating has this been, in the face of state repression?

The main forms of mass struggle in the Valley have been non-violent direct actions—marches, *satyagraha* and civil disobedience. In Sardar Sarovar, for example, in the aftermath of Ferkuwa, hundreds of villages refused to allow any government official to enter. In Maheshwar, those affected by the dam have repeatedly occupied the site in the face of police repression. Other forms of *satyagraha* have involved people staying in their villages despite imminent submergence, or indefinite fasting to arouse the public conscience. State repression and indifference have often left us feeling frustrated and helpless, but I don't see that as a failure of our tactics. In an increasingly globalized world, we have to search for richer and more compelling strategies; but that does not mean compromising on the principle of non-violence, which remains fundamental for the NBA. If we fight for the inalienable right to life, and insist that such concerns should form the basis for assessing any development paradigm, how can we resort to violence? There have been a few unplanned incidents involving self-defence that cannot count as non-violent; situations where people have been pushed beyond the edge. But as a strategy, how could physical violence on our part ever match the armed might of the Indian State, or of imperialist globalization? Most importantly, only a non-violent struggle can provide the silence in which the questions we are asking can be heard. A strategy of violence results in a very different kind of political discourse.

But don't activists put their own lives at risk, through fasting and submergence?

The monsoon *satyagrahas*—where people in their hundreds stand ready to face the waters that enter their homes and fields—have to be distinguished from the practice of immersion, or *jal samarpan*. *Satyagraha* means more than putting pressure on the State—it is also a way of bearing witness to what the State is doing to the people. It affirms the existence of the Valley inhabitants and shows our solidarity. It makes a moral point, contrasting the violence of the development project with the determination of those who stand in its path. In most of the monsoon *satyagrahas* where the waters have actually flooded the houses—as in Domkhedi over the last two or three years—the police have physically dragged people out of the areas being inundated, in an attempt to rob the agitation of its symbolic power. As I have said, many of us are very critical of such methods as *jal samarpan*. We need to be alive to fight. We also need to assess whether the State can twist the issue to its own advantage by claiming that, since we are not willing to be rehabilitated, it is the protesters' own fault if we drown. Fasting is more gradual and allows us time to awaken the public conscience. But if you use the same weapons again and again, they become blunt and ineffective.

Many in the Valley now advocate seizing federal land in Madhya Pradesh for self-settlement, and as a way to expose the government. Two and a half thousand acres belong to a state farm, which the Asian Development Bank has recommended should be hived off—it may go to one of India's biggest conglomerates. So there seems to be land for corporations but none for the millions whose homes have been taken away from them in the name of the 'public interest'. Not a single person in Madhya Pradesh has been given the legally required equivalent for his land. The record is also very poor in the other two states. They say 4,000 families are being rehabilitated in Gujarat and 6,000 in Maharashtra. But there are 25 million in the Valley whose lives will be adversely affected in some way and at least 500,000 displaced by direct submergence.

How does the NBA raise its money?

Almost 40 per cent of NBA funds come from the farmers of Nimad—the relatively wealthy plains area of the Narmada Valley. After the wheat harvest, each farmer contributes a kilogram per quintal produced and there are small cash donations after the cotton harvest, too; though their prosperity is now seriously threatened by the WTO. The other 60 per cent comes from our urban supporters. Several prominent Indian artists have contributed their works to the movement, and Arundhati Roy has consistently supported us through her writings; she donated her entire Booker Prize winnings to us, three years back, and has contributed generously every year since.

We decided very early on that we would take neither government grants—why should they pay for direct opposition to their policies?—nor foreign money, save for travel costs and local hospitality when we're invited to speak. Foreign donations would expose us to all kinds of questions about the autonomy of the movement; it would also allow the Indian government to exercise some control over us, since such finance has to be routed through the External Affairs Ministry. Of course, we defend our right to call for international solidarity; but we also believe that it is possible for the resources of Indian civil society to sustain popular struggles—and that to do so builds and affirms support for the movement.

Gujarat has been the most communally polarized of Indian states—the labo-ratory of Hindutva forces where, in the wake of the most brutal and deliberate

*anti-Muslim pogrom since Independence, the BJP has been returned to power
with its greatest ever majority, over two-thirds of the vote. Is there a connexion
between Gujarati communalization and the opposition of large sections of the
population, especially its upper-caste, middle-class layers, to the NBA?*

This is a real problem in Gujarat. A change took place in the political
complexion of the state during the eighties. Middle and upper castes
came to power after the break-up of the lower-caste alliance of KHAM,
which had previously held sway in electoral politics—composed of
kshatriyas, who are not upper castes in Gujarat, *harijans*, *adivasis* and
Muslims. This new elite is far more communalized and *lumpen* than
other sections of society. There is a lesson here for people's movements
like the NBA. In spite of our work among tribals, we failed to take as seriously as we should have the issue of communalism, and the grass-roots
influence of the Right. The Sangh Parivar's continuous mobilization
among tribals over the last two decades has yielded them a rich—for the
others, a bitter—harvest of hate. This was happening all around us, but
we never fully assessed the Sangh's destructive potential and failed to
counter them. Why? I feel the problem lies in a seeming inability to offer
our own holistic political philosophy as a consistent alternative.

*At a certain point in the nineties, the NBA sought to move in the direction
of developing such a holistic agenda, connecting issues of communalism, mili-
tarization, neoliberal globalization. Was there a gap between intentions and
outcomes? Where does the NBA go from here?*

I must confess that the NBA as a collective entity has not yet sat down
and thrashed these matters out. We have taken some initiatives on
these issues—international questions, anti-globalization struggles—but
we urgently require a more concrete and coherent agenda, a collectively
evolved action plan. In any case, there is no possibility of addressing
these points on our own, without a wider alliance of movements. Since
1994, the NBA has been working with the National Alliance of People's

Movements, of which Medha Patkar is the national convenor. The NAPM has three broad currents: Gandhians, Indian Social Democrats—to the left of Euro-socialism, but unsympathetic to the official Communist parties—and people's organizations from various backgrounds, including Marxist. In Madhya Pradesh, the NBA is also part of the broad front of the Jan Sangarsh Morcha, which brings together numerous progressive organizations to challenge the World Bank and Asian Development Bank on issues such as energy, forestry and the dismantling of the public sector. But both the NAPM and JSM are at the embryonic stage—it remains to be seen whether they can combat the bankruptcy of the country's existing political structures or solve the social and ideological crisis it confronts.

Yet the real challenge is to begin from where we are, with our own constituencies. If we work only at the state or national levels, there is a real danger of losing the organic leaders who have emerged from the Narmada movement and form our real strength. There are hundreds of capable tribals, women, fisherfolk, with high levels of consciousness—the outcome of sixteen years of collective resistance. The real success of our struggle lies not only in stopping dams but in enabling such leaders to play a guiding role in broader struggles, not just against displacement, but against corporate globalization and communalism: to lead the defence of democracy in this country, and shape its economic and political future. It is the marginalized people of the Narmada Valley who know the system at its worst, and have some of the richest experiences in struggling against it. Their lives and tragedies have made them both sensitive to what is needed in the long term and courageous in their willingness to undergo whatever sacrifices prove necessary for prolonged resistance.

NJOKI NJEHU

CANCEL THE DEBT

Africa and the IMF

Where were you born, and how did you first become active?

I was born in a small village in Kenya, in 1965. Although not that far from Nairobi, it's very rural; the dirt roads are impassable when it rains. We grew up—I'm the eldest of six—without electricity, in a hard-working community of subsistence farmers, an extended kinship network of my dad's brothers and their families. People would keep a cow—my parents were unusual in having three—and grow bananas, maize, beans, kale, which we make into *sukuma wiki*, a staple in Kenya; the families that had more land would grow coffee. It has always been an opposition area which meant that, under the two and a half decades of Daniel Arap Moi's presidency, there was virtually no money for development.

I first became politically active as a teenager. My mother used to send me along to her women's group meetings, when she couldn't get to them. She would say, 'Go and tell them I'm not going to make it—and once you're there, why not stay so you can tell me what they talk about?' The women used to discuss family issues: teenage pregnancy, violence in the home, kids, the challenges they were having with their daughters; all the problems of scarce resources, and the way they had never had the opportunities for education their brothers did. I became politicized by learning what the issues were. I got to understand the environmental concerns that women had about firewood, and the loss of trees. My mum—all the women in the community—had been involved with the Greenbelt movement for tree-planting from early on: 1981 or '82. As kids, we all had our own trees by the path leading to the land. Our youngest sister's was closest to the track; as the eldest, mine was the farthest. We competed to see whose tree did best. If the rains didn't come, we'd fetch water from the river or the well to keep them growing. Some of the trees were for fruit—avocados and papayas—but they were there as windbreakers and for soil protection, too.

From 1983 onwards, I got involved with other young people in a translating project for rural women who didn't speak English, who were participating in the 1985 UN 'Decade for Women' conference in Nairobi. Though we spoke Kachchi at home, at primary school the lessons were all taught in English; that continued at the boarding school I went to, run by nuns. After that I worked as a teaching assistant in a local school in our community.

How did you first come to the United States?

As a teenager, I wanted to be a journalist. But up until about 1992 at least, the media at home was under very tight control. Working for Kenyan radio or TV meant being a mouthpiece for the Moi government. I started to explore ways of getting an education abroad. My mother had been involved in a training programme sponsored from the US by the Episcopalian Church, and I applied through their scholarship programme. I got a place on the third attempt and came to the US in 1986, when I was 21, majoring first in English and then Third World and Women's Studies, at William Smith College in Geneva, New York; followed by graduate school at Cornell. After two years there, I'd changed my mind about journalism. My mother's Episcopalian friends were in Alexandria, Virginia, so I came down here and started doing environmental organizing, in Washington DC. I worked at Greenpeace for three years, on the toxic trade campaign—a great education.

Greenpeace was one of the founding members of the '50 Years Is Enough' network in 1994—the fiftieth anniversary of the World Bank and the IMF. I remember coming back from a visit to Kenya in July that year and getting up, incredibly jetlagged, to go to a 50 Years banner-hang. Through Greenpeace, I got involved with the gender caucus here. I was appointed public-outreach coordinator of 50 Years Is Enough in 1996, and became director at the end of 1998.

Who were the other founding members of the 50 Years Is Enough network, and what other organizations are affiliated to it?

Most of the groups that were involved at the start had already been campaigning around aspects of World Bank and IMF policy. There was the Development Group for Alternative Policies (D-Gap), the International Rivers Network, Global Exchange, Friends of the Earth, Greenpeace and Oxfam America—with whom we disagreed on several points, and who have now left the network. The Colombian Justice and Peace Office, a religious group, was one of the six original founders; the Maryknoll Office for Global Concerns is also now quite involved. Catholic orders and NGOs such as the Quixote Centre have been very strong in the social and economic justice movement in the US, and around the world. People like Marie Dennis from Maryknoll, and Susan Thompson now with Medical Mission Sisters, are some of our key supporters. Their missionaries, mainly in countries of the global South, know first-hand what is happening on the ground; they are there primarily to fight the things we are talking about: structural adjustment programmes, the effect of international debt, the lack of good political administration locally, due to these external pressures.

What is the internal structure of the 50 Years network? How is it funded?

A new structure was put in place last year, one of the requirements of our becoming a 501(c)(3) tax-exempt organization. We now have an

IRS-required board, which will set broad policies. This consists of five representatives from US organizations, seven from the global South, two from elsewhere—Canada or Europe, for instance—and the director. The US-based Steering Committee, made up of colleagues who work on these issues day-to-day, rather than Washington lobbyists, are responsible for implementing the board's policy decisions, with the office staff. Another element is the South Council: people from fifteen countries in the global South, working around the same problems, who are consulted on our positions: 'How would you think about this?'; 'How should we think about this?'. We want to make sure that our practice is informed by their experience of the reality of World Bank and IMF programmes. And of course, we are also in constant touch with member organizations, and a broad layer of individual supporters.

As to funding: more than a third of our money comes from pro-gressive foundations, including the Solidago Foundation and the Public Welfare Foundation. The Unitarian Universalist Veatch Programme, the United Methodist Women's Division, Sisters of The Holy Cross, Catholic and other religious orders give us a variety of grants. Through direct mail appeals, individual donors send us sums from $5 to $100, on a year-to-year basis. Then we have some major donors who give us $5,000; $10,000; $15,000 maybe once or twice a year. Different fund-ing sources have different requirements. For example, the money we get from the Unitarian Universalist Veatch Programme is a general sup-port grant that we use to pay salaries, rent and travel and printing costs. The Dominican Sisters give us money for a specific project called 'Voices of Struggle in the Global South'. Some of that grant goes to ensure that grassroots people, women in particular, can attend or speak at international meetings—the World Social Forum, G8 summits, World Bank/IMF gatherings in Washington. We can also send out a free news-letter to anyone in the global South who wants to receive it. Its purpose is to provide information on programmes and policies to those affected by them, but also to make people aware of struggles in other parts of the world, or even of the same continent—many people in Africa, for instance, know little about the Ogoni people's battle with big oil corporations in the Niger Delta.

Much of what we do on a daily basis is to provide information, to educate people on how the global economy really works—and what the actual levels of exploitation are. The other day I saw bananas on sale here in DC for 30 cents a pound. I grew up on a farm, and I know that it takes two or three years for bananas to grow; they have to be sprayed, tended, harvested, shipped over to the US—how much are the farmers getting, if consumers here are paying that? Nike sneakers can cost $150, and the shoe-workers are paid something like $2 a day. Wal-Mart prices aren't that cheap because Sam Walton 'had an idea'—they are cheap because workers are being exploited.

Could you explain 50 Years' demands vis-à-vis the IMF and World Bank?

Our eight demands are: unconditional cancellation of all debts to the IMF and World Bank; an end to all structural adjustment programmes; reparations for the effects of structural adjustment programmes, and for the social and ecological devastation caused by World Bank-funded projects; that the World Bank stop providing advice and investment facilities to the private sector; that individuals and agencies within the IMF and World Bank group complicit in corruption be prosecuted; that all proceedings and documents of the IMF and World Bank be made publicly available; and, lastly, that the future existence and structure of these organizations be thoroughly reassessed, in a transparent, democratic and participatory process, building on the findings of an independent Truth Commission.

Given Washington's well-documented hold over these institutions, shouldn't Southern popular movements be calling for a boycott, or for their abolition, rather than reform?

50 Years is quite a broad coalition—though I would say that even the right wing of our political spectrum is definitely to the left of centre—and there was great negotiation and consensus building around this question. Some argued that if the World Bank and IMF were to be abolished, they might only be replaced by something worse—pointing to the example of GATT being succeeded by the WTO. The US government could, for instance, fill the vacuum left by the elimination of the World Bank with the Millennium Challenge Account, so that even the World Bank's patina of multilateral oversight would be dispensed with, in favour of an agency controlled by the Bush administration. If this is the alternative, do we have an interest in maintaining some degree of multilateralism, despite its imperfections?

This ambivalence is reflected in the organization's position of calling for the 'profound transformation' of the IMF and World Bank. Personally, I do not think that they can be reformed. Although they are public institutions, funded by taxes, they have a track record of repeatedly failing the public good, on the social, economic, environmental or cultural level. But they have succeeded in their prime function, which has been to serve the purposes of capital—to assist the naked transfer of wealth from public into private hands.

Others within the 50 Years network would not yet go so far as to call for the abolition of the IMF and World Bank, but there is a consensus around opposition to the HIPC Initiative, and around the need to delegitimate these institutions, explaining the connexions between their activities and the interests of capital. The question is whether it's actually possible to change the nature of the global economy and of the international financial institutions—can they be made transparent and accountable, be made genuinely public? For me, this is not an economic argument: it is an argument about values, about rights—about evaluating twenty years of development policy and asking, did it deliver what it promised?

Some of our colleagues in the global South have made the point, at the World Social Forum and elsewhere, that the World Bank and the

IMF are often the lenders of last resort—many nations are trapped into dealing with them. But it could be argued that, since loans are often merely used to service past debt, many governments don't need the foreign capital, or the institutions, so much as a lifting of the debt burden. President Obasanjo of Nigeria noted that in 1978 his country borrowed $5 billion, and by 2000 it had paid back $16 billion, and yet still owed another $31 billion. By the time they pay it off, they will have paid $50 billion more. The inherent injustice of such situations was what led us to advocate debt cancellation and reparations. But we have also suggested alternative paths, such as what we call equitable development, in which priorities would be determined locally, rather than in Washington, Zurich or Tokyo. In my village of Rokobi, for instance, people would decide that electricity was the first requirement, and then a health clinic to tackle HIV-AIDS. But for the most part, the people who currently make these decisions will never have to encounter the depth and range of problems that exist in the global South, or even in parts of Washington DC.

What effect did the November 1999 protests in Seattle have on the campaign?

Seattle really added momentum to the protests against the IMF and World Bank. It was great to be there. I was part of the human chain around the Exhibition Hall, organized by Jubilee 2000 Northwest and modelled on those at previous G7 summits in Cologne and Birmingham. It was headed by John Sweeney of AFL-CIO; Maxine Waters, a Democratic Representative from California; Hannah Petros of Jubilee 2000 Northwest; Ann Pettifor of Jubilee 2000 UK; and me. Inside the hall, only 1,500 WTO delegates showed up at the grand reception—they had been expecting 5,000—while outside, 30,000 people stood in the driving rain chanting 'We're here, we're wet, cancel the debt!' We got thoroughly soaked, but I'm sure we had a much better time.

Since it was set up, 50 Years had always picketed the IMF and World Bank annual spring meetings, and the fall meetings that take place in

Washington DC two out of every three years; but the numbers were quite low—in 1999 we only had between 30 and 35 people, for example. But soon after Seattle, several organizations, including 50 Years, came together to form the Mobilization for Global Justice, and by January 2000 it was clear that between us we would be able to mobilize several thousand people for the demonstrations in Washington on April 16.

How would you describe the achievements of 50 Years Is Enough, up till now?

I think one of our greatest successes is putting the World Bank and the IMF on the map as public institutions that are failing to serve the public good. They have 10,000 employees and a public relations budget of over $21 million, and yet once debate began after the Mexican peso collapse and the Asian Crisis, we found we were winning over more minds. We have made the US Congress instruct US representatives to oppose user fees, and our colleagues in the South have confirmed the difference this has made on the ground.

But we have also failed, because for the most part these institutions haven't really changed. Despite some cosmetic changes, the same model is still in place. An awful lot of work remains to be done, and as long as we are not having a concrete influence on elected and appointed officials, all we are doing is talking.

How would you see the relationship between the economic justice movement and the anti-war movement?

The peace movement, as I would like to call it, comes out of the fraternizing between the two. As Martin Luther King Jr said, peace is not just the absence of war. We're talking about peace on many levels, in talking about economic justice. These movements are not so split—without the World Social Forum and the global movement, there would not have been the massive anti-war demonstrations of February 15.

After September 11, a lot of people woke up to the need—not to bring the world under the control of the United States, as the neo-conservatives would have it—but to realize the ways in which we are connected as people across the planet. We have a real opportunity to deepen and broaden our analysis of what other challenges face us, from perpetual war, to famine, to HIV-AIDS, to international debt. There are also questions of police brutality, environmental racism, union busting—and all the other issues, from lack of health care insurance, to homelessness, to safe drinking water and so on. If we recognize these circumstances as a totality then there are no divisions. The Institute for Policy Studies, the American Friends Service Committee, the Washington Peace Centre and a lot of groups that we work with on all kinds of other issues have taken a lead against the war on Iraq. To me, this means that there is no difference between a peace activist, a global justice activist or an anti-corporate globalization activist. That it is necessary for us to make those connexions. Every time they raise the terror alert level, there is the great sucking sound of civil liberties going out the window, because it becomes the excuse for all kinds of draconian measures. We have to be vigilant. We need to continue to push on the issue of justice, on immigrant rights, in the same way that we are pushing for a cleaner environment and an end to exploitation.

Analysing the role of the IMF and World Bank in Africa, you have pointed to 1980 as the start of a significant downward spiral. What are its causes?

1980 is when structural adjustment programmes began to be introduced around the world, implemented by the World Bank, IMF and, to a lesser extent, regional banks. In Africa, this was a period of ascendancy for the IMF and World Bank, bolstered by the US's aggressive push for Cold War dominance under Reagan. Africans were told to tighten their belts, and that the short-term pain of cuts in expenditure would bring gains in the long term. But twenty years later, those gains haven't materialized—and this is a point that I made in my evidence to

Congress, the year before last. Looking at the periods before and since structural adjustment, you can track the drop in literacy and immunization rates, declining numbers of hospital beds and doctors, and increasing agricultural insecurity, as governments cut credit to farmers who are not producing for export. The numbers are getting worse. Ghana is supposed to be one of the Bank's success stories but, in the 1990s, the Bank itself calculated that it would take the average Ghanaian forty years to regain the standard of living she had had in the 1970s. Imagine what that means for the so-called 'basket-cases' such as Somalia, Sierra Leone or Cameroon.

The World Bank recently released a report containing figures on healthcare provision, literacy rates, and so on. When it was pointed out that the country with the best indicators was Cuba—not a member of the IMF or World Bank, subject to US embargo for 40 years, and not following the policies of the Washington Consensus—Wolfensohn said he wasn't embarrassed to admit this was the case. But these people are so wedded to the orthodoxy that they can't envisage alternatives. This is really the heart of the struggle for Africa's second liberation—we need to examine how these institutions and their policies have become embedded in our communities, our economies, our continent, without the people's consent. The only consent given is that of the finance minister, or the president, or the governor of the Central Bank—themselves usually educated at Harvard, Yale, Chicago or Stanford, and often former employees of the World Bank or IMF.

There is also the HIV-AIDS crisis. In Zimbabwe, the fastest-growing sector is carpentry, because of all the coffins needed for people dying from the pandemic. There is, in fact, a connexion between HIV-AIDS and structural adjustment programmes: by the time the crisis hit, health systems had been completely undermined. Kenya had a network of community or village clinics at local level, and then hospitals at the district, provincial and national levels, with private and church-run hospitals in between. It used to be a place where people from outside Kenya— black South Africans, for instance—would come for treatment. Now it's almost impossible to get into a state hospital, and once you do, you have to share a bed; if you need a prescription the doctor gives it to your family to fill. The same is true of schools, roads and street-crime—you are very likely to get robbed, pick-pocketed or worse in Nairobi today, but this never used to be an issue.

What of the World Bank and IMF claims that corruption is responsible for much of the deterioration of African social services?

They talk a great deal about 'good governance' and the need for anti-corruption initiatives—that was why Richard Leakey and his 'dream team' were seconded to Kenya. They define corruption in a narrow sense—police officers taking bribes on the roads. But if you impose a system whereby governments have to cut public-sector salaries to the bone, if people aren't getting paid, what are they going to do? You can't claim to be fighting corruption and simultaneously reduce people's incomes. There is corruption on an everyday level in Kenya: when you go to government offices, you have to hand over a bit of money to get the right file, to be told what to do next, and so on. But the real corruption lies in the billions of dollars that have been spirited out of the country, into accounts in New York, Zurich, Paris or London—with the collusion of G7 governments, the World Bank and IMF. That was why Kenyans found Leakey's 'corruption-busting' especially hypocritical. In 2000, the World Bank and IMF pushed for the passage of the Kenya Anti-Corruption Authority, which contained a clause amnestying economic crimes committed before 1998. Aid had been cut off in 1997, so after 1998 there was almost nothing left to steal. By this point Kenya owed $8 billion, and yet Leakey was willing to forgive the theft of vast amounts of money, while claiming to be clamping down on petty sums. In fact, Leakey participated in another level of corruption, by pretending that he could get real results.

Certainly, there are plenty of cases in Kenya and elsewhere in Africa where elite individuals have profited. Abacha and Mobutu salted away millions in Swiss bank accounts and bought properties across Europe, and everybody knew it. But the worsening quality of education and healthcare afflicting African countries is also to be found in Haiti, the Philippines, Nicaragua or India—the same policy prescriptions are affecting the everyday lives of people across the global South.

In December 2002, Moi stepped down as Kenya's president after 24 years— much of that time characterized by a brutally enforced one-party rule. All the expectations in the Western media were that his hand-picked successor Uhuru Kenyatta would win the 2002 election. What were the conditions for Mwai Kibaki's victory?

Moi took over in 1978, after the death of Jomo Kenyatta, the country's first president, and banned all parties other than his Kenya African National Union after the first stirrings of dissent in 1982. For the rest of the 1980s he stifled the opposition through arrests, tear gas or assassinations; but he was a loyal supporter of the West in the Cold War, and the international institutions turned a blind eye. In 1991, however, he was forced to amend the constitution to allow other political parties to operate and to restrict the presidency henceforward to two terms. Internal factors played a role—there had been large anti-government demonstrations in 1990—but Moi was more concerned by international pressures, especially from the IMF and World Bank, who threatened to withhold loans unless some gestures were now made towards democratization.

Of course, Moi forward-dated the two-term restriction, and stood in the 1992 and 1997 elections himself. The only reason, electoral fraud apart, that he, and KANU, managed to win was because Moi succeeded in splitting the opposition. This was his speciality—creating and exacerbating ethnic tensions. Between 1991 and '94, for example, there were a lot of what were termed 'tribal clashes'—people who had been neighbours for 30 years apparently woke up one day and started slaughtering each other. The ruling elite claimed it had been instigated by tribal warriors. But eyewitnesses said the aggressors had military haircuts, and were dropped into the area from helicopters. They may have been wearing Masai *shukas* and carrying bows and arrows, but the arrows were imported—'Made in Hong Kong', 'Made in Korea'.

The opposition was once again split between several candidates in the 1997 elections, allowing Moi to win comfortably—though there was once again a great deal of vote-rigging. In 2002, Moi seemed tempted to bust the two-term restriction. A chorus of sycophants was urging him to run again. Eventually he realized he wouldn't be able to get away with it—despite everything, the changes to the constitution had gradually altered the political landscape, giving rise to several new parties and NGOs. Moi kept everyone guessing for a long time about whom he favoured to succeed him. Though he might have been expected to nominate his vice-president, George Saitoti, Moi shunted him aside in March 2002. Various other figures, such as Raila Odinga, a former oppositionist who had joined the government in 2001, and Musalia Mudavadi, a KANU insider, also had aspirations to the candidacy. But Moi then circumvented the nomination procedure and declared that Uhuru Kenyatta, a political newcomer, would stand for KANU—hoping to trade on the dynastic connexion with the first president. He also seemed to believe that by choosing a Kikuyu candidate, he could mop up the votes of an ethnic group that, though the largest in Kenya, was not a core element of KANU.

In effect, Moi, who calls himself the professor of politics, gambled—and went out on an incredibly stupid wager. By choosing Kenyatta before the opposition had settled on their candidate, he allowed them to nullify his ethnic strategy simply by opting for another Kikuyu. The crucial factor differentiating the 2002 elections from those that preceded it was that, for the first time, the bulk of the opposition parties—gathered into the National Rainbow Coalition (NARC)—united behind one candidate. There had been between seven and nine opposition candidates in the two previous elections; this time, there were only three besides Kibaki. Simeon Nyachae, who had been Moi's minister of finance in the late nineties, ran for the Forum for the Restoration of Democracy–People, but really only picked up votes in his district. James Orengo—probably the most progressive and principled politician in Kenya—stood for the Social Democratic Party, and got around 0.4 per cent of the vote. Waweru N'gethe of the Chama cha Umma appeared on the scene at the last minute, but no one really knew him or his party.

Kibaki, a neoliberal economist by training, is a figure with national standing, and was always the most serious challenger. Like Nyachae, he had been very much a part of the old regime—he had been finance minister from 1969–82 and vice-president from 1978–88, and only left the government in 1991, setting up the Democratic Party of Kenya barely in time to run in the 1992 elections. He finished third, and was second in the 1997 elections. His success in 2002 can largely be put down to the unprecedented unity of the opposition—even those Moi had alienated within his own party, such as Saitoti and Odinga, left KANU to join NARC, rather than announcing separate candidacies. NARC's support held together because there was a real momentum to remove KANU from power—after two failed attempts, Kenyans were very focused on the task. KANU was the party that had fought for independence, and many people never thought the day would come when they would have to vote against it. But by now they were fed up. A lot of people were outraged by the Anti-Corruption Authority Moi tried to pass in 2000, for instance—the amnesty for economic crimes committed before 1998 was a particular sticking point. The attraction of Kibaki was not so much any democratic credentials—he had never been part of the struggle, and had once referred to those who spoke of multi-party politics in Kenya as dreamers—but rather the fact that he wasn't tainted by corruption scandals.

There was also a very deep and serious process of re-politicization in the period leading up to the last election. It was agreed that there would be a constitutional review after the elections, and a lot of ordinary people began to educate themselves and others about civic responsibilities and the provisions of the new constitution. These weren't people running for office, they were people who felt that it should not be leaders alone who determined the path of development. They had had too many examples of leaders going astray, and had learned very hard, very bitter and painful lessons. So many lives have been lost, whether through lack of healthcare or from hunger—people have starved in Kenya because we are not growing enough food, and at the same time we are exporting tonnes of coffee, cotton and cut flowers. People are no longer willing to sit back and accept the lip service that is given by political leaders, or believe that the politicians they send to parliament are really going to represent their best interests. They want to determine their own fate. Whether it's electrifying a village, or building a clinic, they realize, 'We can do it, we can draw on our resources.'

I witnessed another aspect of this civic education on polling day, when I took my mother and sister to vote. There had been all kinds of rumours about plans to stuff ballot boxes and carry them away in hearses and coffins, so people were watching like hawks when the ballot boxes were opened, and would make a note of the serial number. Ten or fifteen people did their own election monitoring, declaring results invalid when the serial numbers were missing from official tallies. International observers had proclaimed the previous two elections free and fair—Jimmy Carter vetted the 1997 election—but people in Kenya were very bitter about the double standard. This time around it was not the presence of outside monitors but the vigilance of the locals that made all the difference. It was a huge triumph for the Kenyan people, and the process of organic democratization makes me quite hopeful that it won't be reversed. Although I should note that one of the first things the new parliamentarians did was to award themselves huge raises and all kinds of perks. Not only did this cause great public resentment, it also had implications for the budget deficit. Even cabinet members expressed reservations about the motion, which to a certain extent indicates that there is more accountability now for elected officials—they know they have to answer to the people.

How would you assess the present state of other African nations, in terms of economic and political well-being?

I think they can be divided into two different sets. I would name South Africa as a country that is doing relatively well politically and economically. The only other African state that still attracts significant numbers of economic migrants is Libya—Côte d'Ivoire used to, but obviously no longer does because of the civil war. Libya and South Africa are certainly the only countries where people see opportunity, and to which they might move to make a living instead of going to Europe. But there are also many countries that wouldn't rank in the World Bank's top five, but which are among the more open and democratic states. Mali is quite impoverished, but there is serious and lively debate there on all sorts of issues. Ghana, Botswana, Senegal and, to some extent, Kenya, I would also classify as quite promising in political terms. But most of these countries have been devastated by structural adjustment programmes for two decades now, with terrible consequences for education, healthcare and food security.

At the bottom of the list I would include Somalia, where there is no functioning central government, and Sudan, which has likewise suffered enormously from its long civil war. The Democratic Republic of Congo is descending still deeper into hell, but people are making money from its mineral wealth—diamonds, manganese, cobalt, copper—like there's no tomorrow. Multinational corporations will reap the spoils of diamonds and oil in Angola, which has yet to recover, despite the death of Savimbi. Côte d'Ivoire, Sierra Leone and Liberia are still being torn apart by war. Zimbabwe, meanwhile, is a tragedy of its own special kind. Land reform is an issue that genuinely needs to be resolved, not just in Zimbabwe but in South Africa, Zambia, Namibia, Kenya—in all African countries with a large indigenous population. But Mugabe has exploited the problem in a last ditch effort to perpetuate his oppressive rule.

In nearly all of these places, the aspirations of Africans have been crushed by regimes propped up by the West; their struggles have been overpowered by other interests—those of foreign governments, of multi-national corporations, of bodies such as the IMF, World Bank and WTO. This continent is transferring $15 billion annually to the G8 and international institutions, vast resources that are not being applied to problems here. Women have often had to bridge the gap, managing non-existent resources to give their communities the basic services the system has failed to provide. In a sense, it's the extraordinary things people have done to survive that give grounds for optimism. Even amid the suffering inflicted first by slavery, then by colonialism, neo-colonialism, structural adjustment and now HIV-AIDS, families have somehow managed to feed and educate their children, communities have somehow kept themselves from falling apart. This isn't a matter of romanticizing hardship, it is about recognizing the dignity and tenacity with which people go about their everyday lives.

TREVOR NGWANE

SPARKS IN THE TOWNSHIP

Where were you born and brought up, and what was your family background?

I was born in 1960 in Durban. My father and mother were medical nurses. My grandfathers were both Presbyterian preachers, from Zululand. My father was an ANC supporter. He spent some time in Dar es Salaam when I was small. I'm not sure that he went because of politics: people got out for lots of reasons, for opportunities or dignity. He came back for the sake of the family. But anyone who had been abroad was targeted by the Special Branch once they returned to South Africa. Although he was not really active, they used to visit him every week or so when I was a child; he died more or less a broken man. He definitely had an influence on me. I remember him showing me some political books: there was one in a brown-paper cover, so I never knew the author or title. When I was six we moved to Zululand. My parents worked in a hospital there run by a Scottish missionary, who tried to work along progressive lines. There was a black Jesus in the chapel, for example—that was something in those days; we used to point him out to each other. At that time, Buthelezi was considered quite a hero—he refused to accept 'independent homeland' status for Zululand, toured the country speaking out for black people and met with the ANC. Even my father was fooled when he set up Inkatha with the colours black, green, gold: 'It's the colours of the ANC!' he told me; only the older people knew that then.

After my parents separated, my brother and I were sent to a Catholic boarding school, run by the Dominicans, near Durban. My mother thought it was the best school around but it had a really strict regime, with punishments for everything. The food was terrible, too. I was there for four years—I was expelled after the school strike in 1976. Not that I was particularly political: more of a rebel in a generic sense, getting caught out of bounds, or drinking. But there was a spontaneous strike at our school after the police massacres in Soweto on 16 June 1976. The situation was very tense. Some students came in to talk to us; they had more experience and were at the forefront of the boycott. I didn't play much of a part but these things quickly affect everyone. We felt under very strong pressure. We were all expelled, sent home. A month later, the school authorities handpicked the ones they wanted to return. But they told my brother and me not to come back—they had some problem with me. After that I transferred to a township school in Newcastle, on the other side of Natal, where my father was living. I matriculated there.

In 1979, I started at Fort Hare, in the Eastern Cape. It's the oldest black university in South Africa; Nelson Mandela and Oliver Tambo went there. I studied sociology, although at first I was enrolled for a BA in Personnel Management. When I arrived, there was the normal hulla-baloo about which course to take. We were shoved around and didn't get proper guidance, and this was a special new syllabus that they wanted to recruit students to. We studied sociology, industrial psychology, stat-istics, other social-science subjects. It made a big impact on me—at first, not politically: I was just fascinated by the ideas, and a whole new world opened up. It must have been around this time that I stopped believing in God.

Sociology was a bit better than some of the courses: there were a few black lecturers who tried to put the other side; Eastern Cape was a politi-cal place and Fort Hare has that prestige. We read dependency theory as well as the classics: Durkheim, Weber. There was a special course, 'development policy and administration', where we learned about the Group Areas Act and apartheid policy. It was meant to train young blacks in apartheid administration but it was taught by a good teacher, Mike Sham, who tried to give us a different perspective. He used to lend me books. But there was also the baptism by fire of the grading system.

Many of the courses that were strategic for black students—statistics, anthropology, accounting—had something like a 10 per cent pass rate. Some people got a low mark on their first test and never recovered. But each one counted, and if you didn't get around 50 per cent overall, you failed the course. Come September, all those who didn't make the year mark had to face the ritual of returning home. Typically, some of them were your friends. It was the expulsions, I think, that made for the solidarity among us, when there were outbreaks of defiance.

What was the political atmosphere like?

The country wasn't yet on fire, but there were things going on. When Mozambique got its independence in 1975, there were student demonstrations and class boycotts in support of FRELIMO. A group of students put up a manifesto, signed with a popular name —something with a bit of mystique, like 'The Wolf Man'—and we all read it. This happened three or four times. Then there was a meeting in the Great Hall. Everyone came to listen to the debate; it was quite democratic. I wasn't really political yet, but the atmosphere was so highly charged: not only in the country, in terms of people striving for freedom, liberation; but with FRELIMO showing the way, the possibility. There was hope. But also we felt, at least myself and my friends, that we were so oppressed in that university. Everyone shared a sense of relief and wanted to support the boycott; there was no question of breaking it—perhaps one or two people might have tried, but it was too strong. So we were all expelled for 'political disturbances', as they were called. The same thing was happening at every black university. After a month you could reapply and the authorities would select who they wanted.

By this stage I was starting to develop a more conscious critique of apartheid; there were a couple of guys who used to challenge us to think more constructively. But we weren't discussing politics all the time. For us, it was a question of surviving the courses, passing, failing—and then, if there was a student strike, a boycott, we all went for it; there was

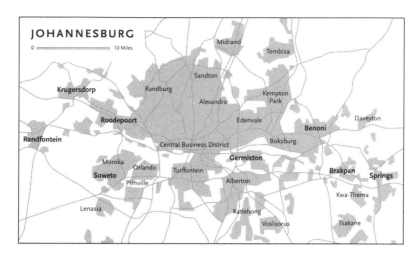

JOHANNESBURG

0 _____ 10 Miles

Midrand

Tembisa

Sandton

Krugersdorp

Randburg

Kempton Park

Alexandra

Roodepoort

Edenvale

Daveyton

Benoni

Randfontein

Central Business District

Boksburg

Moroka

Orlando

Germiston

Soweto

Turffontein

Brakpan

Springs

Pimville

Alberton

Kwa-Thema

Lenasia

Katlehong

Vosloorus

Tsakane

ZIMBABWE

MOZAMBIQUE

BOTSWANA

LIMPOPO PROVINCE

• Pietersburg

NAMIBIA

GAUTENG

Nelspruit

Pretoria •

MPUMA-LANGA

• Mmabatho

Johannesburg •

SWAZI-LAND

NORTH-WEST

• Newcastle

FREE STATE

Ulundi •

Kimberley •

KWAZULU-NATAL

NORTHERN CAPE

Bloemfontein •

LESOTHO

SOUTH AFRICA

• Durban

EASTERN CAPE

Atlantic Ocean

Indian Ocean

EASTERN CAPE

Bisho •

WESTERN CAPE

Cape Town •

Port Elizabeth •

0 _____ 200 Miles

a lot of solidarity. In 1982, there were more protests and they expelled us again. But this time we decided, nearly all of us, that we would not go back because we were so poorly treated. We knew they would exclude all our leaders, the so-called agitators. So we stayed out, apart from a few. They are still known as 'the defenders'. Someone should write a book about them: the black guys who now defend the corporate world betrayed us even earlier.

What did you do after the expulsion from university?

I moved to Soweto. I phoned a research agency that I had worked for during the June holidays and got a job there. Meanwhile, I carried on with my degree by correspondence course through the University of South Africa. The agency turned out to be the research wing of a government parastatal for apartheid engineering, developing personnel management strategies—aptitude tests for mineworkers, supervisors and so on. The pass laws were still in force—they'd ask for your pass and arrest you if you didn't have it—and the 8 o'clock curfew. When I arrived here, I didn't have anywhere to stay. I squatted around in different parts of Soweto, including the Salvation Army, until I found a place. First I was living in a backroom, then I graduated to a backyard garage. That was bigger, but there were insulation problems, what with the roll-down door and everything.

This was the time of the 1984–86 township rebellions. What was your involvement with the movement, and what were its effects on your own political development?

Soweto was burning—it affected everyone. At that stage I was doing a full-time masters degree at Wits University, in downtown Johannesburg. I worked there as a tutor, then junior lecturer, till '88 and it was in those years that I became a Marxist. There was a small group of us who are still close comrades, who would read and talk things through; they've seen me through a lot. Though I was only in my twenties I had my own course, 'Class and Nationalism', lecturing on the youth of the ANC, the Pan-African Congress, Afrikaaner nationalism and the South African Communist Party. Our orientation was towards the ANC: we supported the workers who wanted to fashion it as a weapon of struggle, and always argued against the two-stage theory. 'We unban the ANC!' was one of our slogans. But at that point the link for me was more of an intellectual one than actual involvement on the ground. For example, some youths came to demand my car—that's the kind of thing that would happen—but my room was so full of posters about the struggle that I convinced them I knew their leadership, which saved the car. And I did have Winnie Mandela in one of my classes. Each week, one of the students would present and teach a class and on Winnie's day, she came dressed in full ANC regalia with a prepared speech about the movement. We even managed to use banned material in my course reader—Marx, Mao, Ho Chi Minh, Slovo, the whole lot. During the wave of mass arrests when the State of Emergency was declared in 1986, one of my students, Pascal Moloi, got detained. So we took his course work and all this material into jail. It was a popular thing.

Those were heady days for me. We had radical ideas about reading policy and the role of education. I decided I didn't want to make the students go through the exam system; I would hand them the question papers two or three days before, against regulations. We watched a video once a week, read books, used the amazing library. Then an ex-mine worker who'd come to the department for the 'Sociology of Work' programme, a Lesotho politico, started showing the videos to the university workers, who'd been cleaning the blackboards for twenty years but could barely read or write. Being political, he would give a short talk, before or after; then the workers started interrupting to say their bit. Soon we commandeered the tea room to start teaching them to read and write; my students all joined in. This was what mushroomed into the Wits Workers Literacy Project—it grew and grew, and started attracting railway workers, shop workers. I'd got squeezed out of my department,

though there was a big campaign for my reinstatement, so I started
teaching at the Literacy Project instead.

*What was your assessment of the negotiations that followed Mandela's release
from jail in 1990, and the unbanning of the ANC and SACP? To what extent
were the rank and file privy to what was going on—or did they simply want
to trust the ANC regardless?*

I remember turning on the radio and hearing: 'The ANC announced
today that the armed struggle has been suspended'. We couldn't believe
it—it was like chopping off an arm and a leg. Of course, they never did
anything much but we used to romanticize it; that little bomb at the
Wimpy Bar won them so much support in the country. People wanted
to trust them, naturally, but there was opposition to the direction the
negotiations were taking. Mandela used his gigantic stature to contain
it. In January 1990, he'd announced—in the note smuggled out from
Pollsmoor Prison—that nationalization continued to be the policy of the
ANC; 'growth through redistribution' was the line. By September '93, he
was touring Western capitals with the National Party Finance Minister,
Derek Keys, speaking at the UN, pleading for foreign investment and
guaranteeing the repatriation of profits and capital-protection measures.

   Without detracting from those 27 years in jail—what that cost him,
what he stood for—Mandela has been the real sell-out, the biggest
betrayer of his people. When it came to the crunch, he used his status
to camouflage the actual agreement that the ANC was forging with
the South African elite under the sugar-coating of the Reconstruction
and Development Programme. Basically, the ANC was granted formal,
administrative power, while the wealth of the country was retained in
the hands of the white capitalist elite, Oppenheimer and company.
Mandela's role was decisive in stabilizing the new dispensation; by all
accounts, a daring gamble on the part of the bourgeoisie.

   I was working with the Transport Workers Union at that time,
between '91 and '93, as a political education officer; I'd joined the ANC

in 1990. The feeling in the trade-union movement was triumphant: we were really hitting the bosses, now they felt forced to invite us to sit down, to give us all sorts of things. The reality was just the opposite: because the bosses were on the back foot they had gone on the attack. They deployed the ideology of tripartism—the golden triangle of labour–government–capital—to trap the unions in 'codetermination' discussions on how to maximize company profits and productivity. The way they did it was supremely flattering to the middling union officials. Don't forget South Africa had one of the most unionized working classes in the world—something like 23 per cent of the economically active population in 1994. Between them, the two independent trade-union federations, FOSATU and COSATU, had 3.2 million members and 25,000 elected shop stewards. Their role was going to be vital in stabilizing the new order, supporting what they called the 'export-oriented economy'. Of course, the collapse of the Soviet Union had made a big difference—a disarming and disorienting world event which the bourgeoisie took full advantage of to argue that there was no alternative.

At the same time, there were big struggles going on inside the trade-union movement, between the more 'workerist', plant-based FOSATU faction and the 'populist', UDF-aligned COSATU, with closer ties in the communities. Sometimes it got physical. There were also real fights between the black consciousness forces and the ANC; blood was flowing. The returning ANC leadership had to graft itself onto the mass democratic movement. They started by closing down the other structures, in the name of unity: 'Why do you need your own Youth Congress? We have the Youth League'; 'Why do you need the Transvaal Federation of Women? We have the Women's League'. There was also a lot of destabilization going on: the dirty war organized by the security forces, provoking bloodshed. That strengthened the hand of those calling for 'unity'.

There was opposition in the trade unions to the line the leadership was taking. But, to quite a large extent, this was either bought off or repressed by the ANC–SACP–COSATU officials. For instance, I wrote a paper in 1993 called 'Is Holding Hands with the Bosses the way for

New South Africa?' that was critical of COSATU's codetermination policies. I was expelled, then reinstated after a big campaign, then expelled
again in 1995. That's carried on. John Appolis, the Chemical Workers'
leader, has just been fired by the union for his role in the anti-privatization struggle. Whereas Alec Erwin, once a big trade-union figure and
defender of workers' democracy, is now Minister of Trade and Industry,
pushing neoliberal policies. Moses Mayekiso from the Metalworkers'
Union, who was once *the* socialist leader, has been promoting every
World Bank initiative through the National Civic Organization, SANCO.
Now he's caught up in an investment-company scam.

*The first one-person, one-vote municipal elections in South Africa came a year
and a half after the ANC's watershed victory in 1994. You were elected as a
councillor for the Pimville ward in Soweto, on the ANC ticket. What space
was there then for progressive politics at the municipal level? How much of a
change, with the ending of apartheid?*

It was a real change after apartheid. Before that, local government had
been run strictly along black and white lines, so Soweto had its black
local authority, Sandton a white one. In 1995, that was reorganized so
that the black areas were no longer isolated: Soweto was divided in two,
with Pimville and Orlando East joined to Randburg, in the north, and
the rest linked to the Central Business District, so that redistributive
policies became a real possibility. The same went for the other townships; Alexandra was linked to Sandton. The Johannesburg Metro, a
city-wide municipality, was superimposed overall. The Reconstruction
and Development Programme had a component of 'people-driven development': local labour had to be used for building projects and each
community had to come up with its own development objectives. My
first job in the Pimville ward was to call public meetings, with representatives from the civic, the community organizations, the ANC, to
draw up a participatory budget where the local people could list their
own priorities.

We ran into problems within a matter of months. The contractors tried to turn the local-employment policy against the working class by using casual labour, undocumented migrants. We dealt with that by enforcing a minimum wage of 50 rand per day, around $7, on every contract tendered: 'You can employ casual labour but you have to pay the minimum wage'. The employers complained to the Metro council, claiming this was an 'obstacle to development'. I was 'investigated' over the 50-rand wage; there was a bit of a witch hunt. They would bribe local leaders to soften the rules, so they could pay less. It soon became clear that the bureaucracy was frowning on community control. Officials would talk about 'the contradiction between development and democracy' and the councillors weren't strong enough to question that. A lot of them were naïve and well-meaning, but didn't really know what they wanted to do. The bureaucrats had an interest in undermining them—they would prepare the agendas, decide how many meetings there should be. Of course, this couldn't have happened without the ANC's tacit consent. The mood changed within the ruling ANC caucus: robust debates became muted; decisions were taken away from councillors and we were discouraged from participating in local community forums. There were issues we couldn't discuss.

The crunch came when they announced a big financial crisis for Johannesburg; they had 'just realized' the city was in the red. This was in 1997, a year after the national currency crisis, when the ANC effectively ditched the RDP for GEAR, the Growth, Employment and Redistribution programme—a thoroughgoing privatization-deregulation strategy, involving savage public-sector cutbacks, loosened exchange controls and a regressive sales-tax policy. All the Johannesburg ANC councillors were called to an emergency caucus meeting—you could see it was a coordinated effort—for a long PowerPoint presentation, followed by three minutes of questions. All the 'people's budgets' had to be frozen. I argued, 'But comrades, when there's less money, all the more reason to be democratic'. But they didn't want to hear that. The next budget was put together by experts, special whizz kids. Again, the plan was unveiled with PowerPoint—we joked about how 'the words fall from the sky like rain'; one hour's presentation and a couple of questions. After that they started to target people more systematically, or co-opt them for well-paid committee jobs.

In 1999, just after the second general election confirmed Mbeki in power, the council introduced their comprehensive privatization plan for the city, Igoli 2002. There would be massive cutbacks, around twenty thousand job losses, and everything would be put out to tender—water, electricity, garbage collection, sewage. *Igoli* is the Zulu word for Johannesburg. I called it E. coli 2002, because the water privatization soon had sewage leaking into the water table. At this time, Mbeki was using the phrase, 'The people have spoken', to imply that if people had voted for the ANC they must support its neoliberal policies and shouldn't now oppose them. I wrote a piece for the newspaper called 'The People Have Not Spoken', a debate between the city manager, the trade union—SAMWU, the municipal workers' union, had come out against the plan—and myself, putting the views of my constituents. The piece was by invitation, though I didn't write it without discussing it with my comrades. I decided it had to be done.

Within three days, the ANC suspended me from all my positions, including those in the Council. I faced a disciplinary hearing for bringing the Party into disrepute. They then tried to make a deal, saying, 'OK, if you publicly recant your statements, we'll reduce the two years' suspension to nine months'. The timing was calculated to coincide with the local government elections in 2000. They were offering me the chance to run again. I went to my constituents, and they said 'No, you can't apologise'. It was then that I became an independent.

What sort of problems were Sowetans facing at this stage? What did the city's restructuring programme entail?

The privatizations envisaged in Igoli 2002 were premised on 'cost-recovery': that is, once the basic infrastructure had been set up—with corners often cut in the process—the citizens were supposed to cover whatever costs the utility companies demanded for maintenance and supply. The problems, and the pace of privatization, varied according to the utility. Take electricity. ESKOM—the Afrikaans acronym for the Electricity Supply Commission—had been established as the engine for the apartheid state's mining–mineral complex. It absorbed over half the World Bank's $200 million credits to South Africa during the fifties and sixties, supplying cut-price power to white-owned industries while the majority of blacks went without domestic electricity. To this day, most poor blacks rely for their lighting, cooking and heating on paraffin, coal and wood—you can smell the coal smoke over the settlements when the evening meals are being cooked. Electricity only really reached the townships in the eighties. The main dwellings were supplied with cables and metres, and the backyard shacks and garages would have to run a wire from there.

Under the apartheid regime there was a fixed payment for services. But under the ANC, as ESKOM was readied for privatization, they began to charge per kilowatt hour. In 1999, Soweto electricity prices rose by 47 per cent. In Soweto, average bills in the summer are around 150 rand per month, or $20; in the winter they soar to 500 rand, nearly $70, when the average monthly income for over half Soweto's households is only 1,500 rand, just over $200. From the spring of 2001 ESKOM started to implement a drastic cut-off strategy for households overdue on payments—the company's 'debtor book' was apparently scaring off private buyers and there was disapproving talk of the townships having a 'culture of non-payment', a legacy of the rent and service boycotts of the eighties. In some cases, the Johannesburg Council further tightened the screw by cutting off people's water too.

Was this when the Soweto Electricity Crisis Committee was formed?

It had begun earlier, in June 2000, when we ran a series of workshops on the energy crisis; then we started having mass meetings in the township. We got some research done by Wits University, a project organized by Patrick Bond, Maj Fiil-Flynn and other comrades. Their survey, 'Electricity Crisis in Soweto'—it's on the web at www.queensu.ca/ msp—showed what we already suspected: that most of the residents were working-class pensioners or unemployed, with lots of grannies as heads of households; that most of them did try to pay their bills, though there was such poor service at the local ESKOM offices that they often had to queue all day on payment days. But the prices were out of their range. 89 per cent of them were in arrears, 61 per cent had had their power cut off by ESKOM in the past year alone—they couldn't cook or run refrigerators, it was back to coal and paraffin to heat and light their homes. The draft report came out in April 2001, just when ESKOM was stepping up the cut-offs to around 120,000 households a month nationwide. The ANC had been boasting that they'd brought electricity to millions of black households, but by 2001 more people were losing access every month than were gaining it. We called a Soweto-wide mass meeting and people came in their hundreds.

How is the SECC organized on the ground and what has been the focus of its activities?

We have around 22 branches in Soweto, each one with their own organizing committee—we reckon around 7,000 members in all. We've had a debate about membership cards. At the moment the position is, you can join and get a card for 10 rand a year, or you can just be a member. I don't have a card—my position is, everyone is a member who wants to be. We have an AGM every year on March 1st, and directly elected officials: chair, secretary, treasurer. Every Tuesday there's a committee meeting of representatives from the branches, around 60 people, where we get reports on problems, organize speakers for meetings and so on. We've had funding from War on Want, and this year we've got a US Public Welfare Foundation grant which we're going to use to employ an organizer and open an office, even if it's just for one year.

One of the first things we did was to launch Operation Khanyisa—*khanyisa* means light—where we reconnect people's electricity supply when it's been cut off. We trained local people how to do this. Within six months, over 3,000 households had been put back on the grid. We found that a lot of people were already illegally connected, through bribing ESKOM employees. When we raised the question in mass meetings it would come as a relief to everyone to find that their neighbours were illegally connected too—they'd all been hiding it from each other. We turned what was a criminal deed from the point of view of ESKOM into an act of defiance. It was good tactics and good politics. We organized a lot of protest marches, including going to city councillors' houses to cut off their electricity, to give them a taste of their own medicine, and to the mayor's office in Soweto. When they targeted our leaders for arrest after a councillor's supply was cut, five hundred Sowetans marched to Moroka Police Station to present themselves for mass arrest; the police were overwhelmed.

By October 2001, ESKOM had retreated: they announced a moratorium on cut-offs. That gave us a victory under our belts. In December 2001, Jeff Radebe, the ANC Public Enterprise Minister and a leading SACP member, came to Orlando Hall in Soweto to offer a partial amnesty on arrears. We said that wasn't enough. Our demands are electricity for everyone, including the urban settlements and poor rural villages that don't have any supply yet; scrapping all arrears; the free basic supply the ANC promised in the 2000 municipal elections and a flat-rate monthly price that people can budget for—a demand that we won in the 1980s from the apartheid regime. It's sad that Sowetans are now back to fighting for this from their own democratic government. We also oppose the privatization scheme that Radebe is still trying to push through. Recently, ESKOM has been installing pre-pay meters, a pilot scheme. That's our current campaign: marching to remove the pre-pay meters—or bypassing them, if people prefer—and dumping them at the mayor's office, at ESKOM, at the council. This is giving us new strength.

What led to the march on Mayor Amos Masondo's house?

Masondo had stood in the 2000 municipal elections on Mbeki's pledge of free basic water and electricity and though only a few people went to the polls, that was what they were voting for. By the end of the year, they had got nothing. I was on national TV saying that the promises had just been an election ploy. People were beginning to call them liars. So the ANC announced that they would start a programme on 1 July 2001. On 30 June, we all took a *kombi*—a minibus—to the mayor's house in Kensington and cut off his supply, to remind him that he had to give us the free water and electricity the next day. We know him personally because, though he lives in the suburb now, he comes from Moletsane. In fact, he left his mother there. Our movement has many pensioners, so this is a humiliation for him. At the time, Masondo downplayed the meeting to the press, but the next year, 2002, when we went to his house again after the mayor's office refused to respond to our demands, he was still complaining about it: 'You guys, you're undisciplined! It's very bad when you come to my house'.

The comrades weren't prepared to swallow this. We reported back to the meeting in Soweto and a resolution was passed that we would all go to his house the weekend after Easter. We took a bus this time and, as fate would have it, we got there in a mean mood, even the grannies and the old people. Masondo's bodyguard opened fire and we had to run for our lives. After that, all hell broke loose. Oddly, there was a truck of municipal workers there, collecting garbage, and they let us help ourselves. The comrades poured rubbish in his swimming pool, cut his water, cut his lights. In the end, 87 of us got arrested. They used the law that allows them to keep us for seven days without bail, but we managed to mobilize even more people, each time we appeared in court. We became known as the Kensington 87. It was only in March 2003 that we were finally cleared.

Could you tell us about the Anti-Privatization Forum? Was this set up at the same time as the SECC?

The Anti-Privatization Forum is a broader coalition of several dozen groups, with SECC one of the most active. But both grew out of the campaigns against Igoli 2002. The APF really came together in July 2000, when a lot of different organizations—the Anti-Igoli 2002 Committee, the Municipal Workers' Union, the Education Workers, NGOs, students, even the SACP to begin with—came together to protest against a big international conference on privatization, 'Urban Futures', that was being held at Wits University. We set up the APF with very simple terms of reference: 'We are not here to debate privatization, or find some "third way" to finesse it. Everyone here has decided that privatization is bad, and wants to do something to fight it'. Because at that time there were a lot of think-tanks, debates, NGOs and so on that saw their job as derailing anti-privatization struggles. The ANC instructed the union leaderships to keep away, although the municipal workers stayed with us for longer.

The main campaigns fought by the APF have been around water, electricity, evictions. We have a central office at Cosatu House, in downtown Johannesburg, that gets some funding from War on Want, and clusters of affiliated groups in the communities. In Vaal, to the south, for instance, there is the Bophelong Community Forum, the Working-Class Community Coordinating Committee and three others. In the east, we have the Kathorus Concerned Residents, the United Physics of South Africa, the Vosloorus and Daveyton Peace Committee Civic. Then there's the Johannesburg cluster; Soweto and Orange Farm, the Thembelihle Committee, two affiliates in Alexandra, three new ones in the North West Province. The APF Executive Committee meets fortnightly, with a representative from each affiliated organization, and we have a Coordinating Committee that meets monthly, with five representatives from each group. We are trying to organize regional solidarity committees so that people can come out to support each other immediately they hear about an eviction or a water cut-off. In Thembelihle, an informal shack settlement of some 4,000 stands, they're facing forced removals—often at night. That's when the City Council sends the security men in, the Red Ants as they're known, from the colour of their overalls. Two or three thousand people will turn out to stop the evictions there, because the whole community is under threat. The Council says they have to be moved because the area is dolomitic; but the place they're being shifted to, ten kilometres out, is dolomitic too. Who knows what the real reasons are—it might be class or race: the settlement's next to a middle-class community, largely Asian, that might find the corrugated structures an eyesore.

Emily Nengolo, an activist in the Orange Farm Water Crisis Committee, was shot in her home in February this year in what seems to have been a politically motivated killing. How much violence and harassment does the ANC employ against the poor in the settlements, and against anti-privatization campaigners?

If you want to shift people from the place they've lived in for fifteen years—and from one shack to another, not to proper housing—then you have to bring in the Red Ants, the crowbars, the back-up police. With electricity cut-offs, violence can be unavoidable. People chase away the ESKOM men who've come to do the work, and the police are called; in Soweto, ESKOM employs its own security company. As to harassing campaigners: they arrest us during marches—you have to apply for permission and they can turn you down, or give permission with restrictions. For instance, during the Kensington 87 trials they said we could picket, but only 200 metres from the court, out of sight. Then people defy that, and the police are called. They use tear gas, rubber bullets, water cannon. It's not all-out violence, but you are threatened with it the whole time—it's always there. Emily's killing was clearly politically motivated, but that could be the specificities of the area, rather than the ANC centre; the local leadership is trigger happy.

To what extent do the APF and SECC draw on the townships' established networks of resistance—or is this wave of struggles something new?

It is a new wave, but it uses the traditions, the fire, the experience of the old days. The SECC is becoming more like a civic; people come to us with their problems because we are the official opposition in Soweto now. The ANC promote us, by attacking us as anti-ANC in their speeches. When they call meetings—and it's always councillors, never the party that does so—we go along to picket them; but they would never dare come to ours.

How has the city itself changed since the apartheid era?

The most striking differences have been the mushrooming of the informal settlements, the transformation of the Central Business District and the new 'edge cities' where big business has relocated to the outer suburbs. In Soweto, the changes have been more gradual: new home-loan developments, in-fill building, more overcrowding with backyard shacks springing up behind the old four-room council houses, now transferred to private ownership; though the Council is trying to reduce the shacks to two per yard. During apartheid, you were always under the thumb of the township manager, inevitably an Afrikaner. A house would be allocated to you; you had to register each child as it was born to allow it to live there. At 16, the township manager could say your son had to be sent to a hostel. The idea was total control. A visitor had to have a permit. The Metropolitan Police would check on the Permit List and you could lose the house if their name wasn't on it. They clamped down on overcrowding—influx control, they called it—by sending people back to the homelands. If a husband died, the widow could be sent away. You couldn't put up a shack at the back then without the township manager knowing, though you could get permission for backrooms and garages, where people used to live. Once that repression lifted, people started to build where they could—families growing, people coming in, or spilling over. Shack settlements grew up around Soweto. The Sowetan residents would have first preference, or act as landlord for a whole new area.

The changes in the Central Business District have been far more dramatic. That was an all-white area during apartheid, very hostile, with a lot of harassment of blacks. In the late eighties and early nineties, there was a big shift of business headquarters to Sandton, in the northern suburbs. Symbolically, the Johannesburg Stock Exchange relocated there, although the big banks have tended to stay in the centre. Whites who had been living in the multi-storey apartment blocks moved out in droves. The landlords made a killing, renting out empty flats and offices to black working-class incomers from Ethiopia, Nigeria, Mozambique, Somalia, Zimbabwe. They could crowd ten people into a bachelor flat for 200 rand per month each, without providing proper services. Some of the buildings have been taken over by tenants' committees. Some succeed; others, where the committee takes over the role of the landlord, have been a disaster.

Some people have rejoiced in the emergence of an 'informal city' in central Johannesburg—Saskia Sassen, for instance—hailing it as a 'new space'. This seems to parallel earlier claims that 'black economic empowerment' would sprout from the informal economy.

Formal business has certainly decayed in the city centre, with empty shops, boarded-up office blocks. Maybe a black guy will buy a shop and start selling *pap*, the local food, but there's been no boom of black businesses—prices are still high, and because of the Group Areas Act it's mainly Asians who own the shops and warehouses. There are plenty of traders and hawkers in the streets now, ladies doing other ladies' hair for money and services like that. There are big working-class taxi ranks because the public transport is so bad. But the general economic tendency is very clear: the rich have got richer and the poor poorer. Under the ANC, South Africa has now surpassed Brazil as the most unequal country in the world. According to *Statistics South Africa*, the average African household has got 19 per cent poorer in the past five years, and the average white household 15 per cent richer. Unemployment is now running at 43 per cent of the workforce, with youth unemployment up to 80 per cent in some rural areas. We've lost more than a million jobs. Basic food prices have been soaring. What with the public-spending cuts and the AIDS crisis, the situation in the health service is frightening.

As for the 'informal city', it may look more colourful but power relations haven't gone away. The banks and insurance companies have held on to their real estate there, and built themselves huge, fortified complexes with easy access to the arterial freeways out to the suburbs. Now the Council has decided it wants to clean up the Central Business District again. They've targeted over eighty buildings to clear out, through forced evictions. They're trying to limit the traders to certain streets and they are building huge, multi-storey taxi ranks that look like giant prisons, for the *kombis*. Once again, it's a question of control. The hawkers will be given space inside these blocks, so they can't be seen. The Council has set up a new Metropolitan Police Force—the most hated body from the height of the apartheid era. They've got advisers in from the NYPD to train them in Broken Mirror police theory: zero tolerance. The city is becoming a hostile place again. The ordinary police will stop you, especially if you look too dark, and demand to see your papers, just like before. There's a lot of hostility towards undocumented immigrants. Sometimes the Red Ants are used to cordon off a whole area and if you find yourself inside, without ID, you can get sent off to a detention camp at Lindelani, 50 kilometres from Johannesburg, and processed for deportation. They have trains from there to Mozambique and other places. The camp is run by prominent leaders of the ANC Women's League and operated like a private prison. The government pays per person processed.

How would you compare Mandela's role with that of Mbeki?

Mandela did what many African statesmen try to do: play the role of Caesar. He has freed himself from formal politics so that he can act the grandfather. He can swan in and out, chide the government, cover for Mbeki's stubbornness on AIDS, publicly criticize George Bush—which of course is what Mbeki should be doing. Mandela regularly pops up on TV opening a clinic or a school in the rural areas, sponsored by capital. It shows the great partnership between the private sector, government and people. He likes to behave like Father Christmas: above politics. But whenever there is a crisis, Mandela will be there to oil, smooth and con.

Their styles are very different. Mandela used to run the national ANC meetings like a chief—he would let everyone discuss, and then make the ruling. He's famous for phoning comrades at 3am and calling them 'My boy' in Xhosa, which means you are uncircumcized; an insult, but he gets away with it because of his charisma. Mbeki is much stiffer. He was trained at the Lenin Institute and spent a long time bag-carrying for Oliver Tambo in diplomatic circles in the West. He thinks he is an intellectual but he just talks in convoluted sentences. Internationally, he is seen as the sober African statesman, beloved of the World Bank, who is going to help pull the continent up by its bootstraps. But he is quite widely despised, inside the country. Our march at the World Summit on Sustainable Development on 31 August last year was a humiliation for him, it exposed his weakness in his own home base—we got 20,000 and he could only muster 3,000, even though he had COSATU, the SACP and the South African Council of Churches lined up behind him. He has made a series of blunders: Zimbabwe, AIDS, a corrupt $5 billion arms deal, letting his insecurity and paranoia show in his attacks on Cyril Ramaphosa and Tokyo Sexwale. His supporters are getting worried. Mandela might have to come in and clean up. Because the real point is that their politics are exactly the same: they share a common project, an identical orientation.

Despite the new ground swell against their neoliberal policies, the ANC can still bank on its popular legitimacy from the anti-apartheid days. What are the prospects of building an independent left alternative and what elements might this contain? Are there any signs of cracks in the ANC–SACP–COSATU alliance?

We do need such a force, but this is still a long way off. When Mbeki attacks the COSATU leaders and the SACP, calling them 'ultra-left'—as he did when he felt threatened by the scale of the anti-privatization mobilization around the WSSD summit—he is basically whipping them into line. And it works. The SACP immediately declared, 'This is our government, our ANC. We will defend it'. The president of COSATU, Willie Madisha, announced: 'We must not let our disagreements over-shadow the many areas of agreement'. Mbeki needs COSATU and the SACP to contain the working class and deliver the votes. There's no way he wants to break up the alliance; he just doesn't want them to cross a certain line. There was some vague talk of the SACP running inde-pendent candidates, though not in the 2004 elections—but what politics could they stand on that would be distinct from the ANC's?

Nevertheless, workers are losing jobs and the COSATU leadership are under pressure to respond. That's why they hold their yearly general strike—we now call it an Annual General Meeting, because it's such a regular event. They always reassure Mbeki that they are not attacking the ANC but this year's strike, though smaller, was militantly opposed to the government's privatization policy. The workers burned pictures of Mbhazima Shilowa—a former general secretary of COSATU, now the premier of Gauteng Province, the industrial heartland—and shouted him down when he tried to address them, despite the COSATU bosses on the platform chanting 'Viva ANC, Viva Shilowa'. The leadership has captured the bodies of the workers, but their souls are wandering around. One day they will connect with other bodies.

Some in the anti-globalization movement say that the working class is finished, that the social movements or even 'civil society' itself are now the leading force for change. But if we're honest, some of these social movements consist of nothing more than an office and a big grant from somewhere or other. They can call a workshop, pay people to attend, give them a nice meal and then write up a good report. They build nothing on the ground. 'Civil society' can be even more problematic, extending to the business sector and to NGOs tendering for contracts for privatized government services. Of course the working class faces greater obstacles, both political and organizational, with the neoliberal turn of the ANC and other mass parties, and the casualization and de-unionization of labour. But it remains a key component of any alternative left strategy. The high level of unemployment is a real problem here. It does make workers more cautious. We need to organize both the employed and the unemployed, to overcome capital's divide-and-conquer tactics.

What is your assessment of the World Social Forum?

Many on the Left here were quite sceptical about the anti-globalization movement to begin with. Naturally, it came under attack from the ANC—people like Trevor Manuel, the finance minister, dismissed it as bored rich kids having fun: 'What do they know about covert struggle? They wouldn't last a day in Robben Island'. But though the WSF has its strengths and weaknesses it is important for us to link up to it: this is the movement of the millennium. Personally, I found the discussion of different methods of struggle at Porto Alegre a very useful one. It was an inspiration to meet up with people from La Coordinadora in Bolivia, Oscar Olivera and others, to find out about what's been going on in the fight against water privatization there. That sort of solidarity can be very powerful in terms of keeping you going through pauses in the struggle.

How would you define the main priorities of the movement?

In terms of general questions, I think the issue of political power remains crucial. Some people attack the idea of targeting state power— the argument that globalization undermines the role of the nation-state gets translated into an excuse for avoiding the fight with your own national bourgeoisie. But we in South Africa can't not confront the ANC and Mbeki. American activists can't not confront Bush. The COSATU leaders, the SACP, are happy to fight imperialism everywhere except here at home. It's been good to demonstrate against world summit meetings in Seattle, Genoa, even Doha, but there are problems with following the global elite around—it's not something poor people can afford to do. What if they hold their next conference on the moon? Only millionaire activists will be able to go there.

The point is, we have to build where we are. We have had workshops on the World Bank, the IMF, the WTO and we've got strong people working on those issues. We've set up structures for the Campaign Against Neoliberalism in Southern Africa. But in the end we had to get down to the most basic questions: what are the problems facing people on the ground that unite us most? In Soweto, it's electricity. In another area, it is water. We've learned that you have to actually organize—to talk to people, door to door; to connect with the masses. But you have to build with a vision. From Day One we argued that electricity cuts are the result of privatization. Privatization is the result of GEAR. GEAR reflects the demands of global capital, which the ANC are bent on pushing through. We cannot finally win this immediate struggle unless we win that greater one. But still, connecting with what touches people on a daily basis, in a direct fashion, is the way to move history forward.

NORTHERN VOICES

A FARMERS' INTERNATIONAL?

What was your formation as an activist in France—were you too young to participate in 1968?

I was then in my first years of secondary school, outside Paris, but of course I was affected by what was going on—the May events, the discussions, the whole atmosphere. I didn't do much, apart from an occupation of the school football pitch. It was in the last years at school that I started going on demonstrations. When I was 17 I got involved in the struggle against military service—for the rights of conscientious objectors and deserters. There was a network of groups throughout France. We used to attend the military tribunals every week to offer support for the boys doing military service—and for the regular soldiers, put on trial for stealing or getting into conflict with an officer. We collected all the statistics and publicized what was really going on inside the army. In 1970–71, I moved to Bordeaux with my parents, just after the baccalauréat. I had been born there, but my parents—agricultural researchers, who worked on the diseases of fruit trees—moved around quite a lot. We spent a few years in Berkeley when I was a child.

I could have gone to university in Bordeaux, but I wanted to work full-time with the conscientious objectors. It was then, in the early 70s, that the peasants of the Larzac plateau got in touch with us. The Army had decided to expand the military base there—from 3,000 hectares to 17,000. The local farmers asked for our support in setting up resistance groups. We built up a network of over 200 Larzac committees in France; there were some in Germany and Britain, too. All new construction on the plateau had been forbidden so, in 1973, we started building a sheep barn there, right in the middle of the zone that the Army had earmarked. Hundreds, even thousands came to help—we called it a *manifestation en dur*: a concrete demonstration. We built it completely in stone, in the traditional way. It took nearly two years. At the same time, our network was in touch with a mountain farmers' group in the Pyrenees. We used to take military-service objectors to work up there, on land that's too steep and mountainous for machinery—everything has to be done by hand. That was where I had my first experience of dairy farming and cheese-making. Then, in the winter of 1975–76, the Larzac farmers decided we should squat the empty farms that the Army had bought up around the base. I moved into Montredon, as a sheep farmer—with many close contacts in the region.

What were the main influences on you at that stage?

There were two strands. One was the libertarian thinking of the time—anarcho-syndicalist ideas, in particular: Bakunin, Kropotkin, Proudhon, the anarchists of the Spanish Civil War. There were still a lot of Civil War veterans living in Bordeaux, and we used to have discussions with them. The other was the example of people involved in non-violent action strategies: Luther King and the civil rights movement in the States; César Chávez, the Mexican-American farm-worker who organized the Latino grape-pickers in California. There was a strong Gandhian influence, too: the idea that you can't change the world without making changes in your own life; the attempt to integrate powerful symbolic actions into forms of mass struggle.

In much of Europe and the United States, there was a clear rupture between the struggles of the sixties and seventies and those of today, with big defeats— Reagan, Thatcher—lying in between. In the States, in particular, there seems to be a new generation involved now in the anti-globalization protests. In

France, there has perhaps been less sense of a clear-cut defeat, but less genera-
tional renewal, too?

The seventies were years of powerful militancy in France, coinciding
with a political situation in which there was a possibility of the left parties taking office for the first time. There was a lot of hope in 1981,
when Mitterrand was elected. The ebb came in the eighties. Some people
argued, 'We mustn't do anything that would damage the Socialists'.
Others were disillusioned and quit politics, saying: 'We thought this
would change things, but nothing has changed'. They were the years of
commercialization, of individual solutions, when cash was all-important.
We weren't affected by that so much in the peasants' movement. On the
Larzac plateau, after our victory against the army in '81, we started organizing for self-management of the land, bringing in young people to farm,
taking up the question of Roquefort and intensive farming, fighting for
the rights of small producers, building up the trade-union networks that
eventually came together in the Confédération Paysanne. So for us, the
eighties were very rich years. There was no feeling of a downturn.

As for the young generation: it's true that many of the campaigns of
the nineties were a bit drab. They made their point, but they did not
draw many people in. It was the emergence of another set of issues—the
housing struggles of the homeless, the campaigns of the *sans-papiers*—
that began to create new forms of political activity, crystallizing in the
anti-globalization movement of the last few years. At the trial over dismantling the McDonald's in Millau in June 2000, we had over 100,000
supporters, lots of them young people. Since then, in Nice, Prague,
Genoa, there has been a real sense of a different sort of consciousness.
It comes from a more global way of thinking about the world, where the
old forms of struggle—in the work-place or against the state—no longer
carry the same weight. With the movement against a monolithic world-
economic system, people can once again see the enemy more clearly.
That had been a problem in the West. It's been difficult for people to

grasp concretely what the new forms of alienation involve, in an economy that has become completely autonomous from the political sphere. But at the same time—and this may be more specific to France—the anti-globalization movement here has never cut itself off from other social forces. We've always seen the struggle for the rights of immigrants and the excluded, the *sans-papiers*, the unemployed, the homeless, as part of the struggle against neoliberalism. We couldn't conceive of an anti-globalization movement that didn't fight for these rights at home.

You founded the Confédération Paysanne in 1987. What is its project?

Firstly, it's a defence of the interests of peasants as workers. We're exploited, too—by the banks, by the companies who buy our produce, by the firms who sell us equipment, fertilizers, seeds and animal feed. Secondly, it's a struggle against the whole intensive-farming system. The goals of the multinationals who run it are minimum employment and maximum, export-oriented production—with no regard for the environment or food quality. Take the calf-rearing system. First the young calf is separated from its mother. Then it's fed on milk that's been machine-extracted, transported to a factory, pasteurized, de-creamed, dried, reconstituted, packaged and then, finally, re-transported to the farms—with huge subsidies from the EU to ensure that the processed milk actually works out cheaper than the stuff the calves could have suckled for themselves. It's this sort of economic and ecological madness, together with the health risks that intensive farming involves, that have given the impetus to an alternative approach.

The Right has always tried to control and exploit the farmers' movement in Europe, in accordance with its own conservative, religious aims. The agricultural policy of the traditional Left was catastrophic, completely opposed to the world of the peasants in whose name it spoke. We wanted to outline a farming strategy—autonomous of the political parties—that expressed the farmers' own demands rather than instrumentalizing them for other ends. We're committed to developing forms of sustainable agriculture, which respect the need for environ-mental protection, for healthy food, for labour rights. Any farmer can join the Confédération Paysanne. It's not limited to those using organic methods or working a certain acreage. You just have to adhere to the basic project. There are around 40,000 members now. In the Chambres d'Agriculture elections this year [2001], we won 28 per cent of the vote overall—and much more in some *départements*. It was 44 per cent in Aveyron, and 46 per cent in La Manche.

How did this come to pit you against the junk-food industry—most famously, dismantling the McDonald's in Millau?

During the eighties, we built up a big campaign in France against the pressures on veal farmers to feed growth hormones to their calves. There was a strong boycott movement, and a lot of publicity about the health risks. Successive Ministers of Agriculture were forced to impose restrictions, despite heavy lobbying from the pharmaceutical industry. At the end of the eighties the EU banned their use in livestock-rearing, but it has been wriggling about on the question ever since. In 1996, the US submitted a complaint to the WTO about Europe's refusal to import American hormone-treated beef—exploiting the results of a sci-entific conference, organized by EU Commissioner Franz Fischler, that had concluded, scandalously, that five of the hormones were perfectly safe. But there was so much popular opposition, linked to people's growing anxieties about what was happening in the food chain—mad cow disease, Belgian chickens poisoned with benzodioxin, salmonella scares, GMOs—that the European Parliament actually held firm. When the WTO deadline expired in the summer of 1999, the US slapped a retaliatory 100 per cent surcharge on a long list of European products—Roquefort cheese among them. This was a huge question locally—not just for the sheep's milk producers, but for the whole Larzac region.

When we said we would protest by dismantling the half-built McDonald's in our town, everyone understood why—the symbolism was so strong. It was for proper food against *malbouffe*, agricultural workers against multinationals. The actual structure was incredibly flimsy. We piled the door-frames and partitions on to our tractor trailers and drove them through the town. The extreme Right and other nationalists tried to make out it was anti-Americanism, but the vast majority understood it was no such thing. It was a protest against a form of food production that wants to dominate the world. I saw the international support for us building up, after my arrest, watching TV in prison. Lots of American farmers and environmentalists sent in cheques.

How have you coordinated international solidarity with peasants and farmers in other lands?

From the early eighties, we started thinking about organizing on a European level. We felt we shouldn't stay on our own in France when there were other farmers' networks in Switzerland, Austria, Germany. We needed a common structure in the face of European agricultural policy, which is completely dominated by the interests of agribusiness. That was why we decided to set up the Coordination Paysanne Européenne, with its office in Brussels. It was through this movement that we got in contact with peasants' groups in other continents. It was about ten years ago that the idea of setting up an international structure was born. This was Via Campesina. There are many different peasants' organizations involved: the Karnataka State Farmers' Association from South India, which has played a big role in militant direct-action campaigns against GM seeds—they represent some 10 million farmers; the Movimento Sem Terra in Brazil, who lead land occupations by peasant families, and have an important social and educational programme. There are regional networks in every continent, organizing around their own objectives—Europe, North America, Central and South America, Asia and Africa. And then there is an overall coordinating executive which is based in Honduras at the moment, but will be moving to Asia next year.

You went to Seattle with Via Campesina. What was your critique of the WTO?

It was a big victory for agribusiness when food and agriculture were brought into the GATT process in 1986: a huge step towards regulating agricultural trade and production along neoliberal lines. Countries were no longer free to adopt their own food policies. They were obliged to lower tariffs and take a percentage of imports—which means, effectively, US and EU products: 80 per cent of world food exports come from these two. The process was taken further with the 1994 Marrakesh agreement that set up the WTO. Now a state can only refuse to import agricultural or food produce on the grounds of protecting the health of its population and livestock. The threat to these is determined by the Codex Alimentarius, which is in turn run by the food giants: 60 per cent of its delegates are from the EU and US.

The Marrakesh accords were supposed to be subject to a balance-sheet at Seattle—of course, this never came. Not that we need an official report to know that the countries of the South have been the biggest losers: opening their borders has invited a direct attack on the subsistence agriculture there. For example, South Korea and the Philippines used to be self-sufficient in rice production. Now they're compelled to import lower-grade rice at a cheaper price than the local crops, decimating their own paddy production. India and Pakistan are being forced to import textile fibres, which is having a devastating effect on small cotton farmers. In Brazil—a major agricultural exporter—a growing percentage of the population is suffering from actual malnutrition. The multinationals are taking over, denying large numbers of farming families access to the land and the possibility of feeding themselves.

What were your demands at Seattle?

Firstly, all countries should have the right to impose their own tariffs, to protect their own farming and food resources and maintain a balance between town and countryside. People have a fundamental right to produce the food they need in the area where they live. That means opposing the current relocation of American and European agribusiness—chicken and pig farms, and greenhouse vegetables—to countries with cheap labour and no environmental regulation. These firms don't feed the local people: on the contrary, they destroy the local agriculture, forcing small peasant-farming families off the land, as in Brazil. Secondly, we have to take measures to end the multinationals' dumping practice. It's a well-established tactic used to sweep a local agriculture out of the way. They flood a country with very cheap, poor-quality produce, subsidized by massive handouts in export aid and other help from big financial interests. Then they raise prices again, once the small farmers have been destroyed. In sub-Saharan Africa, livestock herds have been halved as a result of the big European meat companies flooding in heavily subsidized frozen carcasses. The abolition of all export aid would be a first step towards fair trading. The world market would then reflect the real cost of production for the exporting countries.

Thirdly, we absolutely refuse the right of the multinationals to impose patents on living things. It's bio-piracy, the grossest form of expropriation on the planet. Patents are supposed to protect a new invention or a new technique, not a natural resource. Here, it's not even the technique but the products, the genetically modified seeds themselves, that are 'patented' by half a dozen chemical companies, violating farmers' universally recognized right to gather seed for the next year's harvest. The multinationals' GM programme has also been a ferocious attack on biodiversity. For instance, something like 140,000 types of rice have been cultivated in Asia, over the centuries. They've been adapted to particular local tastes and growing conditions—long-grain, short-grain, variations in height, taste, texture, tolerance of humidity and temperatures, and so on. The food companies are working on five or six strains, genetically modified for intensive, low-labour cultivation, and imposing them in areas of traditional subsistence farming. In some Asian countries—the Philippines and China are the worst cases—these half-dozen varieties now cover two-thirds of rice-growing land.

What would be your alternative to the WTO?

We've argued for an International Trade Tribunal—in parallel to the International Court of Human Rights—with a Charter, and judges nominated by the UN. There should be transparency of action, and private individuals, groups and trade unions should be able to bring cases, as well as states. The Tribunal would play a constitutional role, advising on whether international economic accords should be ratified: they would have to concur with the individual and collective rights to which UN members are signatories—the right to food, to shelter, to work, education, health. These rights need to be imposed upon the market; they should be respected not just by states but by economic institutions. It's a similar process to that of the Kyoto accords on the environment.

Kyoto surely doesn't offer a very powerful precedent?

I agree. But these things take time. The call for an International War Crimes Tribunal has now been ratified by 30 or 40 countries, although it's taken almost four decades. But it's essential to ask what structures we do want, for multilateral trade. We have to develop a long-term global vision, without being naïve. That will require a certain balance of forces.

Others in Via Campesina—the MST, for instance—have called for the abolition of the WTO, rather than its reform. Are the experiences of North and South at odds here?

'Food out of the WTO' is Via Campesina's demand. We're all agreed on the three main points—food sovereignty, food safety, patenting. For the people of the South, food sovereignty means the right to protect themselves against imports. For us, it means fighting against export aid and against intensive farming. There's no contradiction there at all. We can stage an action in one part of the world without in any way jeopardizing the interests of the peasants elsewhere, whether it's uprooting genetically modified soya plants with the Landless Movement in Brazil, as we did last January, or demonstrating with the Indian farmers in Bangalore, or pulling up GM rice with them when they came to France, or protesting with the peasants and the Zapatistas in Mexico—effectively, our demands are the same. Of course there are different points of view in Via Campesina—it's the exchange of opinions and experiences that makes it such a fantastic network for training and debate. It's a real farmers' International, a living example of a new relationship between North and South.

Shouldn't the anti-globalization movement oppose globalized forms of military power—NATO, for example, as well as the WTO?

That's more complicated. It's not to say that one shouldn't fight against NATO. But behind the military conflict there is often a far more cunning and destructive form of economic colonization going on, through the programmes imposed by the IMF and World Bank—opening regions up to the multinationals, dismantling public services, privatizing utilities. In Sarajevo in the mid-nineties, for instance, there were people in the French military contingent who weren't officers at all but representatives of the multinational, Vivendi—originally Eaux de France. They spent their whole time studying the water mains and the infrastructure. When the fighting was over, they were on the spot to offer their services in reconstructing Bosnia's utilities. Today, it's Vivendi that runs Sarajevo's water system, as a private service. It's a form of economic domination that we're seeing throughout Latin America, Africa, Asia and elsewhere.

We do need to denounce the role of the sole military superpower as world policeman. But its economic dominance is more important. There tend to be anti-war protests against particular conflicts, rather than around militarism as such. There was quite a big mobilization in France against the Gulf War, although it wasn't easy since it was a Socialist government that was prosecuting the War. But the way the West struck simply in order to control the oil was so brazen that it did generate real protest. In Bosnia and Kosovo, the situation was much more ambiguous. There was a lot of debate inside the movement between those who opposed the NATO intervention and others who said, quite rightly, that Milošević's regime was a rotten, red-brown affair—the old Stalinism in Serb national dress. And people had known what was going on in Kosovo for years. There was a lot of discussion as to what form resistance and solidarity should take. But for me, there can never be a good war. As soon as you reach that stage, it is inevitably the people who lose. I was against both forms of military intervention, as I oppose the American bombardment of Afghanistan.

What is your attitude to the anti-globalization 'republicanism' of Chevènement, which has had its reflections in left thinking elsewhere: Benn in Britain, for example?

I had a public debate with Chevènement on French radio when I was at the anti-globalization conference at Porto Alegre last January. It came down to an opposition of two completely different points of view. Chevènement thinks that the borders of the nation-state can serve as a rampart against globalization. I believe that's an illusion. Multinational corporations, multilateral accords on investment, free-trade rules operate on quite another level, over and above national frontiers. To say one can have a strong state makes no sense in this context. It just gives people the mirage of a satisfactory form of protection. As Interior Minister, Chevènement was responsible for implementing the most restrictive immigration policies, abrogating the basic human right to freedom of movement. Closing the frontiers does nothing to resolve the fundamental issue at stake in immigration—the inequality between North and South.

Surely the one state whose power hasn't lessened in the face of these multi-lateral accords is the USA?

Of course the US completely dominates the IMF and the World Bank, and its will is hegemonic within the Security Council. But the US government, in turn, is just a tool of the big companies. Its political function is simply to relay the economic interests of the major firms—which is why, in the last elections, many people didn't see any choice between Bush and Gore. Ralph Nader's campaign highlighted the real nature of American politics. Candidates are effectively elected to be the representatives of financial or industrial groups. The system is entirely at the service of economic interests, which retain the real power. One can see this happening in detailed ways at the level of the federal administration: the power of the multinationals imposes itself directly on the running of the machine. The US state functions as a motor of support for them, institutionally and ideologically. But neoliberalism is not just an American preserve. It goes right across the board—Europe or America, governments of the Right or Social Democrats. In their negotiations with the WTO, there has been no difference between the current EU commissioner for trade—Pascal Lamy, a member of the French Socialist Party—and his predecessor Leon Brittain, a British Conservative. The same thinking—*la pensée unique*—really is hegemonic everywhere today. It's not just *la pensée américaine*. We need to pay attention to its proponents within our own countries, rather than see only the Stars and Stripes.

Jospin came to power promising a more radical agenda than either Blair or Schroeder—what's the balance-sheet?

There is scarcely any difference between the economic programmes of the Right and Left—if one can call the Socialist Party that. For example, there's been no attempt at a genuine reduction of the working week, just a series of negotiations within each sector. They're trying to take a middle path. They could have gone much further. Now, with their eyes on next year's elections, the PS have been trying to recover votes on the Left by making a show of interest in the autonomous movements. But it's just at the level of talk. They're doing nothing about the movements' programmes at the level of policy. At the WTO talks in Doha the French government will be right behind the EU positions. The main question in the legislative and presidential elections next spring will be the percentage of abstentions. A lot of people have been very disappointed in the policies of the Union of the Left—and they don't necessarily recognize themselves in the hard-left candidates, who will get a few votes in the first round. Chirac and Jospin offer no real choice between alternatives. Their vision of society is the same. We're moving increasingly towards a situation where economic logic is stronger than any political will. Party leaders simply adjust to the prevailing wind. The Confédération Paysanne is not calling for a vote for any of the parties. I myself wonder whether one should vote at all.

There has been talk of your standing in the presidential election yourself?

Never. That's not my role. In fact, it's a condition of membership of the Confédération Paysanne that you cannot stand in an election. Curiously enough, the first person who said I was thinking of standing in the presidentials was Daniel Cohn-Bendit, just after Seattle. A few days later, the Socialist Party repeated it—as if the aim was to break the social movement by saying: they do all this just to serve as a trampoline towards a political party, or to enter office. As if one couldn't have an autonomous movement with a logic of its own, acting as an oppositional force outside the established political domain. I would never see it as my role to act like the leader of a political party, as a professional representative who takes responsibility out of other people's hands. The aim of a social movement or a union like ours is to enable people to act for themselves. The economy has become an autonomous sphere today, imposing laws of its own. If we are going to create a new politics we have to understand this.

You went to the Israeli-occupied territories this summer, to demonstrate with the Palestinian farmers. What did you learn about the situation there?

First of all, I experienced the reality of the Israeli military occupation of Palestine—that it really is a war of colonization. They're trying to impose an apartheid system on both the occupied territories and the Arab population in the rest of Israel. They are also putting in place—with the support of the World Bank—a series of neoliberal measures intended to integrate the Middle East into globalized production circuits, through the exploitation of cheap Palestinian labour. Along the frontier with the occupied territories, they're setting up the same sort of enterprise system you see along the Mexican–US border. So there is a very acute economic dimension to the conflict. The UN resolutions need to be implemented. But there also needs to be a radical reorientation at the economic level, that would offer a viable future to the Palestinians.

The financial press has been triumphantly announcing that September 11 has put paid to the anti-globalization movement. What is your assessment—did the terrorist attacks in the US 'change everything'?

Underneath, nothing has changed. The world situation remains the same. The institutions are unchanged. And the anti-globalization movements, too, are still here. With the bombardment of Afghanistan, we are seeing the domestic propaganda needs of the United States being elevated to war aims, inflicting revenge on an innocent people already suffering miseries of deprivation, while threatening further destabilization in that part of the world. There is also no doubt that the US wants access to oil wells outside the control of OPEC, and may have its eye on reserves in the ex-Soviet republics of Central Asia. The position of the Confédération Paysanne has been: 'No to Taliban, No to Terrorism, No to War'.

We also see a new awareness, born of the economic crisis, of the need for regulation and public intervention. In that sense, the logic of globalization is more on the defensive now. The critique of neoliberalism that we have been developing over the last years is more valid than ever after September 11. But the response of most of the states who've signed up for what they call the 'war against terrorism' is to call for an expansion of neoliberal policies, as if that could resolve the inequalities between different countries, or social layers. They have understood nothing. September 11 should have been a chance to take stock of the sort of social and ideological costs this regime has been exacting, and to call for its radical reform. Instead, they are seeking to reinforce their global domination, escalating the dangers of wider international conflict. As neoliberalism increases the balance of misery in the world, it just augments the numbers of those desperate enough to throw themselves into fanatical, suicidal attacks against it.

BERNARD CASSEN

INVENTING ATTAC

What are the origins of the movement that has developed so strongly in France against neoliberal globalization?

They crystallized with the formation of ATTAC, which was an initiative of *Le Monde diplomatique*. In December 1997, Ignacio Ramonet, who edits the monthly, published an editorial entitled 'Disarming the Markets', in which he discussed the tyranny of financial markets, and ended with an appeal for the creation of a popular association to which he gave the name ATTAC—Association pour la Taxe Tobin pour l'Aide aux Citoyens. I had discussed this with him, having shortly before given a long lecture to the Parti Québécois about Tobin's proposal for a tax on financial transactions. He wrote the article over a weekend and brought it in on Monday, and circulated it to all of us, as we always do at *Le Monde diplo*. When I saw the acronym ATTAC, I thought 'oh, that's great'. The rest of the editorial office was a bit cool, but I thought it a brain wave. When I asked Ignacio later why he had come up with ATTAC, he told me he had been thinking of one of Robert Aldrich's movies, called *Attack*. So he conceived the acronym before he knew what it would stand for—which is the best way round.

The appeal was launched like a bottle into the sea, without any idea of what the reaction might be. But no sooner had the article appeared than we were deluged with phone calls and letters. I have never seen any article produce such a response. Normally, a piece in the paper will generate half a dozen letters, and in rare cases—when the subject is particularly sensitive, often to do with languages—a maximum of, say, 40. This time we were filling boxes with them, day after day. We were at a loss to know what to do. We had thrown out an idea, but it never occurred to us that it would be we ourselves who would create ATTAC. In the following issues, we kept our readers informed and said we were making contacts, partly to gain time. But by March 1998 the pressure from them was so great we realized there was nothing to be done: we would have to take responsibility for setting up the association, since there was such wide demand. As I had some organizational experience behind me, I was assigned the job of taking this in hand.

My first move was to bring together the organizations—not the individuals—that had responded to our appeal. This was a basic strategic choice: to build ATTAC out of existing structures, whether trade unions, civic associations, social movements or newspapers. We also drew in organizations that had not initially responded, such as the Peasant Confederation, with which I was on good terms, and other unions. Within six weeks of our first working session in March, the organizations concerned had agreed on the statutes, a political programme, and a provisional leadership. ATTAC was officially founded on 3 June 1998. Its founding members were essentially 'legal persons'— that is, collective entities—to whom a few individuals like René Dumont, Manu Chao or Gisèle Halimi were added for symbolic effect. I was astonished by the speed with which the different organizations decided to take part, including trade-union committees not usually quick off the mark, and by the financial commitment that accompanied it, allowing us to set up an office and equip a secretariat. The periodicals involved, besides *Le Monde diplomatique*, included the Catholic weekly *Témoignage chrétien*, *Transversales*, *Charlie hebdo*, *Politis*, and a little later *Alternatives économiques*, a somewhat social-democratic monthly of good quality. So it was a slightly curious mosaic. But it was not conceived and has never operated as an organizational cartel, which would have finished it.

Once the creation of ATTAC was formally announced in the *Diplo*, people started to join it—by October 1998, when we held our first national get-together in La Ciotat, near Marseilles, there were 3,500 members, and the number has grown steadily ever since. We accepted as members 'legal persons', like trade unions, associations, firms or groups, and started to work on the Tobin tax, treating it as a symbolic terrain on which to raise questions about the way in which financial markets function. Since Tobin was an establishment economist, a Nobel Prize-winner in economics from the United States at that, his proposal possessed a certain automatic initial legitimacy, serving to highlight the scandalous character of the flows of global speculation today. So for the purposes of agitation, it makes an excellent weapon. But, of course, we never for a second thought that the Tobin tax was the one solution to the dictatorship of financial markets. It was just one point of entry to attack them.

Today, the national organization of ATTAC has some 30,000 members, but in addition there are also more than 200 local committees all over France, constituted as legal bodies—ATTAC-Pays Basque, ATTAC-Touraine, ATTAC-Marseilles, and so on—in their own right, with democratic rules that we impose on them, in exchange for use of the acronym. They sprang up spontaneously, and a bit chaotically. So one might have 500 members, another 50. But a compact will shortly be signed by each committee with the national association, regulating relations between them. The national leadership—the executive committee of ATTAC—sets the political framework, issues statements, animates campaigns, etc. But if it decides to organize a day of demonstrations against the WTO, nothing will happen unless the local committees want it to. In that sense they are the backbone of the organization.

The result is a situation of dual power. The local committees are independent of us. Each has a president, a secretary, a treasurer. Likewise we are independent of them. A kind of dynamic tension exists between the two poles. The dream of some of the committees would be to constitute themselves into a federation, more or less like a party or a trade union. Although I was far from anticipating everything—indeed I didn't foresee the emergence of the committees themselves—I did sense that problems could arise here, and so I proposed national statutes that on first sight may seem undemocratic, but in my view are by no means so. There are 30 members of the national executive, of whom 18 are elected by the 70 founders of ATTAC, and 12 by the 30,000 membership at large. The reason for this structure is that the founders themselves were very diverse. They include the Peasant Confederation, civil-service trade unions, social movements like Droits Devant!, or the unemployed. There is no movement in the streets that is not a founder member of ATTAC. We reckoned that if all these forces agreed on a line of action and a leadership, they would give balance and stability to ATTAC, thus creating a framework that allowed smaller movements at regional level to develop freely. In the localities, you may find the phenomenon of 'entryism'—organized political groups joining the local committees to try to take them over. So far, they have always failed. But with our national structure, power is not there to be taken; it is proof against raids. It was crucial to make it clear from the start that tactics of that kind wouldn't work. So, last November, we elected a new executive—18 people picked by the founders, forming a blocked list on which the individual members could only vote yes or no, and 12 chosen by the membership, voting for whoever they wanted.

Since its foundation in 1998 ATTAC has not only seen an impressive growth in France, it has also spread spontaneously outside the country. Today, ATTAC groups exist in all EU member states, and in some of the countries that will join in 2004—Poland, Hungary. Its growth has been particularly strong in the Nordic countries, which was a major surprise for us, since this zone has such strong free-trade traditions. But ATTAC has swept through Denmark, Sweden, Norway and Finland. In Germany, ATTAC has some 10,000 members and in Italy it is at the heart of the 'no-globo' movement. In 1999, we convoked the first ATTAC-Europe meeting in Paris, which we have since built into a permanent network. Britain is an exception, since there the ground is already occupied by powerful NGOs like Oxfam, Friends of the Earth and War on Want on the one hand, and by a particularly active far-left group, the SWP—working through Globalize Resistance—on the other. For a British version of ATTAC to be formed, one would need the prior involvement of trade unions and intellectuals outside these sectors. Beyond Europe, ATTAC has already sprung up in Quebec, in Africa, in most Latin American countries and in Japan, and last year in Porto Alegre we organized a world meeting of the different ATTACs—nearly all of which have adopted the same model as the French original. We are meeting again in January 2003.

How do you define the aims of ATTAC?

Some months after we formed ATTAC in France, I proposed a formula which seems to have caught on—ATTAC Italy has even put it in its statutes. I call ATTAC an 'action-oriented movement of popular education'. The notion of popular education is an old one in France, that goes back to the nineteenth century. The Ligue de l'Enseignement was formed in 1866, and many other organizations were created thereafter. By the end of the twentieth century they were suffering an identity crisis, but the idea remains a powerful one, which ATTAC has taken over and adapted to globalized conditions. What does it mean today? Essentially, that militants must be well-informed, intellectually equipped for action. We don't want people turning out on demonstrations without really knowing why. So ATTAC members aren't activists in the French sense of the term, which differs from the English, since its connotation is action for action's sake. Our work is in the first instance—though not the last—educational. If you look at the ATTAC website on any given day, what you'll see is a list of a dozen meetings, conferences and debates. To make sure this mission is properly carried out, we have a scientific committee with very demanding standards that produces or checks the accuracy of the books or leaflets that ATTAC puts out. This is one of the reasons for the high level of credibility that ATTAC enjoys in the media and with politicians.

In the political establishment?

In September 2001, shortly before the Ecofin meeting in Liège, Fabius—then Minister of Finance in the Jospin government—asked us to come and see him about the Tobin tax. When we arrived, there were six senior officials from the Treasury already present in the waiting room. With them, Fabius started to grill us about the tax, enquiring how it could be levied in practice, and suggesting it was technically impossible to do so. We explained that this was far from the case: that there are at least three different ways of enforcing it, and one of the best would be through the European Central Bank itself. Fabius said he had no authority over the ECB, which we of course knew. I replied, 'We are prepared to demonstrate against the ECB in Frankfurt to support you'. He could see that we were well prepared for any question he could throw at us. In general, of course, French politicians are thoroughly ignorant about the realities of globalization. Many ATTAC members know more about the WTO than our parliamentarians.

Do you have relays within the political parties?

Yes, in both the National Assembly and the Senate, as well as in the European Parliament, where we have a coordinating committee of ATTAC members, composed of a representative of each party of the Left—a Socialist, a Communist, a Green, a Radical, a Chevènementiste. We even have a right-wing deputy: Maurice Leroy from the department of Loire-et-Cher. Some, though not all, of these people are viewed with suspicion by the leadership of their respective organizations.

You've given an idea of the scale and organization of ATTAC. How would you describe the social base of its membership?

That's a good question. We don't really have reliable data on the sociology of ATTAC in France, we have at best some opinion polls and samples.

But *grosso modo* you can say that we are an association recruited from the lower-middle classes upwards, above all in the public services, with a significant proportion of students and teachers, but employees and executives of the private sector are also present. We also have a sprinkling of farmers and unemployed. What we do not possess—any more than anyone else—are roots in the working class, or popular sectors more broadly. This is an acute general problem in France, just as I imagine it is in Britain. There is a terrible crisis of working-class representation in the political arena, as you can see from the number of former voters of the Left who now cast their ballots for Le Pen—if they bother to vote at all. We have little or no impact as yet on these categories. We are trying to find ways to do so, via member organizations that work directly on problems of social vulnerability, so we can address those who are the first victims of neoliberal globalization more effectively. But it is still very difficult to explain to an unemployed youngster of 18 all the connexions between his immediate plight and the role of the IMF or WTO. We need to develop ways of getting our message across vividly and accessibly, without denaturing it. Our problem is that our resources—the human energies at our disposal—are still too small for the pressures on us, which are enormous.

What about the age structure of the base of ATTAC?

That's our second weakness. The generational profile of ATTAC is not good. We don't have accurate figures yet—a proper study will be made in 2003—but I would guess that young people, that is, under 35, don't amount to more than perhaps 25–30 per cent of the total membership. Of course, parties and trade unions have the same problem: they fail to attract youth. People say the younger generation will only go to rock concerts, but the truth is more complicated. In June 2000, during a big rally in Millau in support of José Bové and his comrades of the Peasant Confederation, an ATTAC conference on financial institutions—not exactly the sexiest subject—drew 3,000 people, most of them very young. In principle, ATTAC can attract these energies, which you could see in the big anti-Le Pen demonstrations last May. But this is a youth culture that is difficult to capture in any organized form. You see a generation that goes from one big demonstration to another—Genoa, Barcelona, Florence—without ever really engaging in day-to-day activities, in a kind of political zapping. Then in reaction against this channel-surfing sensibility, you get the super-politicization of small nuclei who often take the lead in the streets, as in Genoa or Florence. But a political generation is never formed overnight, so something more durable may arise out of this mixture.

Tracking back a little, what are the origins of Le Monde diplomatique *itself, as the progenitor of ATTAC?*

The paper was created in 1954, as a monthly supplement to *Le Monde*, covering international affairs. By 1973, it had some 40,000 readers. The big change came with the death of the then editor of the paper, François Honti. At that point Claude Julien, the former head of the foreign desk of *Le Monde*, who had taken a sabbatical from the paper, was given the editorship of *Le Monde diplomatique*. Julien promptly made something completely different out of the journal, with a radical line against imperialism, neoliberalism, privatization. I and Ignacio Ramonet joined the staff from that moment onwards. Julien edited the paper for 17 years, retiring in 1990, when Ignacio succeeded him.

Throughout these years, the *Diplo* had no independent legal existence—it was simply an annex of the daily. But by the nineties we were no longer satisfied with this, and in 1995–96 we achieved the goal of a separate status. A new company was formed, in which 49 per cent of the shares were taken by the readers and staff of the journal—a lot of money was raised to help us—while 51 per cent were kept by the daily. Under French law, 33 per cent of the equity of a company constitutes a blocking minority, which can veto changes in its articles of association or capital structure. So our aim was to bolt the independence of the journal securely against any alteration without our consent. The *Diplo* is now a highly successful enterprise. It sells 225,000 a month on average. Like ATTAC, but on a much larger scale, it has grown from a national into an international phenomenon. There are now 23 different editions of the journal abroad: in Europe, Latin America, the Arab world, Korea. There are also more than 20 internet editions, notably in Japanese, Chinese and Russian. In these different versions, the worldwide circulation of the *Diplo* is 1.5 million. We have a global readership.

The political discrepancy between the daily and the monthly has widened over the years?

That's true in many areas. Today, our relationship with *Le Monde* is purely administrative. The daily is the majority shareholder of the monthly, and represented on its board. But it has no power of interference in what we publish, which is occasionally unpalatable to some at *Le Monde*—under French law, it is the editor who is responsible for the contents of a publication. At the same time, while some journalists at the daily may—and do—dislike the radicalism of the monthly, it completely respects our independence. It also benefits financially from the success of the *Diplo*, since we pay the daily a million francs a year for the right to use its name, in a franchise that runs for 25 years, plus the price of the technical services—printing, accounting, distribution—that we buy from it, and of course the dividends. So although some of the shareholders of *Le Monde* are certainly furious at the *Diplo*, and no doubt ask Jean-Marie Colombani—editor of the daily and head of the conglomerate it now controls—why he allows it to be published, it is actually in *Le Monde*'s interest to permit this voice, which sometimes contradicts it, to flourish. Colombani likes to say: '*Le Monde diplomatique* is a journal of opinion; *Le Monde* is a journal of opinions'. Projecting an image of pluralism is not just a personal stand, but an institutional requirement, since *Le Monde* is building a media conglomerate that is increasingly diversified in its interests.

The World Social Forum is often thought to be a joint creation of ATTAC in France and the PT in Brazil. Is that so?

In February 2000, two Brazilian friends visited me in Paris. One, Oded Grajew, was a former entrepreneur. The other, Chico Whitaker, was the secretary to the Commission on Justice and Peace of the Council of Brazilian bishops. They said they had been to Davos, and they asked, 'Why don't *Le Monde diplomatique* and ATTAC organize a counter-Davos?' I replied. 'That's already been tried, at Davos itself. But access to the place is tightly controlled, the Swiss police are murder, and to organize a counter-Davos in France doesn't make much sense.' Then an idea suddenly occurred to me, and I said: 'We need a symbolic rupture with everything Davos stands for. That has to come from the South. Brazil has the ideal conditions for doing so, as a Third World country with gigantic urban concentrations, a wretched rural population, but also powerful social movements and friendly political bases in many cities. Why don't we launch something in Porto Alegre, as a symbol of the alternatives to neoliberalism?' Two years before, I had written an article on the participatory budget of the PT administration and I knew the setting fairly well. Then I added—journalistic instinct speaking—'we should call it the World Social Forum, to challenge the World Economic Forum, and hold it on the same day of the same month of the year'.

That took all of three minutes. My friends said: 'You're right. Let's do it in Brazil'. So they contacted the then mayor of Porto Alegre, Tarso Genro, and the then governor of Rio Grande do Sul, Olivio Dutra, as well as social organizations in São Paulo, to get the project off the ground. In May, I joined them all in Brazil. We still had to decide how best to launch the project publicly. ATTAC alone could not do it. But in June there was the UN Social Summit in Geneva, at which dozens of non-governmental organizations were due to be present, offering an ideal opportunity. So in the closing session of the conference, Miguel Rossetto, then vice-governor of Rio Grande do Sul, launched an appeal for the World Social Forum which provoked an enthusiastic response. (Incidentally, Tarso,

Olivio and Miguel are now members of the Lula government.) Six months later, miraculously, the Forum came into being.

What was the geographical map of the first Forum?

The practical organization of the Forum was at first essentially a Brazilian operation, with the back-up of ATTAC-France. In purely geographical terms, its range was limited. But in media terms, its impact was enormous, because it coincided with the meeting of global elites in Davos. They, of course, assumed that they possessed complete legitimacy and tried to dismiss the meeting in Porto Alegre as a mere leftist rant. But when they had to accept the challenge of televised debates and were trounced, the tables were turned on them. Jospin had sent down two junior ministers to see what was going on—since there were over 300 French participants—and on the first or second day admitted that there were two Forums, one Economic and the other Social, putting them on the same level. So Porto Alegre was a huge success in terms of sheer international publicity.

On the other hand, I said at the time that it should be considered as number zero in the series, which ought properly to start with the sequel as the real first one, because representation from Asia, Africa and even the United States was so weak. I personally made no particular effort to ensure a strong American presence, or to hinder it. But when the American NGOs, who had been informed just like all others throughout the world, arrived only in small numbers, I was not worried. Globalization is an essentially American-led process, and it was important that anti-globalization not be American-led as well. So in my view it was strategically vital that the Forum started along a Franco-Brazilian, and then more broadly Euro-Latin American, axis, which the Americans were welcome to join once the ground was well prepared. Otherwise there was a risk that American NGOs would immediately dominate the proceedings.

The attitude of many of them was summed up by Peter Marcuse from Columbia University, who remarked that since the Forum wasn't a US initiative, not a few American groups thought it couldn't be important, and didn't go. They were mistaken, of course, and next time they showed up in force. But by then the framework of the Forum had been secured. Although most anti-globalization activists come from the North, Western Europe or America, for our purposes it was crucial to kick off from the South. We could then incorporate American contingents in a movement that already had its own vocabulary, concepts and slogans, and could draw on support from Latin American forces, for a homogeneous outlook. Our problem now, of course, is to extend that to Africa, Asia and Eastern Europe.

What has been the role of the PT in all this?

At first, the PT was a bit uneasy about the Forum, because its tradition is quite 'vertical', and it was afraid that a Forum organized in Porto Alegre, which it did not control, might somehow be used against it. On one of my trips to Brazil, Lula asked to see me. We met in the Hotel Gloria in Rio. He had his aide Marco Aurelio Garcia (now his foreign policy adviser) with him, who did most of the talking with me. Instead of discussing the Forum and its relationship with the PT, I talked about ATTAC and its relation to political parties in France. Each of us knew that we were talking about the same thing. I explained that ATTAC was an association, not a party, and kept its distance from organized political forces, though it was not against them. He got the message, and the next day I was informed by Marco Aurelio that he supported the Forum. But the PT as such has never played any role—none whatever—in the leadership of the Forum. On the contrary, the Brazilian committee contains people thoroughly hostile to any interference from political parties or groups, even if some, if not all of them, are members of the PT themselves. A couple of times Olivio Dutra, as PT governor of Rio Grande do Sul, asked one of his aides to ring me in France to find out what the

Brazilian committee was up to. So the PT has had no part in either the concept, or the content, of the World Social Forum.

Nevertheless, PT control of the administration in Rio Grande do Sul and Porto Alegre was presumably of material importance for the infrastructure of the Forums. Is this now threatened by the party's loss of power in Rio Grande do Sul?

It's too early to say. The support of the city, where the PT is still in power, remains. Rigotto, the new PMDB governor, has said he will continue to help the Forum, but it must become 'more open'. Obviously, there is no question of changing it, so in practice this means he will drastically reduce the level of assistance to it. Perhaps the new federal government will step into the breach, but all speakers in the Third Forum have been told that they must pay their own expenses. There will be difficulties, but the Forum itself is not at risk. Rigotto is well aware that shopkeepers, hotels, taxis in Porto Alegre—services in general—benefit hugely from the Forum. A move against it would be very unpopular locally.

How do you assess the impact September 11 and the war on terrorism have had on the Social Forum?

Only four months elapsed between September 11 and the second Forum in January 2002, and for a few days after the attentat there was a certain disorientation among ATTAC militants in France. But then Bush did us a service by explaining that anti-globalization movements were anti-American movements. After that there were twice as many participants in the second Forum, where some 3,000 organizations were represented. So in that sense, the war on terrorism just strengthened our determination not to be intimidated. The more belligerent Bush becomes, the more violent the reaction he is liable to provoke. In France too, steps are being taken to criminalize social movements and NGOs—not terrorists—while in Italy anti-globalization militants are already being arrested. The attack on the WTC has given Bush and hawks everywhere a chance to restrict civil liberties, and cover up bad economic news. The movement understood that quite quickly, and has resisted this pressure pretty well.

To what extent do you think it possible to separate the original agenda of the World Social Forum from the global military offensive of the United States?

The theme of war has entered the prospect of the Forum, and it is important—but not all-important. War or peace, the problems of globalization remained essentially the same on September 10 and September 12: hunger, debt, inequality, AIDS. What we see now is a reconfiguration within the neoliberal order to the advantage of the United States. Europe and Japan, of course, are embarked on the same boat of globalization as the US. But aboard it, there are people who have tried to adopt measures that have nothing to do with neoliberalism, like the 35-hour week. The new conjuncture has allowed America to reassert control over its allies—I would even say that the principal target of the current American offensive is less Iraq than its 'partners'. All this has its place in the Forum, but it will not monopolize it. If the first Forum was an occasion for analysis and critique, and the second for proposals, the third will be for strategy. The questions will be much more operational: what is to be done? The issue of war will be very important, but it will not be as dominant as it was in Italy, at the European Forum in Florence, where it overshadowed everything else.

Were you really surprised by that?

The prospect of war is a much more burning issue in Italy than in France, not least because there are US military bases there, which is not the case in our country. At Florence it was sometimes said that there was no anti-war mobilization in France because ATTAC prevented one, which is ridiculous. The fact is that Chirac has made protest difficult here by appearing to resist American pressures. That has made him very popular in the Arab world, and reduced the potential for French demonstrations against him, though this may not last very long. In Italy, the situation is quite different. War is an absolutely central issue there, but against a background of major social struggles, wide detestation of Berlusconi, and a powerful trade-union movement led by the CGIL. The context is much more effervescent than in France, and the theme of war has become a virtual obsession. Knowing that the Forum would be held in Italy, and that Rifondazione would mobilize around the issue, we all agreed that war would be a leading theme in Florence, alongside its original slogan: 'We Need a Different Europe'. But then we discovered that all the posters for the march spoke only of war, without mentioning Europe. I can't say I was entirely surprised. But if the Forum had been held in France, it would not have gone like this. War would have been on the agenda, but not an obsession with war. Because whether war breaks out or not, B-52s and special forces will not alter poverty in Brazil or hunger in Argentina.

Isn't the contrast you've drawn a bit paradoxical? After all, the Italian state—even under Berlusconi—plays a very minor role in the current wave of Western military interventions, whereas the French state has participated full-bore in every one of them: in the Gulf, the Balkans, Afghanistan and maybe tomorrow Iraq. An Italian might say: this may not be ATTAC's issue, but the fact is that the French Left has a very weak record of resistance to wars of any kind, from Indochina and Algeria onwards.

True enough. In France, the conversion of the Communist Party to the nuclear *force de frappe* in the 1970s—when it was still the largest and most powerful party of the Left—was a watershed. Pacifist traditions of any kind are virtually non-existent in Paris, and there were never any mass struggles against nuclear weapons, as you had in Britain. Today, there is unanimity in the political establishment behind the French nuclear arsenal. On the other hand, if there is a war against Iraq, there will be mass protests—I am completely sure of that. Chirac has little to gain and a lot to lose if he takes part in an American expedition, because he has gained quite a bit by appearing to oppose one so far. But, judging by his past behaviour, he is quite capable of doing so.

How would you situate ATTAC historically? For a long time France was the country in Europe to which nearly all others—the Italians were perhaps an exception—looked for a political lead. This is a tradition that goes back to 1789, 1830, 1848, 1871, right on down to 1968. Thereafter it appeared to fade away. Should one see ATTAC as in its own way a revival of this lineage—a French creation and initiative, in a period of deep reaction, that rapidly acquired a broad international resonance?

I've emphasized the way in which it was made possible by the impact of *Le Monde diplomatique*, which had already gained an international audience before ATTAC was created. But it is also rooted in another and much older tradition within French society, which is *la fonction publique*. In France, public services—education, transport, utilities—are not only a technical mode of delivering goods to citizens, but a bond of social solidarity: what makes possible the 'republican pact' that creates national cohesion. Attachment to these services lies very deep in French culture, as one could see in the great strike movement of 1995, which was essentially a public-sector phenomenon. When the Paris metro shut down, it would take people here about three hours every day to get from Vincennes, where I live, to work in the city, and another three to get home again. But—this was the fantastic thing—it was as if the public-sector workers were striking for everyone else. It was a kind of proxy strike. Far from there being any complaints, the movement was hugely popular. That was why the government had to beat a retreat.

What one could see very clearly was that in popular consciousness, the public services are the first line of defence of the citizenry. They knew immediately that if these services were taken apart, they would be next for the chop. Of course, the battle over these services is worldwide. The drive to privatize them has two aims, which the European Commission scarcely takes the trouble to conceal. What are they? First, to put an end to a situation where banks and insurance companies see large sums of money circulating under their nose, in pension or security systems over which they have no control. The very thought of it makes them ill. Second, to whittle down the forces of resistance to neoliberalism. Public-sector employees have legal rights to strike and use them. If you can reduce their numbers, you weaken the possibility of any resistance to the neoliberal order.

ATTAC comes to a large extent out of this world, as its composition suggests—we are in our own way heirs of its traditions, and belong to its logic. But, of course, there was also the global conjuncture of the late nineties. Ignacio Ramonet wrote his editorial of December 1997 at the height of the Asian financial crisis, which was like a life-size illustration of all the texts against globalization the paper had ever published. That too gave powerful credibility to the launching of ATTAC.

The great strikes of 1995 in France, followed by the Asian financial crisis in 1997, explain why ATTAC was born well before Seattle. But there is still one puzzle about its emergence. If one looks at the official varieties of French politics over the past 20 years, from Mitterrand onwards, their centre of gravity has moved steadily to the right. Ironically, it was Chirac who popularized the notion of la pensée unique as a stifling consensus, before becoming one of its most prominent examples. Whether governments have been nominally of the Left or Right, the policies have remained the same. With every election, the voters rejected the government that pursued this programme, and the new government then carries on as before. How do you explain this strange paradox: a radical tradition that is far from spent, and finds expression in one of the strongest movements of protest in Europe, yet apparently has no impact on the immovable cupola of French politics?

That's a very complex question, to which I can do no more than give a few elements of an answer—it really demands a longer and more theoretical reflection. But in the first instance you have to remember the weight of the historic division between Right and Left in French life—it is virtually consubstantial with our political tradition. These are categories that live on after their content has declined or disappeared. So there is always a sector of opinion for which a bad government of the Left— any such government—is preferable to a good government of the Right. You can see this reflex at work in every municipal and legislative election in France. It is powerfully reinforced by the two-round voting system. There is no chance of changing this overnight.

Then there has been the enthusiastic neoliberal turn of social-democracy in France, as elsewhere, which has often made governments of the Left as zealous for deregulation and privatization as governments of the Right. Part of the reason for that difference is that the number one pressure for liberalization has come from the European Union, to which social-democrats were in many cases more favourable than conservatives. In France, as Alain Touraine candidly admitted, the word 'liberal' could for a long time not be spoken. So a substitute was found for it: 'Europe'. Things could be done in the name of Europe that would never have got through otherwise. In this sense, Europe was the Trojan horse of neoliberalism in France. You can see this very clearly in the case of Mitterrand's presidency. In 1988, after he was re-elected President, the first European directive on the free movement of capital in the EU came into force. It had been approved by Balladur as Minister of Finance during the cohabitation of the previous government. Now the PS was back in office again, and Bérégovoy went to Mitterrand and asked him: '*Monsieur le Président*, what should I do? Ought I to fight for a directive harmonizing taxation of capital in the Community, as a safeguard?' To which Mitterrand simply replied: 'Bérégovoy, are you for Europe or against it?' Bérégovoy understood he had no choice. Mitterrand deliberately opted for a neoliberal Europe rather than no Europe at all. But he had, after all, a conception of Europe that dated from the immediate post-war period.

This kind of outlook influenced all the parties, including the Communists. *Le Monde diplomatique* and ATTAC have developed a consistent critique of it, with arguments that have crystallized into an active framework of education and action, in an international context where they have real resonance. It is perfectly true that we have had little impact on the French governments to date. But we always thought of a medium-term strategy, and never paid much attention to the electoral cycle in France. The elites don't care much about us, but movements and citizens do. Still, our target audience is ultimately international, rather than national. Our fundamental aim, as I have often said, is to decontaminate people's minds. Our heads have been stuffed with neoliberalism, its virus is in our brain cells, and we need to detoxify them. We have to be able to start thinking freely again, which means believing that something can be done. For the overwhelming conviction at present is that, politically speaking, nothing can be done. That is why our slogan, 'Another world is possible', amounts to something like a cultural revolution. It means that we are not condemned to neoliberalism, we can envisage other ways of living and organizing society than those we have at present. So our task is to persuade the largest number of people possible of the viability of such alternatives, and prepare the ground for a Gramscian hegemony that would allow different policies to be realized.

For the moment, our influence is considerable at the level of public opinion in general, and finds some echo in the political parties, even of the Right. But there is still very little advance there. This morning I had to give a talk to a conference of the PS, whose first session was devoted to the question: 'what forms of organization do we need?', while the second asked 'what kind of ideas do we need?' As if you could decide matters in that order! I told them that for us the basic line of division is what attitude one takes to neoliberal globalization. So long as you are not clear about that, you might as well give up—there is no *juste milieu* that will allow you to evade the issue: saying yes to the Commission and no to the IMF is a farce that no longer fools anyone. The majority of the audience was openly hostile, of course. But a strong minority is beginning to listen, and to ask questions. Intellectually, we have by and large won the game, as you can see from the titles that sell in French bookshops.

What explains the strange default of the French political class as a whole in the arena of foreign policy, where in the last years it seems to have lost its strategic capacity completely? The current enlargement of the EU is a dramatic example. What can the French elites gain from a Europe of 25 members— with the United States openly demanding that Turkey, as the launching pad for a war on Iraq, be admitted in short order too? It is no mystery why the English elites are happy with this prospect, since they have always wanted to dilute the Community. But what has happened to their French counterparts, that they accept it so passively?

The debate on Europe has always been very different in France from every other continental country, where there was a consensus in favour of integration, uniting Christian and social democrats. That did not exist in France, where there was a sharp division between most social-democrats and the local equivalent of Christian democrats, on the one hand, and Gaullists and Communists on the other. This is a structural cleavage which put paid to the European Defence Community in 1954, and has to a large extent persisted to this day. The partisans of Europe have never commanded a secure majority, and so they never wanted Europe to be really discussed. They feared that any concrete, detailed debate might give weapons to their adversaries, and so they always avoided it. Because they were always on the defensive, there was very little public discussion of Europe in France, till the late eighties. Then, in 1992, Mitterrand decided to stage a referendum on the Treaty of Maastricht. There was a tremendous political and media barrage in favour: practically every newspaper called for a yes vote, every television channel pummelled the same message home, most public figures declared their support. Yet in the end, 49 per cent of those who voted rejected the Treaty. So it squeaked through by a miracle. For good reasons and bad, popular opinion did not follow instructions from on high.

That is why none of the succeeding treaties—Nice and the like—have been submitted to a referendum. The chances of losing were too high.

So there was no debate about Europe in France because the pro-Europeans regarded themselves as a fortress under siege, and did not want to air issues that might expose divisions among them, or assist their opponents. Today, there is zero discussion of enlargement—absolutely zero—because that is what makes life easy for transnational companies and financial markets. ATTAC defines enlargement as a structural-adjustment plan, along IMF lines, for Eastern Europe. The Washington Consensus comes by different names these days: in Western Europe we have the ECB and the Stability Pact, in the South it is structural adjustment, in Eastern Europe it is the incorporation of the *acquis communautaire*. Since the Nice summit of December 2000, ATTAC has had many workshops on Europe in progress. We have produced documents and demonstrated for another vision of Europe, and will certainly intervene on the terrain of the Constitution that Giscard's convention in Brussels is now confecting.

In the theoretical debates over global neoliberalism, what was Pierre Bourdieu's role—has the organization he created, Raisons d'Agir, played a significant flanking part alongside ATTAC?

Raisons d'Agir is one of the founding members of ATTAC, and Bourdieu's work has always been a key point of reference for us. Institutionally, however, he kept his distance. We asked him, without success, to address one general assembly of ATTAC. He had his own circle, not to speak of a court, and hoped to inspire a European social movement. Actually, his idea of a European Estates-General came true, but at the Social Forum in Florence, out of a movement he had not foreseen. I saw him once at Millau, but never had a conversation with him. Sadly, just before he died, we had finally arranged to have lunch together. It's a great pity that a closer connexion between Bourdieu and ATTAC was never made, because it would have had a lot of impact.

How do you assess the balance of forces on the wider French intellectual scene, where a whole series of bestsellers attacking la pensée unique *coexist with the ubiquitous media prominence of its chief exponents, not least in* Le Monde *itself?*

On television and in the press and leading publishing houses, you continue to see the same familiar faces and names everywhere: Philippe Sollers, Alain Minc, Bernard-Henri Lévy, André Glucksmann, Alexandre Adler—not to speak of Cold War veterans like Jean-François Revel. But this media galaxy plays for a middle-brow public, it has little credibility in the intelligentsia proper, based mainly in the educational system. It operates as a mutually supportive mafia, which has been very well described by Serge Halimi in his book *Les nouveaux chiens de garde*—it sold a quarter of a million copies, which gives you an idea of how this coterie is viewed by the great majority of what Régis Debray has called the *bas-clergé* of the French intellectual class. In this layer, my guess is that opinion has been moving strongly in our direction—especially perhaps among economists. Whereas the neoliberal paradigm was completely hegemonic up to a few years ago, now it is strongly challenged, as you can see from the widespread reception of the Fitoussi Report.

How do you see the next phase of development for ATTAC and the World Social Forum?

The World Social Forum is not an entity, but a process—a snowballing momentum that is bringing together forces which, though developing in the same direction, were without mutual contact and often completely unaware of each other. A global constellation is coming into being that is beginning to think along the same lines, to share its strategic concepts, to link common problems together, to forge the chains of a new solidarity. All this is now moving with astonishing speed. There has just been an Asian Social Forum in India, an area with which we hitherto had virtually no contact. In Brazil, the government's agenda is set by all the problems identified at Porto Alegre. What will Lula do about the enormous debt that is crushing the country? He has said, of course, that Brazil will be meticulous in meeting its obligations. But will it actually be able to? I believe that a moment of truth is arriving in Argentina and Brazil, which could create the conditions for a radical, worldwide revision of the neoliberal order. If the President of Brazil were to say, 'we are no longer going to pauperize our citizens to pay foreign bond-holders', and Argentina and other Latin American countries followed him, what would happen? Wall Street could do very little about it, since as a leading banker has admitted privately, 'Brazil is too big to fail'. The banks would have little alternative but to 'save the furniture', and accept losses of 30 or 40 per cent rather than write off 100 per cent of their investments.

As for France, Chirac got less than a fifth of the electorate in the first round of the Presidential elections, and the Right that is now in power only just over a third. The political base of the new regime is very, very weak. The government is already extremely nervous, as it sees signs of social tension mounting, particularly about pensions. It is not looking for a confrontation. Growth is slowing to a crawl, the Stability Pact is strangling consumption, fixed costs are rising. If Chirac tries to increase taxes to cover the deficit, there will be an outcry at his betrayal, after so many electoral promises not to; if he tries to slash public expenditure, he will be heading once again for a show-down in the streets. The Right is caught in this dilemma, and its logic is explosive.

What we are seeing today is a movement that, for the first time, is adopting the same perspectives, hitting at the same targets, and developing all over the world, linking local struggles to global objectives. History has accelerated so rapidly in the last ten or fifteen years that there is no reason to think it will stabilize now. I cannot help feeling that what we have achieved together so far will have some effect on what is to come.

RAISING A RUCKUS

How did you get into political protest—what were your starting-points?

I wanted to be an activist since I was a little kid. My parents were pretty concerned people—my mom was a teacher and my pop was a United Rubber worker in a Goodrich tyre plant, till they closed it down. So I grew up in somewhat of an activist house. I remember when I was ten or eleven watching a Greenpeace story on *Sixty Minutes*—all these lunatics with long hair in little inflatable rubber boats, zipping round the ocean and putting themselves in front of explosive whale harpoons. I guess that's when I decided I wanted to do that, some day. That would have been around 1977, in the heyday of Greenpeace. After college in west Pennsylvania, I went backpacking around the South Pacific for about a year. There my commitments were reinforced by seeing the environmental devastation of the region, particularly in Australia. My uncle managed one of the largest oil refineries in the southern hemisphere for Caltex outside Sydney, and Greenpeace was regularly plugging his outfalls into the Cronulla Bay. I would see these images on the news and feel inspired. Then my uncle would come home and say, 'Those green bastards! You know, they flooded my pipes today!'

When I got back to the United States, I started to work for Greenpeace in Philadelphia in the winter of 1990, and got into my first action in the spring of 1991. I then moved down to Washington to be the Assistant Director there in the summer. I became a Director a few months later, and ran the DC office of Greenpeace for about five years. At the time it was pretty healthy economically, but soon afterwards it started to crumble—I was constantly saying goodbye to friends as it downsized and downsized. By 1996 I decided I wanted to work more on rivers and forests anyway, and to see the North-West. Greenpeace wasn't working on forests at all, and wasn't focusing on rivers as much I wanted. So I left and pretty soon afterwards got involved in a bunch of EarthFirst actions in the Headwaters forest in northern California. One of the things I wanted to do was take the ethic of excellence and the technological sophistication of Greenpeace actions, and spread it around. Greenpeace had an amazing training regime, but it was only for an elite cadre inside the organization. My idea was to dumb this down technologically, so it would be cheaper, and then popularize it.

Who created Ruckus?

Mike Roselle, my non-violence trainer at the last Greenpeace action camp and one of the founders of EarthFirst, was the key person. He had been the first direct-action coordinator for Greenpeace in the United States. In the early nineties, he and Twilly Cannon were living out in Montana, where they were up against a really nefarious piece of legislation called the Timber Salvage Rider, which was opening up some of the biggest roadless areas left unlogged in our national forests, on the pretext of clearing the three Ds—down, dead or dying, and diseased trees. This was antithetical to everything that a real biologist would tell you about an ecosystem—in fact, dead and dying trees are of vital importance to any kind of forest. It was just a rationalization to destroy some of the last wilderness left. There was big struggle against it, that drew in a whole new generation of activists. Mike, who comes from Kentucky, grew up on and off in orphanages because his mom couldn't afford to have the kids at home. He was like a living legend, a veteran of actions involving hundreds of arrests, that I'd read about while growing up. In 1995, he and Twilly and a few others founded the Ruckus Society.

Basically they took the Greenpeace direct-action model, threw away the little rubber boats, and imposed it on the forests. Instead of teaching how to steer inflatables, they taught people technical tree-climbing for doing tree sit-ins, tripods, and tree villages, to defend wilderness areas. Then they built a large scaffolding to teach urban climbing techniques. The rest of the skills were very traditional: non-violence training, media training, direct action planning and strategy, and scouting.

Where did you come in?

At the time I was still working for Greenpeace; so far as I recall, when Roselle, Cannon and the others held their first informal camp, I was on the Rainbow Warrior. But I was soon working as one of their lead climb trainers, even before leaving Greenpeace. I took over as Director two years ago.

How was the name Ruckus picked?

At some point during the campaign against the Timber Salvage Rider, Howie Wolke—one of the founders of EarthFirst—made an off-hand comment to Roselle that we don't need a wilderness society any more, we need a ruckus society. That really resonated with Roselle. Ruckus, as the definition on the back of our T-shirts says, is a loud, angry interruption, a hullabaloo, a disruption. It's not an acronym, it doesn't stand for anything. It just announces what we're about: strategically, non-violently raisin' hell, because we don't like what's happening to the planet. Some people claim it's too provocative and we need to change it, that people are going to misunderstand us because of it. 'When your name is the Ruckus Society, they're going to believe just about anything they are told about you'. But it suits us.

What kind of an outfit is Ruckus—is it right that it's primarily a training organization, that doesn't have an actual membership?

The Ruckus Society is in many respects anomalous, in that we have some attributes of EarthFirst, and some attributes of a movement, while organizationally we in some ways resemble Greenpeace or Rainforest Action Network. But we're not actually any of these things—we're not an institution, and we're not a movement, we operate in some middle ground. We like to think of ourselves, if you will, as a volunteer fire department for the movement. What we want to do is hold a place in the centre, which offers the resources and contacts and political opportunities for people to come together. You can think of Ruckus as a set of concentric rings. We have a very small staff; then we have probably twenty or thirty volunteers that really orbit close to that; and about a hundred and twenty who probably come to one camp a year, or once every couple of years; and then we have close to three thousand people who have graduated from our programme, with whom we keep in close touch. Who are they? Demographically they're still fairly homogeneous, but getting more diverse. When we first started, it was almost entirely folks from Greenpeace or Rainforest Action Network, with a few EarthFirsters. But in the five short years we've been around, an entire generation of Ruckus trainers has had the torch passed on to them, and as we've gotten more involved with the human rights movement, with social justice and fair trade organizations, and labour groups—so we're seeing a slow but steady diversification of that general population. We have a couple of grandmothers that are trainers, though no grandfathers yet. But most Ruckus trainers are somewhere between 22 and 35.

What's your response to those who say these activists are white middle-class kids with authority complexes about their parents?

We are who we are. We can't escape where we've come from. Five years ago, we were an organization composed predominantly of white tree-huggers. We've come along since then. One of our priority pushes this year is the Schools Not Jails campaign on the West Coast, and supporting youth-led communities of colour struggling against the expansion of the prison–industrial complex. In our pre-convention camps in 2000, things were really changing—before the Republican Convention in

Philadelphia the white trainers were the minority, and for the Democratic one in LA I'd say the camp was about 50–50. I was in Greenpeace when it was trying to diversify its stock in a really tokenistic and unstrategic way, and asking a lot of the wrong questions—such as 'How do we bring more brown-skinned people out into our movement, out onto the streets with us?' Ruckus is asking: 'How do we get more white faces standing in solidarity with movements and struggles that are central to people of colour? How do we support those campaigns?'

How is Ruckus funded?

Ruckus started out with the generosity of one individual, essentially. For a couple of years he carried Ruckus on his back, but he asked us to use those two years to diversify our funding base, and wean ourselves off him. Ruckus did that with only very limited success, and was struggling by the third year—which was when I came in as Director. We had one institutional support in the Turner Foundation, which was giving us five or ten thousand bucks a year. We ended up having a decent run with Turner—the last year they funded us we got fifty thousand dollars from them. But in 2000 we asked for a hundred and they said, politely, 'No thank you'—we were told that we weren't operating as a forest organization any more and that we had too much of a WTO residue on our proposal and resumé. Ted is a big fan of free trade. Since that time, we've diversified considerably. We get about 40 per cent of our funding from small but pretty radical foundations, in five-, ten- and twenty-thousand-dollar chunks. We don't receive anything from Ford, Rockefeller or Hewlett-Packard, of course. Currently we're getting about 40 per cent of our budget from individuals, and most of that money comes from a pretty small number of people. We also get some 15 per cent or so from other NGOs that co-sponsor our camps, or contract us out as an action team for hire, or as consultants; and the other 5 per cent comes from merchandise.

How does the decision-making process work?

Obviously, those who are closest to the centre get more input than people who are further away from it. For example, I took the decision to hold the WTO camp, and that's how a lot of the decisions have been made since. We're not a consensus organization. But we're not an overwhelming hierarchy either—it's a pretty flat management structure. We don't even like to use the word management, preferring to be called coordinators. But we try to communicate as a society, with a lot of transparency and availability to a larger community around us.

You've spoken of media training—what do you mean by that?

It's mostly nuts and bolts of media for activists: how to write a good press release; how to flack your story; how to identify and develop friendly media ties. But the most important thing we teach is how to distil very complex campaign themes into very simple messages, that can pass through the filter of corporate-controlled media and still make it out the other side into the homes of the American or global public, in a form that you would still consider effective—and can begin to create the political will we need to turn things around.

Do you see any problems here? At the demonstrations outside the Democratic Convention in Los Angeles, it often seemed too many messages were being put on the streets, sometimes cancelling each other out.

We were driven into a false competition between messages, between campaigns, with far too little time to talk about a people's platform which had lots of diverse planks to it. They were all based on social justice, but they were different and there was no chance to talk properly about any of them. The reporters would sanitize the scene even more completely by just labelling us 'protesters', without mentioning any of the issues we were acting on. Still, we knew this was going to happen—

we've seen how the media work, and know the pathology of these giant corporations, which will always try to marginalize and stereotype us. So there needs to be smarter planning of our messages to the world. At Seattle a great effort was made to bring lots and lots of different people under the tent, and not discount anyone's campaign or slogans. In Philadelphia and LA, we could have framed matters better.

Does the search for consensus among very disparate groups become a real difficulty?

Because we exist in symbiosis with lots of different kinds of organisms in this movement, Ruckus moves in and out of situations where we have to help make decisions in a consensual framework. When that happens we try to demand transparency and accountability, since there is often a tyranny of endurance—the last ones left at the table get to make the decision. When the process of consensus is being tweaked in the direction of some hidden agenda, it can be a very disempowering experience. We try to ensure not only that good decisions are made, but that whatever the decision, those who take it are accountable.

How do you see the role of Ruckus, as distinct from groups like Global Exchange, Amazon Watch, Rainforest Action Network, or EarthFirst?

I would say we differ starkly from EarthFirst, and from Rainforest Action Network. These are campaigning organizations, who target very specific political issues. We are more of a strategic and tactical clearing-house and support network. I'm not saying that's all we do. We're evolving and looking at how Ruckus operates, and whether or not we are in fact doing something like campaigning—and the answer we keep coming up with is 'Yes'.

What's been the overall evolution of Ruckus, then?

We started out as an environmental group, with a very specific focus on forest issues. Then, as we gained notoriety, we moved into other bio-regions. The first time we went down to the South-East, into Appalachia, a lot of different activists came out to our camp—not just folks working on chip mills, but also environmental justice types. That began to happen more and more, so we started going into a region and asking 'What are the most compelling issues round here? Let's bring every-body together, talk about common adversaries and build solidarity, so that when one campaign needs support and help, additional numbers and resources, it can count on others who've met at our camps coming out and heeding the call.'

Then we took another step about two years ago, when I became Director. We were in some serious financial straits, and we realized we could go to foundations concerned with human rights, if we organized around these issues. We set up our first human rights camp in 1998, and another in 1999. So we ceased to be just an environmental group; we diversified our portfolio, if you will. It was at a 1999 camp that we first began to discuss setting our sights on the WTO as a concrete politi-cal target. We could see there were different constituencies we could approach, and show how useful the set of skills we had to offer could be to them—the human rights community, the fair trade community, the labour movement, the social justice movements.

The confluence of movements that came together against the WTO was possible because it was such an all-encompassing adversary to so many different people, so evil and nefarious on so many levels. For Ruckus, targeting the WTO was a way to force open the larger issues of corporate globalization—it was an entry point, to gain traction and pique the American public. Since the WTO campaign, we've seen Citigroup as the perfect target because if you look at Citi, you find it's number one, two or three in almost every sector of extraction you could think of—oil, forests, mining; and if you consider red-lining and predatory lending in disenfranchised communities of colour, they're way up there too; or if you take sweatshop labour and exploitation, Citi also casts a long shadow. They're virtually a poster child for corporate globalization. So now we're going after them. Likewise, we want to work on biotech and Schools Not Jails.

Do you see this kind of activity as a break from the past, or as following a consistent trajectory?

Well, I think that it is a fairly logical progression. It is an expansion of our world-view; we're seeing more and more people coming into the fold. A lot of people that were big-time wilderness defenders five years ago have now moved into urban environments, working on social justice issues. I was blown away to see how many young students, high-school-age activists working on Schools Not Jails, who come from inner-city communities in Los Angeles, have a real environmental sensitivity. Something very exciting and dynamic is happening right now: a general recognition that people can cut across traditional boundaries of race, class, culture and gender, by building a sense of community that creates reciprocity—the knowledge of each group that when its time comes, it will need and can get the support of the others as well.

How would you assess Ruckus's role at Seattle?

I think that we made a very important contribution to the battle against the WTO. All kinds of organizations pitched in, and I wouldn't say that our role was any more or less significant than anyone else's. But we brought together a lot of the direct action community and leadership for the action in Seattle. In fact, the Direct Action Network was born at our camp two months before Seattle, and it was great to see all the different tools and gear that we granted out for the action being put to such good use by people in the streets, the lock-down devices and well-trained people who put the blockade in place. Beforehand, we planned to hang this giant banner from a crane, so you could see the Space Needle behind it. We went back and forth for weeks about what this damn flag should say. Finally, we settled on a pair of one-way street signs pointing in opposite directions—one to the WTO, the other to Democracy. It was very simple and beautiful, and stark: people got it. I jumped into the banner-hanging action on 30 November, not even expecting to get to the streets the next day. But the cops let me out on bail, so I got to make a complete circumnavigation of the Convention Centre, while 13 simultaneous actions made an incredible festival of resistance before the cops attacked and all hell broke loose. It was an amazing week. I'm very proud of our share in it.

What about the following demonstrations in DC, Philly and LA? In Seattle, the police weren't really ready, but in the next cities the authorities already had a siege mentality.

Yes, no question. In DC, I think we made a tactical mistake. We were so inspired by the incredible victory of shutting down the WTO conclave in Seattle, that we announced we were going to close down the World Bank/IMF meeting in Washington. That gave the authorities the opportunity to win, by keeping it open. Our success or failure should be defined by the vision of the world we develop, and the kind of solutions for it we offer, rather than by whether we can tactically out-manoeuvre the most powerful combined police forces in the world—in DC they have fifteen different agencies in a multi-jurisdictional task-force. In Seattle, we told them exactly what we were going to do. I had dinner with the captain in charge of the entire downtown area, and the lieutenant in charge of the Convention Centre itself. They literally didn't believe us. They just couldn't credit that thousands of people were going to come out there and risk arrest to intervene against the most powerful business meeting in the history of the planet. But in DC they believed us: and they were willing to launch COINTELPRO-like operations, to engage in surveillance, in pre-emptive strikes, suspension of free speech and constitutional guarantees, to make sure it didn't happen again. They were quite ready to throw the Constitution into the Potomac, if need be.

In Philadelphia and Los Angeles, it was much harder. A lot of activists knew that in the States political conventions are a black hole as far as media coverage of any quality goes. The Democratic and Republican parties are far more entrenched in the American psyche than an institution like the WTO. They have intimate connexions with the media, and can silence dissent around them in a much more chilling and effective way. Also, by then people were tired. It was a long year to go from Seattle to the World Bank/IMF four months later, to the political conventions in the summer. That's a lot of ground to cover, and begs the question of how many mass actions we can mount effectively in a year. I'd rather we organized one great action every two or three years than three mediocre ones every year. It's true that police behaviour is getting more and more outrageous each time we show up. But that goes with the territory. I don't want us to be distracted from our own aims into campaigning against COINTELPRO conduct by the authorities. The police are a symptom, not the real problem. We have to keep our eye on the prize. To be truly radical, you've got to go for the roots, and the cops aren't the roots.

What recent actions have been inspirational for Ruckus outside your own participation?

Two weeks before Seattle, fourteen thousand-plus people marched in Fort Benning, Georgia, to demonstrate against the US counter-insurgency training centre, the School of the Americas. If Seattle could be considered a hotbed of progressive consciousness in the United States, Fort Benning is really its polar opposite. The fight to eliminate the Confederate flag in South Carolina, where 10,000 marched in Columbia, was also inspiring. If you keep your ear to the ground, you can hear a kind of unrest, a dissent that is building against the dominant elite. Another very effective action was the campaign against Home Depot, as the largest corporate player in the market for ancient forest products. It was turned back within a very short space of time by a grass-roots movement that won not because it cut into corporate earnings, but because of a psychological campaign it waged against the CEO and Board of Directors of Home Depot. The message was: 'If you don't watch out, we're going to make you into the leper of every cocktail party that you go to—we're gonna turn you into an oil executive'. It worked. Then there has been the fight around factory trawlers, and the biotech campaign that bloodied Monsanto's nose in public. We can be proud of all these.

How far is the unity achieved at Seattle based just on anti-globalization, and how far does it have an anti-capitalist undertow—if you accept such a separation?

Certainly, there are different tribes within the movement. There's some classic Marxist, anti-capitalist energy, and a lot of the most thoughtful and intellectual material comes from these people. But there's also a lot of input from college students and outfits wanting to create more sustainable and responsible corporations, more stable forms of capitalism, who aren't going to have the same kind of systemic critique. They're willing to take radical action to bring about a world with benign corporations, but they see the solution to our economic nightmare in something that would still look pretty much like it to people who want to get rid of the whole thing.

What thinkers most inform the agenda of Ruckus?

I think it's really important to study all kinds of different historical movements and social philosophies. I like to read Gandhi and King, so if I were to pick out two particular thinkers I guess it would probably be those two. Marx's critique of capital is terrific, but I've always thought Weber was right that human beings can find some way to exclude and oppress one another, without necessarily involving capital. At the moment I'm reading *Parting the Waters* by Taylor Branch, about America during the King years, which spends some time dissecting the decisions and calls that were made during the Civil Rights movement—questions like why was Rosa Parks chosen? What was her background? This is an important type of political analysis for me, and I think for Ruckus. We're trying to create powerful symbols that will help to build a movement of populist resistance. We need to be funny, and smart. We want the kind of grass-roots social revolution that people will be attracted to. So I look at the Yippies and Merry Pranksters, and the early culture-jamming those guys were pioneering. I like to read *Adbusters* magazine and look at the culture-jamming of *The Onion* today. I don't read as much as I should. I don't read a lot of social philosophy, but I watch a fair bit of corporate news to figure out how that medium functions.

Media coverage of anti-globalization actions often likes to raise the spectre of anarchism. What's your view of the black flag?

Anarchism has got a really bad rap, like communism. There are probably a lot of trainers in Ruckus who, if you forced them to identify themselves with anything, would say maybe they were anarchists—though they would never use the term to the media, because of the way the American public perceives it. I meet great anarchists all the time. It is a beautiful philosophy to believe that we can take care of one another without centralized institutions that take on a life of their own, and impose their will on us. When Ruckus is ready to develop a sense of its own intellectual place and push for solutions, we will have to think about how practical such a conception might be. For the moment, what we're good at is saying to the corporate world: 'Stop—you're wrong, turn back', but we do a very poor job of describing the sort of world we envisage. In my view, this has to start at the local level, in the effort to build sustainable communities that can provide for their own needs without exploiting others, that don't depend on giant highways and massive infrastructure, that can recreate green space and cover their own energy needs. That kind of vision is pretty anarchistic. The reputation of anarchism, however, has sometimes been damaged by unstrategic and potentially dangerous acts. Ruckus holds very near and dear the idea that you can be as radical and non-violently confrontational as you want, so long as you don't scare people or endanger them.

In Europe, a distinction is often drawn between vandalism and violence, which doesn't seem to have played out in American consciousness.

I get asked about this all the time. You're right—Americans, even though we actually have a rich tradition of political acts of property destruction, starting with the Boston Tea Party, are very slow to grasp that. In Europe there have been major labour struggles and large-scale political riots in cities in much more recent times than in the States. But I also think there is a difference of intellectual tradition. In this country, we have so skewed a concept of private property—it's such a sacred, inviolate value that people think any harm done to it is inherently violent; it's actually written in our criminal code as violence to property. *Time* magazine even thought it worth quoting when I once simply remarked that violence can only be done to living beings.

Having said that, violence is in my view a lot like obscenity—I don't have a hard and fast definition for it, but I can tell you what it looks like when I see it. There is a big difference to me between José Bové and his French farmer friends, and some of our anarchists here. They dismantled a McDonald's with their tractors while the whole town including kids had a picnic and a band played, with the community out in force to support them in this largely symbolic action. To a corporation like McDonald's, this was nothing, it was less than a drop in the bucket. There's a big difference between an action like that and four or five people in black masks suddenly emerging from a crowd of people celebrating a positive, forward-looking movement, and smashing a few windows at a McDonald's. This kind of gesture can incite a violent reaction from the cops, in which people who didn't come to take part in or even witness the action could be hurt. Here you can really speak of a violent act, which may harm others and let the cops label us as 'terrorists'.

It's very important for Ruckus that what we do is understood by the public, that people connect with our intentions and accept the tactics we adopt. I've engaged in property destruction. When I sailed with the Rainbow Warrior in 1995, we were attacked by the French navy while we were confiscating a French driftnet in the Mediterranean, which I cut with a pocket-knife. It was illegal in length, but was someone's private property. The net belonged to a fisherman, but the global public knew why I was doing it. They were ready to understand why industrial strip-mining of our oceans is wrong, and to identify with people that were cutting the nets—but that took lead-time, outreach, and educational work.

Greenpeace always made an effort to explain the context in which its actions made sense. So they *did* make sense, to a great many people. In Philadelphia, on the other hand, during a day of action against the prison–industrial complex, I saw a lot of cop cars being beaten up, and at some level, I can understand that—some people are living in neigh-bourhoods where an urban police force is more like an occupying army. But then I also saw Department of Recreation vehicles getting smashed up, right next to the police cars, and I thought to myself, how are we ever going to get the American public to understand why we're stopping inner-city youth from going to parks? What kind of message is that sending to anyone? Isn't it just going to alienate people? I think all of us, whether we self-identify as anarchists or revolutionaries, revisionists or Marxists, Taoists or whatever, have to look at the message that we send and ask ourselves who is our audience—how can we speak to their set of values?

How do you assess the role of new technology in organizing and getting your message out? Do you think Independent Media Centres, or groups like FENAMAD in Peru, linking up indigenous people with the internet, offer hopeful tools for social change?

Ruckus is very interested in exploring digital tactics for the various chal-lenges that face us as activists. Our last camp of this year will be called 'e-genius', and half of it will be dedicated to analyzing and refining the emerging model of independent media centres. The reason is obvious: you have only to look at the potential here for reaching the public. The website of the Independent Media Centre was getting a million and a half hits during the week of the WTO protests in Seattle, which dwarfed even CNN during that time. That's an amazing feat. If we could create alternative institutions to which people can turn for credible news and analysis of what's happening on the planet, then more power to us. The pitfall, of course, is the informational overload that comes from this electronic world. That threatens to become an anarchist's nightmare. But I think we have to develop some portals with a critical mass, that we can project as *the* places to be. Then we would have the kind of listenership, or viewership, or readership that we need to compete with the corporate media.

You don't fear that the internet will ultimately fall under the control of the same corporations?

My friend Han Shan is fond of what he calls the slave adage: use the master's tools to tear down the master's house. We need to make the most of the net, it's a very powerful medium. It allows Subcomandante Marcos to communicate with Mumia Abu-Jamal, and with sympathizers in Prague at the same time. That's power—the ability to build a truly global resistance to what is a completely global system of exploitation.

What do you see as the future for Ruckus, over the next decade—do you have any plans to move overseas, as more struggles break abroad?

The movement against globalization started way before anything much happened in the United States, and long before Ruckus existed. Today, we get requests from all over the world to set up our training-camps for tactics of resistance. But to tell you the truth, we've resisted the urge to travel because we feel we've got more to learn from those movements than we have to teach them. We were invited to South Africa, but what would we instruct them in there? The South African movement toppled apartheid. So many of the engines of global oppression reside here in the United States, where our government supplies the political basis for its corporate citizens to extract the natural wealth of the world, that we believe the most profound political act of which we are capable is to mobilize resistance in the belly of the beast itself. People all over the world were so inspired by Seattle, partly because it was the most heavily televised protest in history—there is probably more celluloid on that week than on any political action of all time—but also because most people had no idea that there was real dissent here in the United States. But when they saw tens of thousands of people in the streets, and the façade of democracy peel away to reveal armed storm troopers with shields, grenades and gas, wielding chemical weapons against unarmed crowds, it really drove home the fact that there are all kinds of different opinions in this country, and that there can be a true, sweeping social movement in the United States. Since then we've gone to a couple of camps in Canada, and consider ourselves in many ways a North American group. We would definitely be interested in working in Mexico, and Central America next. But it's going to be a long time—if ever— before we set up a Ruckus action camp overseas. We are where we are.

No Qatar camp?

When the WTO chose Qatar for its next meeting, I enjoyed playfully hinting to the *Wall Street Journal* that we were planning to train for the desert, and we were looking for desert camouflage. But we're proud to be North American, and we know this pathological corporate culture that rules our lives better than any people in the world. We have the best tools to tear it down and start rebuilding something in a more compassionate and sustainable way. That's where we've got to concentrate our efforts.

BHUMIKA MUCHHALA

STUDENTS AGAINST SWEATSHOPS

Could you tell us about your background, and how you came to be an anti-sweatshop activist?

I was born in India but grew up in Jakarta from the age of five. My father, an Indian accountant, worked for multinational companies there. I attended an American international school that was completely Eurocentric—they never taught us anything about Indonesian language, culture, or politics. I learned Bahasa from hanging out with the street vendors. I used to sneak out to the street corner and eat *boso*, noodle soup. I came to the US to study at Carnegie Mellon University, in Pittsburgh, and also took a lot of classes at the University of Pittsburgh itself. I had been apolitical as a teenager. But that changed during the ousting of Suharto in 1998—I turned on the TV and watched as my city went up in flames. It shook every fibre in my being to see all these buildings that I knew so well on fire, to see the riots in the streets. I kept hearing references to the International Monetary Fund, and student activists crying out against Suharto's corruption and cronyism, and Chinese–Indonesian dominance of the economy. It was then that I started reading the paper and searching the internet to learn more about the IMF. I learned a lot from the website for Global Exchange, the human-rights and environmental NGO set up in 1988. I decided to double my major, to learn about US foreign policy and US imperialism.

I became involved with Students in Solidarity, a large group of student activists at the University of Pittsburgh, and also got in touch with Robin Alexander at United Electric, an independent union. She had started an organization called PLANTA (Pittsburgh Labor Action Network for the Americas), which introduced me to labour organizing, and all the issues surrounding it. At the same time, Students in Solidarity were doing actions with the janitors at the AT&T buildings in downtown Pittsburgh, as well as with campus workers at the UP. Through an organization called Pugwash, I also got involved in debates on ethical issues in science with students in public policy, science, engineering and environmental departments.

But my main entry into activism came in my senior year, after a summer at Global Exchange. I applied by a fluke, because I really liked the website. They invited me to do an internship, which mostly involved logistical work for the speaking tours of international activists. I translated some information from Bahasa to English for their Gap campaign. I also petitioned outside Gap stores. Back at college, I launched a Gap campaign in Pittsburgh with Robin Alexander from UE. We did a number of Gap actions, as well as a fair-trade coffee campaign. I began to feel, though, that there were a lot of problems with the whole approach to Gap. Many people wanted to turn it into an all-out boycott, but that means people losing their jobs. Far more important is to find a way to make these corporations accountable, and responsible. We don't want them out of Indonesia, we want them to treat their workers with respect and adhere to codes of conduct. It's more about understanding the power structures—the racism, imperialism and neo-colonialism— than seeing the world in black and white terms. I also remember that my initial reaction to the Gap protests was that my friends in Indonesia would never do anything like this—not simply because they were more interested in hanging out at the mall, but because they don't have the do-gooding impulses of many activists here. I wasn't driven by the same sentiment—I wanted more debate, more facts.

How did you end up in Seattle?

I was going to a lot of Global Exchange workshops, including those on the WTO, that were run in conjunction with JustAct. I got involved with national recruiting and organizing, and decided to go out to Seattle because I knew a lot of my colleagues were going to be there. I didn't do direct action, though, because I'm not a citizen. After that, I compiled an oral history of students who were active around the WTO protests—*Student Voices: One Year After Seattle*—while working at the Institute for Policy Studies. The original plan was to conduct a few interviews as preparation for a workshop we put on with STARC—Students Transforming and Reforming Corporations. That was cancelled, but I was asked to do a report instead. At first, my goal was to interview 15 students, but that turned into 30, then 50—I ended up with 60-plus students. Looking at the report now, what strikes me is how blind it was to the demographics: almost all the students were white. At the same time, that makes it a pretty representative cross-section of the students who were at Seattle, or the April 16 demonstrations in Washington DC, or at the Republican National Convention.

How did you become involved with Students Against Sweatshops?

My involvement began with an eight-month trip to Indonesia. I was approached to do some fact-finding by the Workers' Rights Consortium, an organization set up in 2000 by student activists, labour experts and university administrations to pressure the manufacturers of clothing bearing college logos into adhering to a code of conduct for their workers. It was conceived as an alternative to the Clinton administration's Fair Labor Association, set up in 1996, in which corporate interests predominate. Currently, 116 colleges are affiliated, and pay dues to fund the WRC's activities. Its board of directors consists of five independent labour-rights experts, including Linda Chavez-Thompson of the AFL–CIO and Mark Barenberg, a Columbia law professor; five representatives from universities; and five from USAS. It also has an advisory council, which includes US-based NGOs, academics, George Miller—a Democratic congressman—and international representatives.

I was technically an independent researcher—the WRC provided me with a place to stay in Indonesia, an office and transportation, but no salary. The AFL–CIO's Solidarity Centre was a point of contact for people who would introduce me to the various Indonesian trade unions. I interviewed more than 200 workers, over a period of eight months, in assembly plants for Reebok, Nike, Champion, Gear, Gap, Banana Republic—mostly US multinationals, but also a lot of European labels and knock-offs. Initially, it was a startling experience, but I found it easy to strike up a rapport with the workers, because they were mainly women between seventeen and twenty-six—close to my age—who were curious, fun and energetic. They came from all over Indonesia—from Sumatra, Sulawesi, Kalimantan, Java. Local chiefs often pick young women to be sent to work in industrial centres, and the women consider themselves lucky and honoured. They make friends and learn about Indonesia's patchwork of different cultures. They tend to get 600,000 rupiah a month—around $60—and send up to a third of that home to their villages, which means they're living on little more than a dollar a day. They usually run out of money before the end of the month, but they're very resourceful—friends lend money to each other, women's cooperatives pool their incomes, and everyone makes incredible econo-mies, cutting down an already meagre diet.

What happens to the women after the age of 26?

They just get worn down: they develop arthritis or respiratory problems. In the hat factories, for example, they burn a lot of coal and use thinners and other solvents. Once they can no longer work, they are laid off and return to the village, or else become street vendors, selling vegetables, cigarettes or shampoo from stalls or kiosks; others become homeless. Some dream of returning to school, others get married and settle down to raise a family.

What did the workers think was most exploitative about the process?

They were very aware that they were being exploited—they would work for 15 hours at a stretch and come home with stomach pains and headaches. Some of them told me about having to work till 2 or 6 in the morning, having to clean toilets, about suffering verbal and sexual abuse. They were in no sense passive victims, but they responded to some of the questions with astonishment—they had never really considered air temperature in the factory as something that they were deprived of or denied. They were amused and surprised that somebody cared so much about tiny, inane details of their lives, such as what the bathrooms were like. But when I started explaining to them how the monitoring process works, and how we could negotiate with the retailers who had power over their supervisors, they became more interested.

What did you, and the Workers' Rights Consortium, learn from the experience?

I found we had a common interest, along with Indonesian and US unions and activists, in working out how to channel this power through the current corporate structure—how to effect real changes among the Korean management, US retailers, contractors and institutional purchasers such as universities, and secure real improvements for the workers. Being able to meet the workers and Indonesian union organizers face-to-face was an important step. The WRC hierarchy are busy flying from one meeting to another, and don't have time to spend weeks or months in one place; activists and union organizers in producing regions, meanwhile, can't easily be reached by phone, and tend not to have email, so it's hard to make people aware of what we're trying to do without making contact in person. I made a few connexions, and after I left, four USAS activists flew in and started operating in some of the same factories, which has helped to keep the momentum going.

You became active in USAS on returning from your stint with the WRC. Can you tell us about the origins and structure of USAS?

There had been various campaigns against sweatshops, starting with groups of immigrant workers in the US garment industry in New York, California and Texas in the late 1980s; there were also campaigns in the early 1990s by the National Labor Committee, and the Coalition to Eliminate Sweatshop Conditions in California. Students began to focus on the issue of sweatshop labour during summer internships at the AFL–CIO in 1996, and at UNITE, the United Needle and Textile Workers Union. Some Duke students, including Tico Almeida, who spent the summer of 1997 researching the question for UNITE, returned to campus and began lobbying the university to make manufacturers of university apparel sign up to a code of conduct. The campaign was successful, and encouraged students who had been thinking along similar lines to start campaigns on their own campuses. USAS was founded in the spring of 1998, as an informal network of campus anti-sweatshop groups.

The first national conference was held in New York in July 1998. Over 200 campus delegates attended the second conference in 1999, when it was decided to set up a permanent office in Washington, DC. Our national conferences—now held in August—last three days, and feature keynote speakers, workshops on labour action and anti-white supremacy training, as well as panel discussions and meetings of the various caucuses.

As far as structure is concerned, the leadership consists of a coordinating committee, democratically elected at the annual conference, plus the student representatives to the WRC. There are seven regional representatives, four from the identity caucuses—women, people of colour, working-class people, LGBTQ—and three members-at-large. In addition to the committee, there are seven regional organizers who report to the committee, and coordinate with organizers on individual campuses. Then, there is the national office with three permanent staff—a field organizer, a programme coordinator, and a person responsible for fundraising and communications. There are also standing committees on individual issues, such as international solidarity, alliance-building and solidarity with farmworkers. As programme coordinator, I primarily liaise with the international solidarity committee—organizing letter-writing and solidarity campaigns with workers in the Gap factory in El Salvador, for instance.

Does the national office determine what your campaigns are going to be, or do groups at particular universities become aware of an issue, which then percolates upwards?

It's primarily campus-based—different groups decide to do different things. Some are involved in mobilizing research or teaching assistants for rallies, some have taken part in local living-wage campaigns for campus workers, notably those employed by Sodexho–Marriott. Other campaigns have come about through contacts initially made by USAS activists. For example, in late 2000 USAS members were part of a delegation that went to the Kukdong factory in Puebla, and which also included people from AFL–CIO, United Electric and the Mexican union Frente Auténtico de Trabajo. The following January around 850 workers at the factory went on strike to protest the sacking of five of their co-workers, who were trying to organize an independent union. That spring, USAS sent out more activists to talk to the workers and find out how best to support their action. Nike and Reebok contract to the Korean-run *maquiladora*, so USAS organized pickets of their stores in the US, put pressure on university administrations and commissioned the WRC to investigate. Within two months, the workers had been reinstated, and by September the governor of Puebla made a public promise to give recognition to the Kukdong workers' new union, SITEKIM.

A similar process took place with the campaign at the New Era cap factory in Derby, New York where, in early 2001, two-thirds of the workforce was laid off after affiliating with the Communication Workers of

America. USAS sent a delegation there in March 2001, and then began working in tandem with CWA, getting colleges to cut contracts with New Era, putting pressure on major-league baseball teams, for whom New Era are the exclusive supplier. After a long strike, the workers came to a bargaining agreement with the company, and were reinstated—it was a big victory. USAS had a similar success with a cap factory in the Dominican Republic called BJ&B. Apart from that, there have been campaigns against Taco Bell—working with the Coalition of Immokalee Workers in Florida—and Mount Olive pickles, as well as a general campaign against cap producers such as Nike, Adidas, Reebok and Gap over the past few years.

What about the composition of USAS?

The anti-sweatshop coalition is pretty specific to a certain class and culture. There is a considerable level of working-class to upper-class diversity in USAS, but the majority are middle class, suburban—rabble-rousing in actions, but they get good grades. In a 1999 survey of USAS by a researcher called Peter Siu, more than a third of activists stated their family income was over $100,000, and only 8 per cent said it was under $40,000. As with the mobilizations at Seattle and elsewhere, it's predominantly a white movement. Though the conditions in sweatshops resonate with Latinos and the Asian diaspora, these people aren't yet as politically active on campuses—perhaps because they don't feel comfortable in organizing culture. Black students are more focused on civil rights, and they often have other priorities that occupy them in their own neighbourhoods—for working-class students of colour, the prison–industrial complex hits home more than the IMF or World Bank. USAS does have good relations with the Prison Moratorium Project, and maintains a presence at their annual conference; but beyond that, it's left up to individual campuses to decide which struggles to adopt. At the moment, USAS is trying to start up dialogue on the subject of race and culture, but so far it's proceeded along the lines of 'how can we recruit more people of colour?' Personally, I find that culturally insensitive and tokenistic.

You mentioned working with the CWA. What are USAS's relations with the unions like?

On the New Era campaign we definitely worked hand-in-hand with the CWA—a progressive union compared with some others—but for the most part we work pretty autonomously. The unions have a strong presence at our national conferences, and AFL–CIO and UNITE make important financial contributions—the former gave $50,000 in the academic year 2000–2001. It is quite a contentious issue. The AFL does take up a lot of the centre-ground of our campaign work, and people often ask us if we're being used as their youth wing, pointing to the fact that many USAS students go on to become organizers in the Service Employees International Union or Hotel Employees and Restaurant Employees Union. There's also the question of whether we're being steered in a particular direction—some people in USAS feel the AFL is protectionist, which is not something we would want to be associated with. It's true that part of the struggle at New Era was to protect the workers' jobs, since the company threatened to shift production overseas if they made trouble. But similar conditions applied at the Kukdong factory in Puebla, where we made Nike and Reebok promise not to 'cut and run'. As I mentioned earlier with regard to the Gap boycott, it's not about shutting down manufacturing in the developing world, it's about making companies treat their workers with respect.

Are there tensions between the unions and USAS with regard to international versus national campaigns?

Yes, because USAS chapters try to address both. A lot of activists look at international campaigns such as Kukdong, and ask, 'what about the workers on our own campuses, serving us food, cutting our lawns or cleaning our homes?' Living-wage campaigns have been very promi-nent on scores of campuses for this reason. Our rank and file are, after all, predominantly white, upper-middle class, liberal college students attending elite institutions; their engagement with labour issues is in many ways the product of privilege, and they make use of their status to focus media attention on those issues.

What other campaigns would you see as models?

One that has brought enormous inspiration is the campaign against the Narmada Dam—Medha Patkar and Arundhati Roy have been very influential. Of US-based campaigns, I would name those focusing on the prison–industrial complex, especially in California. USAS is also a member of the National Student Youth Peace Coalition, which was formed in the wake of September 11, and opposed the assaults on Afghanistan and Iraq.

DAVID GRAEBER

THE NEW ANARCHISTS

It's hard to think of another time when there has been such a gulf between intellectuals and activists; between theorists of revolution and its practitioners. Writers who for years have been publishing essays that sound like position papers for vast social movements that do not in fact exist seem seized with confusion or worse, dismissive contempt, now that real ones are everywhere emerging. It's particularly scandalous in the case of what's still, for no particularly good reason, referred to as the 'anti-globalization' movement, one that has in a mere two or three years managed to transform completely the sense of historical possibilities for millions across the planet. This may be the result of sheer igno-rance, or of relying on what might be gleaned from such overtly hostile sources as the *New York Times*; then again, most of what's written even in progressive outlets seems largely to miss the point—or at least, rarely focuses on what participants in the movement really think is most important about it.

As an anthropologist and active participant—particularly in the more radical, direct-action end of the movement—I may be able to clear up some common points of misunderstanding; but the news may not be gratefully received. Much of the hesitation, I suspect, lies in the reluc-tance of those who have long fancied themselves radicals of some sort to come to terms with the fact that they are really liberals: interested in expanding individual freedoms and pursuing social justice, but not in ways that would seriously challenge the existence of reigning institu-tions like capital or state. And even many of those who would like to see revolutionary change might not feel entirely happy about having to accept that most of the creative energy for radical politics is now coming from anarchism—a tradition that they have hitherto mostly dismissed—and that taking this movement seriously will necessarily also mean a respectful engagement with it.

I am writing as an anarchist; but in a sense, counting how many people involved in the movement actually call themselves 'anarchists', and in what contexts, is a bit beside the point.[1] The very notion of direct action, with its rejection of a politics which appeals to governments to modify their behaviour, in favour of physical intervention against state power in a form that itself prefigures an alternative—all of this emerges directly from the libertarian tradition. Anarchism is the heart of the movement, its soul; the source of most of what's new and hopeful about it. In what follows, then, I will try to clear up what seem to be the three most common misconceptions about the movement—our supposed opposition to something called 'globalization', our supposed 'violence', and our supposed lack of a coherent ideology—and then suggest how radical intellectuals might think about reimagining their own theoretical practice in the light of all of this.

The phrase 'anti-globalization movement' is a coinage of the US media and activists have never felt comfortable with it. Insofar as this is a movement against anything, it's against neoliberalism, which can be defined as a kind of market fundamentalism—or, better, market Stalinism—that holds there is only one possible direction for human historical development. The map is held by an elite of economists and corporate flacks, to whom must be ceded all power once held by institutions with any shred of democratic accountability; from now on it will be wielded largely through unelected treaty organizations like the IMF, WTO or NAFTA. In Argentina, or Estonia, or Taiwan, it would be possible to say this straight out: 'We are a movement against neoliberalism'. But in the US, language is always a problem. The corporate media here

---

[1] There are some who take anarchist principles of anti-sectarianism and open-endedness so seriously that they are sometimes reluctant to call themselves 'anarchists' for that very reason.

is probably the most politically monolithic on the planet: neoliberalism is all there is to see—the background reality; as a result, the word itself cannot be used. The issues involved can only be addressed using propaganda terms like 'free trade' or 'the free market'. So American activists find themselves in a quandary: if one suggests putting 'the N word' (as it's often called) in a pamphlet or press release, alarm bells immediately go off: one is being exclusionary, playing only to an educated elite. There have been all sorts of attempts to frame alternative expressions—we're a 'global justice movement', we're a movement 'against corporate globalization'. None is especially elegant or quite satisfying and, as a result, it is common in meetings to hear the speakers using 'globalization movement' and 'anti-globalization movement' pretty much interchangeably.

The phrase 'globalization movement', though, is really quite apropos. If one takes globalization to mean the effacement of borders and the free movement of people, possessions and ideas, then it's pretty clear that not only is the movement itself a product of globalization, but the majority of groups involved in it—the most radical ones in particular—are far more supportive of globalization in general than is the IMF or WTO. It was an international network called People's Global Action, for example, that put out the first summons for planet-wide days of action such as J18 and N30—the latter the original call for protest against the 1999 WTO meetings in Seattle. And PGA in turn owes its origins to the famous International Encounter for Humanity and Against Neoliberalism, which took place knee-deep in the jungle mud of rainy-season Chiapas, in August 1996; and was itself initiated, as Subcomandante Marcos put it, 'by all the rebels around the world'. People from over 50 countries came streaming into the Zapatista-held village of La Realidad. The vision for an 'intercontinental network of resistance' was laid out in the Second Declaration of La Realidad: 'We declare that we will make a collective network of all our particular struggles and resistances, an intercontinental network of resistance against neoliberalism, an intercontinental network of resistance for humanity':

> Let it be a network of voices that resist the war Power wages on them.

A network of voices that not only speak, but also struggle and resist for humanity and against neoliberalism.

A network that covers the five continents and helps to resist the death that Power promises us.[2]

This, the Declaration made clear, was 'not an organizing structure; it has no central head or decision maker; it has no central command or hierarchies. We are the network, all of us who resist'.

The following year, European Zapatista supporters in the Ya Basta! groups organized a second *encuentro* in Spain, where the idea of the network process was taken forward: PGA was born at a meeting in Geneva in February 1998. From the start, it included not only anarchist groups and radical trade unions in Spain, Britain and Germany, but a Gandhian socialist farmers' league in India (the KRRS), associations of Indonesian and Sri Lankan fisherfolk, the Argentinian teachers' union, indigenous groups such as the Maori of New Zealand and Kuna of Ecuador, the Brazilian Landless Workers' Movement, a network made up of communities founded by escaped slaves in South and Central America—and any number of others. For a long time, North America was scarcely represented, save for the Canadian Postal Workers' Union—which acted as PGA's main communications hub, until it was largely replaced by the internet—and a Montreal-based anarchist group called CLAC.

If the movement's origins are internationalist, so are its demands. The three-plank programme of Ya Basta! in Italy, for instance, calls for a universally guaranteed 'basic income', global citizenship, guaranteeing free movement of people across borders, and free access to new technology—which in practice would mean extreme limits on patent rights (themselves a very insidious form of protectionism). The no-border network—their slogan: 'No One is Illegal'—has organized week-long campsites, laboratories for creative resistance, on the Polish–German and Ukrainian borders, in Sicily and at Tarifa in Spain. Activists have

---

[2] Read by Subcomandante Marcos during the closing session of the First Intercontinental *Encuentro*, 3 August 1996: *Our Word is Our Weapon: Selected Writings*, Juana Ponce de León, ed., New York 2001.

dressed up as border guards, built boat-bridges across the River Oder and blockaded Frankfurt Airport with a full classical orchestra to protest against the deportation of immigrants (deportees have died of suffocation on Lufthansa and KLM flights). This summer's camp is planned for Strasbourg, home of the Schengen Information System, a search-and-control database with tens of thousands of terminals across Europe, targeting the movements of migrants, activists, anyone they like.

More and more, activists have been trying to draw attention to the fact that the neoliberal vision of 'globalization' is pretty much limited to the movement of capital and commodities, and actually increases barriers against the free flow of people, information and ideas—the size of the US border guard has almost tripled since the signing of NAFTA. Hardly surprising: if it were not possible to effectively imprison the majority of people in the world in impoverished enclaves, there would be no incentive for Nike or The Gap to move production there to begin with. Given a free movement of people, the whole neoliberal project would collapse. This is another thing to bear in mind when people talk about the decline of 'sovereignty' in the contemporary world: the main achievement of the nation-state in the last century has been the establishment of a uniform grid of heavily policed barriers across the world. It is precisely this international system of control that we are fighting against, in the name of genuine globalization.

These connexions—and the broader links between neoliberal policies and mechanisms of state coercion (police, prisons, militarism)—have played a more and more salient role in our analyses as we ourselves have confronted escalating levels of state repression. Borders became a major issue in Europe during the IMF meetings at Prague, and later EU meetings in Nice. At the FTAA summit in Quebec City last summer, invisible lines that had previously been treated as if they didn't exist (at least for white people) were converted overnight into fortifications against the movement of would-be global citizens, demanding the right to petition their rulers. The three-kilometre 'wall' constructed through the centre of Quebec City, to shield the heads of state junketing inside from any contact with the populace, became the perfect symbol for what neoliberalism actually means in human terms. The spectacle of the Black Bloc, armed with wire cutters and grappling hooks, joined by everyone from Steelworkers to Mohawk warriors to tear down the wall, became—for that very reason—one of the most powerful moments in the movement's history.[3]

There is one striking contrast between this and earlier internationalisms, however. The former usually ended up exporting Western organizational models to the rest of the world; in this, the flow has if anything been the other way around. Many, perhaps most, of the movement's signature techniques—including mass non-violent civil disobedience itself—were first developed in the global South. In the long run, this may well prove the single most radical thing about it.

In the corporate media, the word 'violent' is invoked as a kind of mantra—invariably, repeatedly—whenever a large action takes place: 'violent protests', 'violent clashes', 'police raid headquarters of violent protesters', even 'violent riots' (there are other kinds?). Such expressions are typically invoked when a simple, plain-English description of what took place (people throwing paint-bombs, breaking windows of empty storefronts, holding hands as they blockaded intersections, cops beating them with sticks) might give the impression that the only truly violent parties were the police. The US media is probably the biggest offender here—and this despite the fact that, after two years of increasingly militant direct action, it is still impossible to produce a single example of anyone to whom a US activist has caused physical injury. I would say that what really disturbs the powers-that-be is not the 'violence' of the movement but its relative lack of it; governments simply do not know how to deal with an overtly revolutionary movement that refuses to fall into familiar patterns of armed resistance.

The effort to destroy existing paradigms is usually quite self-conscious. Where once it seemed that the only alternatives to marching

---

[3] Helping tear it down was certainly one of the more exhilarating experiences of this author's life.

along with signs were either Gandhian non-violent civil disobedience or outright insurrection, groups like the Direct Action Network, Reclaim the Streets, Black Blocs or Tute Bianche have all, in their own ways, been trying to map out a completely new territory in between. They're attempting to invent what many call a 'new language' of civil disobedience, combining elements of street theatre, festival and what can only be called non-violent warfare—non-violent in the sense adopted by, say, Black Bloc anarchists, in that it eschews any direct physical harm to human beings. Ya Basta!, for example, is famous for its *tute bianche* or white-overalls tactics: men and women dressed in elaborate forms of padding, ranging from foam armour to inner tubes to rubber-ducky flotation devices, helmets and chemical-proof white jumpsuits (their British cousins are well-clad Wombles). As this mock army pushes its way through police barricades, all the while protecting each other against injury or arrest, the ridiculous gear seems to reduce human beings to cartoon characters—misshapen, ungainly, foolish, largely indestructible. The effect is only increased when lines of costumed figures attack police with balloons and water pistols or, like the 'Pink Bloc' at Prague and elsewhere, dress as fairies and tickle them with feather dusters.

At the American Party Conventions, Billionaires for Bush (or Gore) dressed in high-camp tuxedos and evening gowns and tried to press wads of fake money into the cops' pockets, thanking them for repressing the dissent. None was even slightly hurt—perhaps police are given aversion therapy against hitting anyone in a tuxedo. The Revolutionary Anarchist Clown Bloc, with their high bicycles, rainbow wigs and squeaky mallets, confused the cops by attacking each other (or the billionaires). They had all the best chants: 'Democracy? Ha Ha Ha!', 'The pizza united can never be defeated', 'Hey ho, hey ho—ha ha, hee hee!', as well as meta-chants like 'Call! Response! Call! Response!' and—everyone's favourite—'Three Word Chant! Three Word Chant!'.

In Quebec City, a giant catapult built along mediaeval lines (with help from the left caucus of the Society for Creative Anachronism) lobbed soft toys at the FTAA. Ancient-warfare techniques have been studied to adopt for non-violent but very militant forms of confrontation: there were peltasts and hoplites (the former mainly from the Prince Edwards Islands, the latter from Montreal) at Quebec City, and research continues into Roman-style shield walls. Blockading has become an art form: if you make a huge web of strands of yarn across an intersection, it's actually impossible to cross; motorcycle cops get trapped like flies. The Liberation Puppet with its arms fully extended can block a four-lane highway, while snake-dances can be a form of mobile blockade. Rebels in London last Mayday planned Monopoly Board actions—Building Hotels on Mayfair for the homeless, Sale of the Century in Oxford Street, Guerrilla Gardening—only partly disrupted by heavy policing and torrential rain. But even the most militant of the militant—eco-saboteurs like the Earth Liberation Front—scrupulously avoid doing anything that would cause harm to human beings (or animals, for that matter). It's this scrambling of conventional categories that so throws the forces of order and makes them desperate to bring things back to familiar territory (simple violence): even to the point, as in Genoa, of encouraging fascist hooligans to run riot as an excuse to use overwhelming force against everybody else.

One could trace these forms of action back to the stunts and guerrilla theatre of the Yippies or Italian 'metropolitan Indians' in the sixties, the squatter battles in Germany or Italy in the seventies and eighties, even the peasant resistance to the expansion of Tokyo airport. But it seems to me that here, too, the really crucial origins lie with the Zapatistas, and other movements in the global South. In many ways, the Zapatista Army of National Liberation (EZLN) represents an attempt by people who have always been denied the right to non-violent, civil resistance to seize it; essentially, to call the bluff of neoliberalism and its pretenses to democratization and yielding power to 'civil society'. It is, as its commanders say, an army which aspires not to be an army any more (it's something of an open secret that, for the last five years at least, they have not even been carrying real guns). As Marcos explains their conversion from standard tactics of guerrilla war:

We thought the people would either not pay attention to us, or come together with us to fight. But they did not react in either of these two ways. It turned out that all these people, who were thousands, tens of thousands, hundreds of thousands, perhaps millions, did not want to rise up with us but . . . neither did they want us to be annihilated. They wanted us to dialogue. This completely broke our scheme and ended up defining *zapatismo*, the *neo-zapatismo*.[4]

Now the EZLN is the sort of army that organizes 'invasions' of Mexican military bases in which hundreds of rebels sweep in entirely unarmed to yell at and try to shame the resident soldiers. Similarly, mass actions by the Landless Workers' Movement gain an enormous moral authority in Brazil by reoccupying unused lands entirely non-violently. In either case, it's pretty clear that if the same people had tried the same thing twenty years ago, they would simply have been shot.

However you choose to trace their origins, these new tactics are perfectly in accord with the general anarchistic inspiration of the movement, which is less about seizing state power than about exposing, delegitimizing and dismantling mechanisms of rule while winning ever-larger spaces of autonomy from it. The critical thing, though, is that all this is only possible in a general atmosphere of peace. In fact, it seems to me that these are the ultimate stakes of struggle at the moment: one that may well determine the overall direction of the twenty-first century. We should remember that during the late nineteenth and early twentieth century, when most Marxist parties were rapidly becoming reformist social-democrats, anarchism and anarcho-syndicalism were the centre of the revolutionary Left.[5] The situation only really changed with World

---

[4] Interviewed by Yvon LeBot, *Subcomandante Marcos: El Sueño Zapatista*, Barcelona 1997, pp. 214–5; Bill Weinberg, *Homage to Chiapas*, London 2000, p. 188.
[5] 'In 1905–1914 the Marxist left had in most countries been on the fringe of the revolutionary movement, the main body of Marxists had been identified with a de facto non-revolutionary social democracy, while the bulk of the revolutionary left was anarcho-syndicalist, or at least much closer to the ideas and the mood of anarcho-syndicalism than to that of classical Marxism.' Eric Hobsbawm, 'Bolshevism and the Anarchists', *Revolutionaries*, New York 1973, p. 61.

War I and the Russian Revolution. It was the Bolsheviks' success, we are usually told, that led to the decline of anarchism—with the glorious exception of Spain—and catapulted Communism to the fore. But it seems to me one could look at this another way.

In the late nineteenth century, most people honestly believed that war between industrialized powers was becoming obsolete; colonial adventures were a constant, but a war between France and England, on French or English soil, seemed as unthinkable as it would today. By 1900, even the use of passports was considered an antiquated barbarism. The 'short twentieth century' was, by contrast, probably the most violent in human history, almost entirely preoccupied with either waging world wars or preparing for them. Hardly surprising, then, that anarchism quickly came to seem unrealistic, if the ultimate measure of political effectiveness became the ability to maintain huge, mechanized killing machines. This is one thing that anarchists, by definition, can never be very good at. Neither is it surprising that Marxist parties—who have been only too good at it—seemed eminently practical and realistic in comparison. Whereas the moment the Cold War ended, and war between industrialized powers once again seemed unthinkable, anarchism reappeared just where it had been at the end of the nineteenth century, as an international movement at the very centre of the revolutionary Left.

If this is right, it becomes clearer what the ultimate stakes of the current 'anti-terrorist' mobilization are. In the short run, things do look very frightening. Governments who were desperately scrambling for some way to convince the public we were terrorists even before September 11 now feel they've been given *carte blanche*; there is little doubt that a lot of good people are about to suffer terrible repression. But in the long run, a return to twentieth-century levels of violence is simply impossible. The September 11 attacks were clearly something of a fluke (the first wildly ambitious terrorist scheme in history that actually worked); the spread of nuclear weapons is ensuring that larger and larger portions of the globe will be for all practical purposes off-limits to conventional warfare. And if war is the health of the state, the prospects for anarchist-style organizing can only be improving.

A constant complaint about the globalization movement in the progressive press is that, while tactically brilliant, it lacks any central theme or coherent ideology. (This seems to be the left equivalent of the corporate media's claims that we are a bunch of dumb kids touting a bundle of completely unrelated causes—free Mumia, dump the debt, save the old-growth forests.) Another line of attack is that the movement is plagued by a generic opposition to all forms of structure or organization. It's distressing that, two years after Seattle, I should have to write this, but someone obviously should: in North America especially, this is a movement about reinventing democracy. It is not opposed to organization. It is about creating new forms of organization. It is not lacking in ideology. Those new forms of organization *are* its ideology. It is about creating and enacting horizontal networks instead of top-down structures like states, parties or corporations; networks based on principles of decentralized, non-hierarchical consensus democracy. Ultimately, it aspires to be much more than that, because ultimately it aspires to reinvent daily life as a whole. But unlike many other forms of radicalism, it has first organized itself in the political sphere—mainly because this was a territory that the powers that be (who have shifted all their heavy artillery into the economic) have largely abandoned.

Over the past decade, activists in North America have been putting enormous creative energy into reinventing their groups' own internal processes, to create viable models of what functioning direct democracy could actually look like. In this we've drawn particularly, as I've noted, on examples from outside the Western tradition, which almost invariably rely on some process of consensus finding, rather than majority vote. The result is a rich and growing panoply of organizational instruments—spokescouncils, affinity groups, facilitation tools, break-outs, fishbowls, blocking concerns, vibe-watchers and so on—all aimed at creating forms of democratic process that allow initiatives to rise from below and attain maximum effective solidarity, without stifling dissenting voices, creating leadership positions or compelling anyone to do anything which they have not freely agreed to do.

The basic idea of consensus process is that, rather than voting, you try to come up with proposals acceptable to everyone—or at least, not highly objectionable to anyone: first state the proposal, then ask for 'concerns' and try to address them. Often, at this point, people in the group will propose 'friendly amendments' to add to the original proposal, or otherwise alter it, to ensure concerns are addressed. Then, finally, when you call for consensus, you ask if anyone wishes to 'block' or 'stand aside'. Standing aside is just saying, 'I would not myself be willing to take part in this action, but I wouldn't stop anyone else from doing it'. Blocking is a way of saying 'I think this violates the fundamental principles or purposes of being in the group'. It functions as a veto: any one person can kill a proposal completely by blocking it—although there are ways to challenge whether a block is genuinely principled.

There are different sorts of groups. Spokescouncils, for example, are large assemblies that coordinate between smaller 'affinity groups'. They are most often held before, and during, large-scale direct actions like Seattle or Quebec. Each affinity group (which might have between four and twenty people) selects a 'spoke', who is empowered to speak for them in the larger group. Only the spokes can take part in the actual process of finding consensus at the council, but before major decisions they break out into affinity groups again and each group comes to consensus on what position they want their spoke to take (not as unwieldy as it might sound). Break-outs, on the other hand, are when a large meeting temporarily splits up into smaller ones that will focus on making decisions or generating proposals, which can then be presented for approval before the whole group when it reassembles. Facilitation tools are used to resolve problems or move things along if they seem to be bogging down. You can ask for a brainstorming session, in which people are only allowed to present ideas but not to criticize other people's; or for a non-binding straw poll, where people raise their hands just to see how everyone feels about a proposal, rather than to make a decision. A fishbowl would only be used if there is a profound difference of opinion: you can take two representatives for each side—one man and one woman—and have the four of them sit in the middle, everyone else surrounding them silently, and see if the four can't work out a synthesis or compromise together, which they can then present as a proposal to the whole group.

This is very much a work in progress, and creating a culture of democracy among people who have little experience of such things is necessarily a painful and uneven business, full of all sorts of stumblings and false starts, but—as almost any police chief who has faced us on the streets can attest—direct democracy of this sort can be astoundingly effective. And it is difficult to find anyone who has fully participated in such an action whose sense of human possibilities has not been profoundly transformed as a result. It's one thing to say, 'Another world is possible'. It's another to experience it, however momentarily. Perhaps the best way to start thinking about these organizations—the Direct Action Network, for example—is to see them as the diametrical opposite of the sectarian Marxist groups; or, for that matter, of the sectarian Anarchist groups.[6] Where the democratic-centralist 'party' puts its emphasis on achieving a complete and correct theoretical analysis, demands ideological uniformity and tends to juxtapose the vision of an egalitarian future with extremely authoritarian forms of organization in the present, these openly seek diversity. Debate always focuses on particular courses of action; it's taken for granted that no one will ever convert anyone else entirely to their point of view. The motto might be, 'If you are willing to act like an anarchist now, your long-term vision is pretty much your own business'. Which seems only sensible: none of us know how far these principles can actually take us, or what a complex society based on

---

[6] What one might call capital-A anarchist groups, such as, say, the North East Federation of Anarchist Communists—whose members must accept the Platform of the Anarchist Communists set down in 1926 by Nestor Makhno—do still exist, of course. But the small-a anarchists are the real locus of historical dynamism right now.

them would end up looking like. Their ideology, then, is immanent in the anti-authoritarian principles that underlie their practice, and one of their more explicit principles is that things should stay this way.

Finally, I'd like to tease out some of the questions the direct-action networks raise about alienation, and its broader implications for political practice. For example: why is it that, even when there is next to no other constituency for revolutionary politics in a capitalist society, the one group most likely to be sympathetic to its project consists of artists, musicians, writers, and others involved in some form of non-alienated production? Surely there must be a link between the actual experience of first imagining things and then bringing them into being, individually or collectively, and the ability to envision social alternatives—particularly the possibility of a society itself premised on less alienated forms of creativity? One might even suggest that revolutionary coalitions always tend to rely on a kind of alliance between a society's least alienated and its most oppressed; actual revolutions, one could then say, have tended to happen when these two categories most broadly overlap.

This would, at least, help explain why it almost always seems to be peasants and craftsmen—or even more, newly proletarianized former peasants and craftsmen—who actually overthrow capitalist regimes; and not those inured to generations of wage-labour. It would also help explain the extraordinary importance of indigenous people's struggles in the new movement: such people tend to be simultaneously the very least alienated and most oppressed people on earth. Now that new communication technologies have made it possible to include them in global revolutionary alliances, as well as local resistance and revolt, it is well-nigh inevitable that they should play a profoundly inspirational role.

ANALYTICS

NAOMI KLEIN

RECLAIMING THE COMMONS

What is 'the anti-globalization movement'?[1] I put the phrase in quote-marks because I immediately have two doubts about it. Is it really a movement? If it is a movement, is it anti-globalization? Let me start with the first issue. We can easily convince ourselves it is a movement by talking it into existence at a forum like this—I spend far too much time at them—acting as if we can see it, hold it in our hands. Of course, we have seen it—and we know it's come back in Quebec, and on the US–Mexican border during the Summit of the Americas and the discussion for a hemispheric Free Trade Area. But then we leave rooms like this, go home, watch some TV, do a little shopping and any sense that it exists disappears, and we feel like maybe we're going nuts. Seattle—was that a movement or a collective hallucination? To most of us here, Seattle meant a kind of coming-out party for a global resistance movement, or the 'globalization of hope', as someone described it during the World Social Forum at Porto Alegre. But to everyone else Seattle still means limitless frothy coffee, Asian-fusion cuisine, e-commerce billionaires and sappy Meg Ryan movies. Or perhaps it is both, and one Seattle bred the other Seattle—and now they awkwardly coexist.

This movement we sometimes conjure into being goes by many names: anti-corporate, anti-capitalist, anti-free-trade, anti-imperialist. Many say that it started in Seattle. Others maintain it began five hundred years ago—when colonialists first told indigenous peoples that they were going to have to do things differently if they were to 'develop' or be

---

[1] This is a transcript of a talk given at the Center for Social Theory and Comparative History, UCLA, in April 2001.

eligible for 'trade'. Others again say it began on 1 January 1994 when the Zapatistas launched their uprising with the words Ya Basta! on the night NAFTA became law in Mexico. It all depends on whom you ask. But I think it is more accurate to picture a movement of many movements—coalitions of coalitions. Thousands of groups today are all working against forces whose common thread is what might broadly be described as the privatization of every aspect of life, and the transformation of every activity and value into a commodity. We often speak of the privatization of education, of healthcare, of natural resources. But the process is much vaster. It includes the way powerful ideas are turned into advertising slogans and public streets into shopping malls; new generations being target-marketed at birth; schools being invaded by ads; basic human necessities like water being sold as commodities; basic labour rights being rolled back; genes are patented and designer babies loom; seeds are genetically altered and bought; politicians are bought and altered.

At the same time there are oppositional threads, taking form in many different campaigns and movements. The spirit they share is a radical reclaiming of the commons. As our communal spaces—town squares, streets, schools, farms, plants—are displaced by the ballooning marketplace, a spirit of resistance is taking hold around the world. People are reclaiming bits of nature and of culture, and saying 'this is going to be public space'. American students are kicking ads out of the classrooms. European environmentalists and ravers are throwing parties at busy intersections. Landless Thai peasants are planting organic vegetables on over-irrigated golf courses. Bolivian workers are reversing the privatization of their water supply. Outfits like Napster have been creating a kind of commons on the internet where kids can swap music with each other, rather than buying it from multinational record companies. Billboards have been liberated and independent media networks set up. Protests are multiplying. In Porto Alegre, during the World Social Forum, José Bové, often caricatured as only a hammer of McDonald's, travelled with local activists from the Movimento Sem Terra to a nearby Monsanto test site, where they destroyed three hectares of genetically modified soya beans. But the protest did not stop there. The MST has occupied the land and members are now planting their own organic crops on it, vowing to turn the farm into a model of sustainable agriculture. In short, activists aren't waiting for the revolution, they are acting right now, where they live, where they study, where they work, where they farm.

But some formal proposals are also emerging whose aim is to turn such radical reclamations of the commons into law. When NAFTA and the like were cooked up, there was much talk of adding on 'side agreements' to the free-trade agenda, that were supposed to encompass the environment, labour and human rights. Now the fight-back is about taking them out. José Bové—along with the Via Campesina, a global association of small farmers—has launched a campaign to remove food safety and agricultural products from all trade agreements, under the slogan 'The World is Not for Sale'. They want to draw a line around the commons. Maude Barlow, director of the Council of Canadians, which has more members than most political parties in Canada, has argued that water isn't a private good and shouldn't be in any trade agreement. There is a lot of support for this idea, especially in Europe since the recent food scares. Typically these anti-privatization campaigns get under way on their own. But they also periodically converge—that's what happened in Seattle, Prague, Washington, Davos, Porto Alegre and Quebec.

What this means is that the discourse has shifted. During the battles against NAFTA, there emerged the first signs of a coalition between organized labour, environmentalists, farmers and consumer groups within the countries concerned. In Canada, most of us felt we were fighting to keep something distinctive about our nation from 'Americanization'. In the United States, the talk was very protectionist: workers were worried that Mexicans would 'steal' away 'our' jobs and drive down 'our' environmental standards. All the while, the voices of Mexicans opposed to the deal were virtually off the public radar—yet these were the strongest voices of all. But only a few years later, the debate over trade has been transformed. The fight against globalization has morphed into a struggle against corporatization and, for some, against capitalism itself. It has also become a fight for democracy. Maude Barlow spearheaded the campaign against NAFTA in Canada twelve years ago. Since NAFTA became law, she's been working with organizers and activists from other countries, and anarchists suspicious of the state in her own country. She was once seen as very much the face of a Canadian nationalism. Today, she has moved away from that discourse. 'I've changed', she says, 'I used to see this fight as saving a nation. Now I see it as saving democracy.' This is a cause that transcends nationality and state borders. The real news out of Seattle is that organizers around the world are beginning to see their local and national struggles—for better funded public schools, against union-busting and casualization, for family farms, and against the widening gap between rich and poor—through a global lens. That is the most significant shift we have seen in years.

How did this happen? Who or what convened this new international people's movement? Who sent out the memos? Who built these complex coalitions? It is tempting to pretend that someone did dream up a master plan for mobilization at Seattle. But I think it was much more a matter of large-scale coincidence. A lot of smaller groups organized to get themselves there and then found to their surprise just how broad and diverse a coalition they had become part of. Still, if there is one force we can thank for bringing this front into being, it is the multinational corporations. As one of the organizers of Reclaim the Streets has remarked, we should be grateful to the CEOs for helping us see the problems more quickly. Thanks to the sheer imperialist ambition of the corporate project at this moment in history—the boundless drive for profit, liberated by trade deregulation, and the wave of mergers and buyouts, liberated by weakened anti-trust laws—multinationals have grown so blindingly rich, so vast in their holdings, so global in their reach, that they have created our coalitions for us.

Around the world, activists are piggy-backing on the ready-made infrastructures supplied by global corporations. This can mean cross-border unionization, but also cross-sector organizing—among workers, environmentalists, consumers, even prisoners, who may all have different relationships to one multinational. So you can build a single campaign or coalition around a single brand like General Electric. Thanks to Monsanto, farmers in India are working with environmentalists and consumers around the world to develop direct-action strategies that cut off genetically modified foods in the fields and in the supermarkets. Thanks to Shell Oil and Chevron, human rights activists in Nigeria, democrats in Europe, environmentalists in North America have united in a fight against the unsustainability of the oil industry. Thanks to the catering giant Sodexho-Marriott's decision to invest in Corrections Corporation of America, university students are able to protest against the exploding US for-profit prison industry simply by boycotting the food in their campus cafeteria. Other targets include pharmaceutical companies who are trying to inhibit the production and distribution of low-cost AIDS drugs, and fast-food chains. Recently, students and farm workers in Florida have joined forces around Taco Bell. In the St Petersburg area, field hands—many of them immigrants from Mexico—are paid an average $7,500 a year to pick tomatoes and onions. Due to a loophole in the law, they have no bargaining power: the farm bosses refuse even to talk with them about wages. When they started to look into who bought what they pick, they found that Taco Bell was the largest purchaser of the local tomatoes. So they launched the campaign *Yo No Quiero Taco Bell* together with students, to boycott Taco Bell on university campuses.

It is Nike, of course, that has most helped to pioneer this new brand of activist synergy. Students facing a corporate takeover of their campuses by the Nike swoosh have linked up with workers making its branded campus apparel, as well as with parents concerned at the commercialization of youth, and church groups campaigning against child labour—all united by their different relationships to a common global enemy. Exposing the underbelly of high-gloss consumer brands has provided the early narratives of this movement, a sort of call-and-response to the very different narratives these companies tell every day about themselves through advertising and public relations. Citigroup offers another prime target, as North America's largest financial institution, with innumerable holdings, which deals with some of the worst corporate malefactors around. The campaign against it handily knits together dozens of issues—from clear-cut logging in California to oil-and-pipeline schemes in Chad and Cameroon. These projects are only a start. But they are creating a new sort of activist: 'Nike is a gateway drug', in the words of Oregon student activist Sarah Jacobson.

By focusing on corporations, organizers can demonstrate graphically how so many issues of social, ecological and economic justice are interconnected. No activist I've met believes that the world economy can be changed one corporation at a time, but the campaigns have opened a door into the arcane world of international trade and finance. Where they are leading is to the central institutions that write the rules of global commerce: the WTO, the IMF, the FTAA, and for some the market itself. Here too the unifying threat is privatization—the loss of the commons. The next round of WTO negotiations is designed to extend the reach of commodification still further. Through side agreements like GATS (General Agreement on Trade and Services) and TRIPS (Trade-Related Aspects of Intellectual Property Rights), the aim is to get still tougher protection of property rights on seeds and drug patents, and to marketize services like healthcare, education and water-supply.

The biggest challenge facing us is to distil all of this into a message that is widely accessible. Many campaigners understand the connexions binding together the various issues almost intuitively— much as Subcomandante Marcos says, 'Zapatismo isn't an ideology, it's an intuition.' But to outsiders, the mere scope of modern protests can be a bit mystifying. If you eavesdrop on the movement from the outside, which is what most people do, you are liable to hear what seems to be a cacophony of disjointed slogans, a jumbled laundry list of disparate grievances without clear goals. At the Democratic National Convention in Los Angeles last year, I remember being outside the Staples Centre during the Rage Against the Machine concert, just before I almost got shot, and thinking there were slogans for everything everywhere, to the point of absurdity.

This kind of impression is reinforced by the decentralized, non-hierarchical structure of the movement, which always disconcerts the traditional media. Well-organized press conferences are rare, there is no charismatic leadership, protests tend to pile on top of each other. Rather than forming a pyramid, as most movements do, with leaders up on top and followers down below, it looks more like an elaborate web. In part, this web-like structure is the result of internet-based organizing. But it is also a response to the very political realities that sparked the protests in the first place: the utter failure of traditional party politics. All over the world, citizens have worked to elect social-democratic and workers' parties, only to watch them plead impotence in the face of market forces and IMF dictates. In these conditions, modern activists are not so naïve as to believe change will come from electoral politics. That's why they are more interested in challenging the structures that make democracy toothless, like the IMF's structural adjustment policies, the WTO's ability to override national sovereignty, corrupt campaign financing, and so on. This is not just making a virtue of necessity. It responds at the ideological level to an understanding that globalization is in essence a crisis in representative democracy. What has caused this crisis? One of the basic reasons for it is the way power and decision-making have been handed along to points ever further away from citizens: from local to provincial, from provincial to national, from national to international institutions, that lack all transparency or accountability. What is the solution? To articulate an alternative, participatory democracy.

If you think about the nature of the complaints raised against the World Trade Organization, it is that governments around the world have embraced an economic model that involves much more than opening borders to goods and services. This is why it is not useful to use the language of anti-globalization. Most people do not really know what globalization is, and the term makes the movement extremely vulnerable to stock dismissals like: 'If you are against trade and globalization, why do you drink coffee?' Whereas in reality the movement is a rejection of what is being bundled along with trade and so-called globalization—against the set of transformative political policies that every country in the world has been told they must accept in order to make themselves hospitable to investment. I call this package 'McGovernment'. This happy meal of cutting taxes, privatizing services, liberalizing regulations, busting unions—what is this diet in aid of? To remove anything standing in the way of the market. Let the free market roll, and every other problem will apparently be solved in the trickle down. This isn't about trade. It's about using trade to enforce the McGovernment recipe.

So the question we are asking today, in the run-up to the FTAA, is not: are you for or against trade? The question is: do we have the right to negotiate the terms of our relationship to foreign capital and investment? Can we decide how we want to protect ourselves from the dangers inherent in deregulated markets—or do we have to contract out those decisions? These problems will become much more acute once we are in a recession, because during the economic boom so much has been destroyed of what was left of our social-safety net. During a period of low unemployment, people did not worry much about that. They are likely to be much more concerned in the very near future. The most controversial issues facing the WTO are these questions about self-determination. For example, does Canada have the right to ban a harmful gasoline additive without being sued by a foreign chemical company? Not according to the WTO's ruling in favour of the Ethyl Corporation. Does Mexico have the right to deny a permit for a hazardous toxic-waste disposal site? Not according to Metalclad, the US company now suing the Mexican government for $16.7 million damages under NAFTA. Does France have the right to ban hormone-treated beef from entering the country? Not according to the United States, which retaliated by banning French imports like Roquefort cheese—prompting a cheese-maker called Bové to dismantle a McDonald's; Americans thought he just didn't like hamburgers. Does Argentina have to cut its public sector to qualify for foreign loans? Yes, according to the IMF—sparking general strikes against the social consequences. It's the same issue everywhere: trading away democracy in exchange for foreign capital.

On smaller scales, the same struggles for self-determination and sustainability are being waged against World Bank dams, clear-cut logging, cash-crop factory farming, and resource extraction on contested indigenous lands. Most people in these movements are not against trade or industrial development. What they are fighting for is the right of local communities to have a say in how their resources are used, to make sure that the people who live on the land benefit directly from its development. These campaigns are a response not to trade but to a trade-off that is now five hundred years old: the sacrifice of democratic control and self-determination to foreign investment and the panacea of economic growth. The challenge they now face is to shift a discourse around the vague notion of globalization into a specific debate about democracy. In a period of 'unprecedented prosperity', people were told they had no choice but to slash public spending, revoke labour laws, rescind environmental protections—deemed illegal trade barriers—defund schools, not build affordable housing. All this was necessary to make us trade-ready, investment-friendly, world-competitive. Imagine what joys await us during a recession.

We need to be able to show that globalization—this version of globalization—has been built on the back of local human welfare. Too often, these connexions between global and local are not made. Instead, we sometimes seem to have two activist solitudes. On the one hand, there are the international anti-globalization activists who may be enjoying a triumphant mood, but seem to be fighting far-away issues, unconnected to people's day-to-day struggles. They are often seen as elitists: white middle-class kids with dreadlocks. On the other hand, there are community activists fighting daily struggles for survival, or for the preservation of the most elementary public services, who are often feeling burnt-out and demoralized. They are saying: what in the hell are you guys so excited about?

The only clear way forward is for these two forces to merge. What is now the anti-globalization movement must turn into thousands of local movements, fighting the way neoliberal politics are playing out on the ground: homelessness, wage stagnation, rent escalation, police violence, prison explosion, criminalization of migrant workers, and on and on. These are also struggles about all kinds of prosaic issues: the right to decide where the local garbage goes, to have good public schools, to be supplied with clean water. At the same time, the local movements fighting privatization and deregulation on the ground need to link their campaigns into one large global movement, which can show where their particular issues fit into an international economic agenda being enforced around the world. If that connexion isn't made, people will continue to be demoralized. What we need is to formulate a political framework that can both take on corporate power and control, and empower local organizing and self-determination. That has to be a framework that encourages, celebrates and fiercely protects the right to diversity: cultural diversity, ecological diversity, agricultural diver-sity—and yes, political diversity as well: different ways of doing politics. Communities must have the right to plan and manage their schools, their services, their natural settings, according to their own lights. Of course, this is only possible within a framework of national and international standards—of public education, fossil-fuel emissions, and so on. But the goal should not be better far-away rules and rulers, it should be close-up democracy on the ground.

The Zapatistas have a phrase for this. They call it 'one world with many worlds in it'. Some have criticized this as a New Age non-answer. They want a plan. 'We know what the market wants to do with those spaces, what do *you* want to do? Where's your scheme?' I think we shouldn't be afraid to say: 'That's not up to us'. We need to have some trust in people's ability to rule themselves, to make the decisions that are best for them. We need to show some humility where now there is so much arrogance and paternalism. To believe in human diver-sity and local democracy is anything but wishy-washy. Everything in

McGovernment conspires against them. Neoliberal economics is biased at every level towards centralization, consolidation, homogenization. It is a war waged on diversity. Against it, we need a movement of radical change, committed to a single world with many worlds in it, that stands for 'the one no and the many yesses'.

MICHAEL HARDT

TODAY'S BANDUNG?

Rather than opposing the World Social Forum in Porto Alegre to the World Economic Forum in New York, it is more revealing to imagine it as the distant offspring of the historic Bandung Conference that took place in Indonesia in 1955. Both were conceived as attempts to counter the dominant world order: colonialism and the oppressive Cold War binary in the case of Bandung, and the rule of capitalist globalization in that of Porto Alegre. The differences, however, are immediately apparent. On one hand, the Bandung Conference, which brought together leaders primarily from Asia and Africa, revealed in a dramatic way the racial dimension of the colonial and Cold War world order, which Richard Wright famously described as being divided by the 'colour curtain'. Porto Alegre, in contrast, was a predominantly white event. There were relatively few participants from Asia and Africa, and the racial differences of the Americas were dramatically underrepresented. This points toward a continuing task facing those gathered at Porto Alegre: to globalize further the movements, both within each society and across the world—a project in which the Forum is merely one step. On the other hand, whereas Bandung was conducted by a small group of national political leaders and representatives, Porto Alegre was populated by a swarming multitude and a network of movements. This multitude of protagonists is the great novelty of the World Social Forum, and central to the hope it offers for the future.

The first and dominant impression of the Forum was its overflowing enormity; not so much the number of people there—the organizers say 80,000 participated—but rather the number of events, encounters and happenings. The programme listing all the official conferences, seminars and workshops—most of which took place at the Catholic University—was the size of a tabloid newspaper, but one soon realized that there were innumerable other unofficial meetings taking place all over town, some publicized on posters and leaflets, others by word of mouth. There were also separate gatherings for the different groups participating in the Forum, such as a meeting of the Italian social movements or one for the various national sections of ATTAC. Then there were the demonstrations: both officially planned, such as the opening mass May Day-style parade, and smaller, conflictual demonstrations against, for example, the members of parliament from different countries at the Forum who voted for the present war on terrorism. Finally, another series of events was held at the enormous youth camp by the river, its fields and fields of tents housing 15,000 people in an atmosphere reminiscent of a summer music festival, especially when it rained and everyone tramped through the mud wearing plastic sacks as raincoats. In short, if anyone with obsessive tendencies were to try to understand what was happening at Porto Alegre, the result would certainly have been a complete mental breakdown. The Forum was unknowable, chaotic, dispersive. And that overabundance created an exhilaration in everyone, at being lost in a sea of people from so many parts of the world who are working similarly against the present form of capitalist globalization.

This open encounter was the most important element of Porto Alegre. Even though the Forum was limited in some important respects—socially and geographically, to name two—it was nonetheless an opportunity to globalize further the cycle of struggles that have stretched from Seattle to Genoa, which have been conducted by a network of movements thus far confined, by and large, to the North Atlantic. Dealing with many of the same issues as those who elsewhere contest the present capitalist form of globalization, or specific institutional policies such as those of the IMF, the movements themselves have remained limited. Recognizing the commonality of their projects with those in other parts of the world is the first step toward expanding the network of movements, or linking one network to another. This recognition, indeed, is primarily responsible for the happy, celebratory atmosphere of the Forum.

The encounter should, however, reveal and address not only the common projects and desires, but also the differences of those involved—differences of material conditions and political orientation. The various movements across the globe cannot simply connect to each other as they are, but must rather be transformed by the encounter through a kind of mutual adequation. Those from North America and Europe, for example, cannot but have been struck by the contrast between their experience and that of agricultural labourers and the rural poor in Brazil, represented most strongly by the MST (Sem Terra Movement)—and vice versa. What kind of transformations are necessary for the Euro-American globalization movements and the Latin American movements, not to become the same, or even to unite, but to link together in an expanding common network? The Forum provided an opportunity to recognize such differences and questions for those willing to see them, but it did not provide the conditions for addressing them. In fact, the very same dispersive, overflowing quality of the Forum that created the euphoria of commonality also effectively displaced the terrain on which such differences and conflicts could be confronted.

The Porto Alegre Forum was in this sense perhaps too happy, too celebratory and not conflictual enough. The most important political difference cutting across the entire Forum concerned the role of national sovereignty. There are indeed two primary positions in the response to today's dominant forces of globalization: either one can work to reinforce the sovereignty of nation-states as a defensive barrier against the control of foreign and global capital; or one can strive towards a non-national alternative to the present form of globalization that is equally global. The first poses neoliberalism as the primary analytical category, viewing the enemy as unrestricted global capitalist activity with weak state controls; the second is more clearly posed against capital itself, whether state-regulated or not. The first might rightly be called an anti-globalization position, in so far as national sovereignties, even if linked by international solidarity, serve to limit and regulate the forces of capitalist globalization. National liberation thus remains for this position the ultimate goal, as it was for the old anti-colonial and anti-imperialist struggles. The second, in contrast, opposes any national solutions and seeks instead a democratic globalization.

The first position occupied the most visible and dominant spaces of the Porto Alegre Forum; it was represented in the large plenary sessions, repeated by the official spokespeople, and reported in the press. A key proponent of this position was the leadership of the Brazilian PT (Workers' Party)—in effect the host of the Forum, since it runs the city and regional government. It was obvious and inevitable that the PT would occupy a central space in the Forum and use the international prestige of the event as part of its campaign strategy for the upcoming elections. The second dominant voice of national sovereignty was the French leadership of ATTAC, which laid the groundwork for the Forum in the pages of *Le Monde diplomatique*. The leadership of ATTAC is, in this regard, very close to many of the French politicians—most notably Jean-Pierre Chevènement—who advocate strengthening national sovereignty as a solution to the ills of contemporary globalization. These, in any case, are the figures who dominated the representation of the Forum both internally and in the press.

The non-sovereign, alternative globalization position, in contrast, was minoritarian at the Forum—not in quantitative terms but in terms of representation; in fact, the majority of the participants in the Forum may well have occupied this minoritarian position. First, the various movements that have conducted the protests from Seattle to Genoa are generally oriented towards non-national solutions. Indeed, the centralized structure of state sovereignty itself runs counter to the horizontal network-form that the movements have developed. Second, the Argentinian movements that have sprung up in response to the present financial crisis, organized in neighbourhood and city-wide delegate assemblies, are similarly antagonistic to proposals of national sovereignty.

Their slogans call for getting rid, not just of one politician, but all of them—*que se vayan todos*: the entire political class. And finally, at the base of the various parties and organizations present at the Forum the sentiment is much more hostile to proposals of national sovereignty than at the top. This may be particularly true of ATTAC, a hybrid organization whose head, especially in France, mingles with traditional politicians, whereas its feet are firmly grounded in the movements.

The division between the sovereignty, anti-globalization position and the non-sovereign, alternative globalization position is therefore not best understood in geographical terms. It does not map the divisions between North and South or First World and Third. The conflict corresponds rather to two different forms of political organization. The traditional parties and centralized campaigns generally occupy the national sovereignty pole, whereas the new movements organized in horizontal networks tend to cluster at the non-sovereign pole. And furthermore, within traditional, centralized organizations, the top tends toward sovereignty and the base away. It is no surprise, perhaps, that those in positions of power would be most interested in state sovereignty and those excluded least. This may help to explain, in any case, how the national sovereignty, anti-globalization position could dominate the representations of the Forum even though the majority of the participants tend rather toward the perspective of a non-national alternative globalization.

As a concrete illustration of this political and ideological difference, one can imagine the responses to the current economic crisis in Argentina that logically follow from each of these positions. Indeed, that crisis loomed over the entire Forum, like a threatening premonition of a chain of economic disasters to come. The first position would point to the fact that the Argentinian debacle was caused by the forces of global capital and the policies of the IMF, along with the other supranational institutions that undermine national sovereignty. The logical oppositional response should thus be to reinforce the national sovereignty of Argentina (and other nation-states) against these destabilizing external forces. The second position would identify the same causes of the crisis, but insist that a national solution is neither possible nor desirable. The alternative to the rule of global capital and its institutions will only be found at an equally global level, by a global democratic movement. The practical experiments in democracy taking place today at neighbourhood and city levels in Argentina, for example, pose a necessary continuity between the democratization of Argentina and the democratization of the global system. Of course, neither of these perspectives provides an adequate recipe for an immediate solution to the crisis that would circumvent IMF prescriptions—and I am not convinced that such a solution exists. They rather present different political strategies for action today which seek, in the course of time, to develop real alternatives to the current form of global rule.

In a previous period, we could have staged an old-style ideological confrontation between the two positions. The first could accuse the second of playing into the hands of neoliberalism, undermining state sovereignty and paving the way for further globalization. Politics, the one could continue, can only be effectively conducted on the national terrain and within the nation-state. And the second could reply that national regimes and other forms of sovereignty, corrupt and oppressive as they are, are merely obstacles to the global democracy that we seek. This kind of confrontation, however, could not take place at Porto Alegre—in part because of the dispersive nature of the event, which tended to displace conflicts, and in part because the sovereignty position so successfully occupied the central representations that no contest was possible.

But the more important reason for a lack of confrontation may have had to do with the organizational forms that correspond to the two positions. The traditional parties and centralized organizations have spokespeople who represent them and conduct their battles, but no one speaks for a network. How do you argue with a network? The movements organized within them do exert their power, but they do not proceed through oppositions. One of the basic characteristics of the network form is that no two nodes face each other in contradiction; rather, they are always triangulated by a third, and then a fourth, and then by an indefinite number of others in the web. This is one of the characteristics of the Seattle events that we have had the most trouble understanding: groups which we thought in objective contradiction to one another—environmentalists and trade unions, church groups and anarchists—were suddenly able to work together, in the context of the network of the multitude. The movements, to take a slightly different perspective, function rather like a public sphere, in the sense that they can allow full expression of differences within the common context of open exchange. But that does not mean that networks are passive. They displace contradictions and operate instead a kind of alchemy, or rather a sea-change, the flow of the movements transforming the traditional fixed positions; networks imposing their force through a kind of irresistible undertow.

Like the Forum itself, the multitude in the movements is always overflowing, excessive and unknowable. It is certainly important then, on the one hand, to recognize the differences that divide the activists and politicians gathered at Porto Alegre. It would be a mistake, on the other hand, to try to read the division according to the traditional model of ideological conflict between opposing sides. Political struggle in the age of network movements no longer works that way. Despite the apparent strength of those who occupied centre-stage and dominated the representations of the Forum, they may ultimately prove to have lost the struggle. Perhaps the representatives of the traditional parties and centralized organizations at Porto Alegre are too much like the old national leaders gathered at Bandung—imagine Lula of the PT in the position of Ahmed Sukarno as host, and Bernard Cassen of ATTAC France as Jawaharlal Nehru, the most honoured guest. The leaders can certainly craft resolutions affirming national sovereignty around a conference table, but they can never grasp the democratic power of the movements. Eventually, they too will be swept up in the multitude, which is capable of transforming all fixed and centralized elements into so many more nodes in its indefinitely expansive network.

TOM MERTES

GRASS-ROOTS GLOBALISM

Reply to Michael Hardt

Chaotic, dispersive, unknowable . . . Michael Hardt's uncertainty in the face of the multilingual mass of global oppositionists—'a sea of people'—thronging to Porto Alegre for the World Social Forum last spring is entirely understandable. There were anywhere between 50,000 and 80,000 participants, and at least 10,000 official delegates—activists, students, intellectuals, trade-unionists, environmentalists, rural workers, Argentinian *piqueteros*, plus the representatives of scores of NGOs—crowding into seminars, round-table sessions and workshops, or marching through the sweltering streets in celebratory parades or ad-hoc protest demonstrations. Twenty-seven conferences on broad socio-economic themes were running simultaneously, together with over a hundred seminars on more specific questions—food sovereignty, 'the illusion of development', the World Bank and IMF, indigenous peoples and sustainability—and more than five hundred specialist workshops; not to mention the music, the films, the plays.

The first question, in Hardt's view, is how such a widely differentiated mass can begin to work together—for the various movements 'cannot simply connect to each other as they are, but must rather be transformed through the encounter by a sort of mutual adequation . . . not to become the same, or even to unite, but to link together in an expanding network'. The second is to distinguish the major issues they confront. For Hardt, the opponents of neoliberal globalization are faced with a choice between two primary positions: 'either one can work to reinforce the sovereignty of nation-states as a defensive barrier against the control of foreign and global capital; or one can strive towards a non-national alternative to the present form of globalization that is equally global'.[1]

Hardt and Negri have already made a passionate case against the first position in the pages of *Empire*. The modern state—born as a counter-revolutionary, absolutist response to Renaissance humanism, boosted with the toxic ideology of an exclusionary, homogenizing nationalism—has always been a tool for repression, even when posing as the champion of anti-colonial liberation. Over the past two decades, however, the powers of this reactionary instrument have been drained away by the flow of global networks of production and exchange across its borders, while sovereignty is reconstituted at the higher level of a (still somewhat misty) 'Empire'. The authors resolutely refuse any nostalgia for the power structures that preceded the global age. Strategies of local resistance—dreams of liberated zones, outside Empire—'misidentify and thus mask the enemy', just as they obscure the potential for liberation within it. The national-sovereignty defence against the forces of international capital, Hardt now suggests, presents 'an obstacle' to global democracy.[2]

But it was this position, he claims, that dominated the official platforms and plenary sessions at Porto Alegre, promoted above all by the officials of the Brazilian PT and by the *chevènementiste* leaders of the French ATTAC. The other side—the 'democratic-globalization' viewpoint—was represented by the North Atlantic anti-WTO networks, by the more radical base of ATTAC groups and, emblematically, by the Argentinian neighbourhood committees that have sprung up in response to their country's financial collapse. Hardt describes these last as antagonistic to all proposals of national sovereignty, their slogan—*que se vayan todos*—calling for the abolition of the whole political class. To further illustrate the gulf between the two positions he suggests that, if a 'democratic-globalization' solution to the Argentinian crisis exists, it would reject

[1] Michael Hardt, 'Today's Bandung?', above, p. 232.
[2] Michael Hardt and Antonio Negri, *Empire*, Cambridge, MA 2000, pp. 83, 103, 133, 307, 343–6; 'Today's Bandung?', above, p. 235.

any national defiance of the IMF in favour of seeking a 'continuity' between the practical experiments in democracy going on at *barrio* level—the *villa miseria* in Argentina—and the democratization of the global system.

Is he right? There were certainly plenty of *memento mori* at Porto Alegre in the form of Euro-Socialist politicians looking for photo opportunities; but most of these are ardent proponents of the neoliberal cause. Similarly, in the run-up to the Brazilian elections the PT leadership—which certainly hijacked a number of the sessions at Porto Alegre, but did not succeed in controlling its agenda—has been notable not so much for demanding sovereign control over capital flows as for its alacrity in complying with IMF demands on debt repayment. But the experience presented by activists at Porto Alegre—especially those from Latin America, where the neoliberal crisis is at its most intense—proposed a more modulated view of the specific units and gradations of power than Hardt's 'all or nothing' approach. Rather than an intuitive uprising of the multitude against Empire, they suggested a more differentiated field.

The nation-state, precisely because of its role in pushing through the social engineering required by neoliberalism, remains an essential instrument for global capital—and hence a key zone of contestation. It is against their own governments that both South Africans and Latin Americans have been mobilizing to fight against water and electricity privatizations. Peruvians successfully resisted an electricity sell-off—this time at local-state level, in Arequipa—earlier this year; Bolivian 'water wars' rattled Banzer's regime in April 2000; 'Vivendi, go home!' is the cry in Argentina. CONAIE, the national confederation of indigenous peoples, brought down the Ecuadorian government early in 2000, and after broken promises from the military and the new regime were back on the streets a year later to oppose austerity measures, deforestation, privatization of electricity and oil pipelines. There have been protests along similar lines in El Salvador, India, Nigeria, Ghana, Papua New Guinea. Last spring, the shanty towns of Caracas rallied to the defence of Chávez in order to fight US-backed plans for the privatization of their oil and the still greater reduction of their living standards.

'The first question of political philosophy today', write Hardt and Negri, 'is not if or even why there will be resistance and rebellion, but rather how to determine the enemy against which to rebel'.[3] The Latin American mobilizations of the past few years display not a faith in the transcendent power of national sovereignty but, precisely, a grasp of the immediate enemy—and, often, a clear intuition of the forces that stand behind him. The architecture alone of most Third World US embassies—those massive, reinforced blocks that loom more ominously than any national government buildings—not to mention the plain facts of the local USAF military base, is evidence enough. It is a common enough contradiction today that a willingness to pursue 'the radiant horizons of capitalist wealth' can sit quite easily with a sour dose of home-grown cynicism about the uses of Yanqui power.

This is the great ambivalence at the heart of *Empire*. What is the role—the 'privileged position'—of the US within the coming global sovereign power that Hardt and Negri depict? The actually existing United States constantly threatens to emerge from the pages of *Empire* like the face in a nightmare, and has to be perpetually repressed. Instructed that Empire exercises its control by means of 'the bomb, money and ether', we are warned that 'it might appear as though the reins of these mechanisms were held by the United States . . . as if the US were the new Rome, or a cluster of new Romes: Washington (the bomb), New York (money), and Los Angeles (ether).' But any such certainty is immediately withdrawn: the screen goes fuzzy—world power is much too 'flexible' for us to think of territorializing it in this way.[4] 'Empire', we are continually

---

[3] *Empire*, p. 211.

[4] Although, on the very next page—the decline of the nation-state notwithstanding—we find a cool analysis of the 'imperial' tasks—'the construction of information highways, the control of the equilibria of the stock exchange despite the wild fluctuation of speculation, the firm maintenance of monetary values, public investment in the military-industrial system to help transform the mode of production, the reform of the educational system to adapt to these new productive networks, and so forth'—that currently demand 'big government' in the USA. *Empire*, pp. 347 and 348.

assured, 'has no Rome'—despite the fact that US defence spending is more than that of the next twenty-five governments combined. It has bases in at least 59 countries.[5]

The US is, of course, no transcendent, deterritorialized sovereign force but only a mega-state within an international state system—as is all too clear to those who have felt its force. There are real debates to be had around questions of counter-globalization strategy at national and—more commonly proposed today—at regional level. Via Campesina's campaign for 'food sovereignty', for the right to raise protective tariffs that will prevent multinational companies wiping out local farmers by their dumping practices, is one example.[6] It is widely acknowledged that the ability of the Malaysians and the pre-WTO Chinese to impose controls on capital flow during the 1997–98 financial crisis protected their populations from much of the devastation that ravaged Indonesia. Focus on the Global South has rightly counselled Vietnam against joining the WTO, pointing out the social and economic consequences this would entail. It suggests instead 'deglobalization' to build strong regional markets within the South that would have some autonomy from global financial interests.[7] But the traditional Chevènement position is a straw man, at least at Porto Alegre. The real questions to be asked are not about the nation-states from which sovereignty is draining away, but the one it is being sucked into.

For Hardt, the division at Porto Alegre between the 'national-sovereignty' and the 'democratic-globalization' positions corresponds not to Third World versus First World outlooks, but to a conflict between

---

[5] Center for Defense Information, *World Military Database 2001–2002*, http://www.cdi.org/products/almanac0102.pdf.

[6] See interview with José Bové, 'A Farmers' International?', above, pp. 142–4. While *Empire* famously promotes the subversive effects of mass migration, Hardt and Negri also defend, more poignantly perhaps, the right of the 'multitude' to refuse to move. In this instance, a strategy for Asian and African farmers—some third of the world's workforce—to defend their livelihood through some form of regional counter-sovereignty becomes imperative.

[7] Walden Bello, 'The Global South', above, pp. 60–2.

two different forms of political organization: 'The traditional parties and centralized campaigns generally occupy the national-sovereignty pole, whereas the new movements organized in horizontal networks tend to cluster at the non-sovereign pole'. This, he suggests, may explain why 'an old-style ideological confrontation', a clear debate between the two positions, did not take place at the 2002 WSF. Whereas the formally constituted organizations have spokespeople to represent them, the new groups do not—'Political struggle in the age of network movements no longer works that way':

> How do you argue with a network? The movements organized within them . . . do not proceed by oppositions. One of the basic characteristics of the network form is that no two nodes face each other in contradiction; rather, they are always triangulated by a third, and then a fourth, and then by an indefinite number of others in the web . . . They displace contradictions and operate instead a kind of alchemy, or rather a sea-change, the flow of the movements transforming the traditional fixed positions; networks imposing their force through a kind of irresistible undertow.[8]

One difference Hardt seems to miss is the question of scale. Many seemingly traditional bodies at Porto Alegre were actually mass organizations. The Brazilian Sem Terra is a case in point. It counts in its ranks over a third of a million landless families—and this is not a passive, card-carrying membership but one defined by taking action: risking the wrath of *latifundiários* and the state by occupying land. Within this layer there are, again, around 20,000 activists, the most energetic and committed, who have helped to organize their neighbours and who continue to attend courses and participate in regional and state-level meetings that elect the local leaderships. Over 11,000 delegates attended the MST national congress in 2000. Spokespeople—accountable to the membership—become a necessity with numbers of this size.[9]

The North Atlantic networks, by contrast, are more likely to count their active core as a few dozen or less. The Ruckus Society, for example,

---

[8] 'Today's Bandung?', above, pp. 234–6.
[9] See interview with João Pedro Stedile: 'Brazil's Landless Battalions', above, p. 26–7.

has a full-time staff of four, and between 20 and 30 volunteers in close orbit around that; about 120 people will attend an annual camp. Other organizations like 50 Years is Enough and United Students Against Sweatshops (USAS) are run by less than half a dozen full-timers, who call other organizations into action. Rather than sweeping away and transforming all fixed positions, these networks often feel more at risk of being dissolved themselves into the powerful flows of American capitalism. Does size matter? For the authors of *Empire*, 'we are immersed in a system of power so deep and complex that we can no longer determine specific difference or measure'.[10] To the resounding reply of Sem Terra leader João Pedro Stedile—asked what Northern sympathizers should do to help the landless farmers of Brazil—'Overthrow your neoliberal governments!', their book provides no echo. Yet Stedile's demand surely suggests a scale by which the movements can take stock of their opponents, and reckon their own strength.

Hardt's maritime metaphor—the 'sea' of networks—raises a further question, crucial to the 'mutual adequation' of the current movements: waves do not speak. How, if it cannot argue but only 'sweep away' its opponents, is Hardt's network—or multitude—to hold an internal conversation, to debate and decide its strategy? For the Sem Terra, the question of how to develop democratically accountable forms of leadership and coordination, while avoiding the traps of 'presidentialism' and bureaucratization, has been literally a matter of life and death; militant farmers' leaders in Brazil have traditionally been gunned down by landowners or the state. The attempt to answer it has led them to stress the importance of collective, elected bodies at all levels, from the village occupation committee up.[11] As a result, enormous efforts are put into gathering together the far-flung activists, most of them working farmers, for regional, state and national decision-making meetings.

For North American pressure groups, radical NGOs and networks, while there is often a strong commitment to transparency and to rotating

[10] *Empire*, p. 211.
[11] Stedile, 'Brazil's Landless Battalions', above, pp. 26–7.

leadership, a different sort of process often prevails. Often these are run by a small group of dedicated individuals who tend to lead by default, by dint of their accumulated skills. 'Obviously', as the director of the Ruckus Society puts it, 'those closest to the centre get more input than people who are further away from it. For example, I took the decision to hold the WTO camp [in Seattle in 1999], and that's how a lot of the decisions have been made since'.[12] USAS also embraces consensus building in decision-making, with all of its pitfalls; it has only one annual meeting of its university affiliates. With their relatively small numbers and higher educational level, the North American groups have focused on the quality of consensus-making around specific actions. David Graeber has described the patient and ingenious methods—spokescouncils, affinity groups, facilitation tools, breakouts, fishbowls, blocking concerns, vibe-watchers and so on—that have been developed to devise summit-protest tactics, for instance.[13] But it is not clear how these could be extended to cope with strategic issues, or projected onto the vast scale of Porto Alegre, where the star system—as much that of the new movements as of the traditional parties—posed another set of problems for internal democracy.

Given these disparities, should we welcome Hardt's project of an ever-expanding network as the form that the 'movement of movements' should take? It seems more useful to conceptualize the relation between the various groups as an ongoing series of alliances and coalitions, whose convergences remain contingent. Genuine solidarity can only be built up through a process of testing and questioning, through a real overlap of affinities and interests. The Turtles and Teamsters will no doubt meet again on the streets of North America, but this does not mean they are in the sort of constant communication that a network implies. The WSF provides a venue in which churches and anarchists, punks and farmers, trade-unionists and greens can explore issues of common concern, without having to create a new web.

---

[12] John Sellers, 'Raising a Ruckus', above, p. 180.
[13] Graeber, 'The New Anarchists', above, pp. 213–4.

Focusing on questions of national sovereignty and organization, Hardt neglects other areas where there is perhaps a greater need for 'adequation', in some form. If—in the age of Malaysian skyscrapers and New York slums—the distinction between North and South has more to do with power and elite life-style than geographical location, it still denotes a significant split in current experience and historical perception. One obvious difference for activists is that the repressive nature of capitalist state power is posed much more starkly in the South. In Argentina, at least 30 protestors have been killed since March 2001. At least 14 Sem Terra activists have been murdered and hundreds jailed. Since January 2001 four protestors have been killed in the Ecuadorian Amazon and at least 25 shot and wounded in the highlands. In El Salvador, the death squads are back at work. In June 2001, four Papuans were killed by the state during protests against austerity measures and privatizations.[14] Genoa notwithstanding, Northerners stand a better chance of getting home safely after a demonstration.

In the end, divergences over the economy and the environment may prove more crucial than the Left's organizational forms. The 'green production' laws for which North Atlantic groups have campaigned have, in practice, often worked as a form of protectionism, favouring Northern capital—and labour—while increasing poverty and unemployment in the South. Walden Bello and others have spoken passionately of the need to redress this, calling for a visionary strategy that would protect the jobs of Northern workers at the same time as strengthening the rest of the world's working class—forging a common front against the re-stratification of labour that global capital is currently trying to push through. In place of 'green protectionism', they have called for a positive transfer of green technology to the South, coupled with support for indigenous environmental groups.[15] Significantly, few of the big Northern trade unions were present to hear this case put at Porto Alegre.

---

[14] For further details of numbers of protestors killed—many fighting IMF austerity measures—see *States of Unrest II* (2002) at http://www.wdm.org.uk/cambriefs/Debt/Unrest2.pdf.

[15] Bello, 'The Global South', above, p. 63–4.

Agriculture, of course, remains far more labour-intensive in the South, where a just redistribution of land is still the central issue. The threat of GM terminator seeds menaces the livelihood of hundreds of millions of small farmers across Africa, Asia and Latin America. *Pace* Hardt's strictures on national-sovereign solutions, African governments that have refused to accept the poisoned gift of Monsanto's unmilled, self-sterilizing corn have for once been acting in the interests of their citizens. Via Campesina—itself a North–South alliance of working farmers—held its own mini-forum at Porto Alegre, in a park near the city centre; Monsanto and Coca-Cola logos were ritually burnt at its closing ceremony. First World environmentalists need to listen attentively to these Third World farmers and indigenous groups, who unite powerful ecological concerns with a highly critical perspective on international capital.

A third division—here, no longer on North–South lines—was over the question of global capitalism itself. While almost all the speakers and participants were critical of the IMF, World Bank and WTO, there was disagreement over whether these institutions could be reformed, or whether they were inherently linked to a system that is fundamentally unequal, corrupt and unsustainable. For all the attention paid to these general issues, however, there was far less debate on the current world political situation. When the questions on which any global opposition might be expected to raise its voice were discussed—the US war in Afghanistan, the Middle East, the threat to Iraq—it was often away from the central plenaries and official platforms, though such issues did surface after the initial presentations.

The debate over the WSF needs to remember, too, the exhausting logistical problems that global organizing presents to the dispossessed. Time, money and a daunting sense of distance present real obstacles to students, activists, trade-unionists, the rural and urban poor—in stark contrast to the well-funded global infrastructures of the ruling class. For all his reservations about the Brazilian PT, Hardt must acknowledge that, without its municipal government in Porto Alegre, the WSF would never have taken place. Naturally, most of the participants were from Latin America—Brazil, Argentina and Uruguay between them fielded over 7,000 delegates, Italy and France around 1,200. Travel problems precluded many more. The hard-working interpreters—translating into Portuguese, the host language, and English, although Spanish might have been a more natural *lingua franca* for most of those present—often went unpaid for their skills.

Organizing from below is a fragile process, at threat from numerous different forces. A micro example: when LA-based activists recently sought to get in touch with *maquiladora* workers in Mexico, they first had to negotiate their way through a series of blocking attempts by the moderate NGOs that controlled the funds for transport and translators, and wanted to run the agenda too. When, finally, the Angelenos met with their Tijuana counterparts, they found that what the *maquiladoristas* needed most was computers—to send information out but, above all, to get news in. The US side could come up with the computers; what they couldn't produce was electricity, decent phone lines, Spanish-language software and technical help.

Hard as it is, this sort of grass-roots organizing remains crucial for building up relationships of mutual support, coalitions of resistance. In these nano-level processes of forging solidarity, the WSF—and especially perhaps its informal side: the youth camp, fiestas, lunches, marches—can play a vital role. 'Chaotic, dispersive, unknowable' as they may be, these messy, mass-scale, face-to-face encounters are the life-blood of any movement—an element that telecommunications metaphors can never attain.

EMIR SADER

BEYOND CIVIL SOCIETY

The Left after Porto Alegre

The geography of the current anti-globalization protests signals a new world-political landscape for the Left. In a sense, this is a reversal of that historic shift of which Isaac Deutscher spoke—the relocation of the anti-capitalist movement from its nineteenth-century origins in Western Europe to Russia, then China. Behind this millennial transformation, of course, lies the earthquake that brought down the Soviet bloc; set China on course for a pragmatic integration with the capitalist market; provoked an identity crisis—and then a political one—in social-democracy and the old mass Communist Parties; and led to the selective immiseration of the Third World. An entire topography of the Left was obliterated in that upheaval. From its ruins—in Chiapas or Porto Alegre, Seattle, Genoa, Barcelona and elsewhere—have grown the groups and networks that are now questioning neoliberal globalization. They point towards an entirely new ideological, political and geographical design.

Chiapas: an impoverished region of southern Mexico. Seattle: symbol of the microchip and American postmodernity. Porto Alegre: a 'European' city in Brazil's deep south, run by a party that claims to represent its workers. What kind of movement can arise from such social and geographic diversity? In a country not known for its leftist traditions, Porto Alegre has suddenly emerged as the emblem of the new groupings, the point at which a host of hopes and fears, illusions and questions converge.

I

The development of the Brazilian Left was delayed relative to that of other countries in the region. Although its Communist and Socialist parties were founded at roughly the same time, the late 1910s or early 1920s, Brazil's socio-economic formation—its coffee economy and low level of industrialization—made it impossible for these forces to acquire the critical mass of those in Argentina, Chile or Uruguay. A comparison between the national-populist programmes of Vargas in Brazil and Perón in Argentina points up the distinction. In response to the devastating consequences of the Wall Street crash, Vargas took power in 1930—overthrowing a conservative, primary-exporting government—in an essentially agrarian country. The state had little difficulty in harnessing, both politically and institutionally, the syndicalist structures through which he promoted the rights of a limited urban working class. In Argentina, by contrast, it was a progressive, Radical government, which had played a leading role in university reform in Córdoba in the late 1910s, that fell victim to the 1929 disaster. A military regime that would renegotiate Argentina's dependency on regressive terms was in place throughout the thirties and early forties. When Perón seized power in 1943, it was at the head of a socially constituted working class, with a clear political and ideological trajectory and a distinct set of traditions— Perón had to defeat socialist and communist influence in order to project himself as the people's leader. Vargas had far less difficulty in imposing his rule (as dictator, from 1930–45; as elected president, 1950–54), due to the weakness and political backwardness of the Brazilian working class.

One of the consequences of this fragility was that the nationalist labour-communist coalition that had backed Vargas virtually disappeared after the military coup in 1964. The *trabalhistas*, who owed their strength entirely to the state apparatus, the Labour Ministry in particular, ceased to exist once this had been taken over by the junta, whose first measures decreed the military supervision of all trade unions, a wage freeze, and police persecution of working-class leaders. The Communists' strategy of subordinate alliance with the 'national bourgeoisie' collapsed in ruins, and the Party effectively disappeared.

Thanks to its important geostrategic position, the sixties' coup in Brazil occurred relatively early compared to others in Latin America—1964, the same year as Bolivia's; 1966 saw a failed putsch attempt in Argentina, successfully pushed through ten years later; the military seized power in Chile and Uruguay in 1973. Although the Left was weaker in Brazil than elsewhere, ferment in the countryside on a hitherto unseen scale and the politicization of lower-ranking army officers was considered a risk to national security both by Washington and by the upper echelons of the armed forces, concentrated in the Escola Superior de Guerra.

Coming at this stage, the Brazilian coup allowed the military dictatorship a honeymoon period during the final years of the long post-war boom. An influx of surplus dollars funded economic expansion, albeit based on exports and the luxury-goods sector.[1] Growth rates exceeded 10 per cent per year, right up to the international capitalist crisis of 1973. Even then, while practically every other economy was entering recession, Brazil's rates merely decreased to between 5 and 7 per cent. The expansionist momentum was maintained up to the end of the seventies by loans and dubious public-works projects—football stadiums, the still unfinished Transamazonian highway, large hydroelectric plants and other grandiose affairs. At this point the boomerang of borrowing and state spending came back, bringing to a close five decades of continuous growth that had transformed the country in almost every respect, while leaving it choked with debt, inflation and public deficits. This crisis resulted not just in a 'lost decade', but an era of virtual stagnation, with indices of economic expansion barely exceeding demographic growth.

Left resistance to the military coup mostly took the desperate route of armed struggle between 1967 and 1971, all other methods being ruled out by the repression. Despite a few spectacular actions, this strategy proved unable to accumulate forces on a mass level. Following the Left's defeat, there was a broad liberal hegemony over the opposition to the

---

[1] See Ruy Mauro Marini, *Dialéctica de la dependencia*, Mexico 1973.

dictatorship, ideologically oriented by the 'authoritarianism' theses of Fernando Henrique Cardoso—then gaining prestige as an intellectual trying to start a political career. This force crystallized in a broad party—the Movimento Democrático Brasileiro (MDB)—grouping together all elements of the legal opposition. Alongside it, a grass-roots trade unionism began to develop from the devastation of the earlier syndicalist tradition.

The old unions had been based in state enterprises—oil, transport and public services—with Rio de Janeiro, the former capital, their focal point. The core of the new worker militancy lay in the automobile plants on the outskirts of São Paulo—socio-economically, by this stage, Brazil's most important city. Car production has driven Brazilian industrial growth since the fifties, and still accounts for a quarter of the country's GDP. With their strong class consciousness and visceral hostility to a military regime bent on wage-freeze policies, these unions would forge the nucleus of the largest new party of the Brazilian Left, the Partido dos Trabalhadores. Their leader, Luis Inácio da Silva, known as Lula, a migrant from the impoverished, rural North-East, would be its head.

The PT brought together progressive elements of the Catholic Church—transformed, under the influence of liberation theology, from component of the military regime to haven for social activists—with civil-rights campaigners, Trotskyists, Maoists and former guerrillas, under the hegemony of Lula's militant trade-unionists. Since its foundation, the PT has been the major player on the Brazilian Left. Its role has changed from that of a party of resistance to the dictatorship—and to the subsequent transition to a partial democracy that maintained the world's highest income disparity—into a national alternative to government. Lula has been runner-up in every presidential election since 1989, with the PT consistently gaining a plurality—30 per cent—of the vote; by the time this appears, he could be President-elect of Brazil. The PT has won a series of municipal elections, and has a record of successful local administrations marked by their social policies, their transparency, their engagement with popular movements and, above all—as in Porto Alegre—their participatory budgets.

II

Porto Alegre is the capital of Brazil's southernmost state, Rio Grande do Sul, abutting on Uruguay and Argentina. This frontier character gives it a special status. Despite Brazil's vast territories, debouching onto every country in South America save Chile and Ecuador, nearly all its borders are impassable. Jungle and mountain block the route to Bolivia, Colombia, Peru and Venezuela. The Paraná crossings to Paraguay are the only other exception. Early on, then, Rio Grande do Sul became a military stronghold and, once the Brazilian army began intervening in government, shortly after the vicious war of the Triple Alliance in 1865–70, an important power base in national politics. Many of the country's leading figures have come from here—Getúlio Vargas himself, João Goulart, president from 1961–64, Leonel Brizola, ex-state governor and currently leader of the Partido Democrático Trabalhista—not to mention several high officials of the military dictatorship, including three presidents: Costa e Silva, Garrastazu Médici and João Figueiredo.

The PT has inherited the state's politicized tradition, in a more radical form. In 1988, Olívio Dutra—trade-unionist, bank employee and founder member of the PT—was elected mayor of Porto Alegre. His deputy, Tarso Genro—lawyer and ex-militant of the clandestine opposition, now standing as the PT candidate for state governor—developed the concept of the participatory budget. This consists of shifting decisions on how to allocate municipal resources from the City Council to popular assemblies. The process has politicized budgetary debates, taking them out of the technocratic and legislative sphere, allowing broad public debate about funding priorities and their social and political implications. Throughout the year, a series of assemblies decide where the money should go, follow up on implementation and make a balance-sheet of the results. This process has become the PT's trump card, differentiating and legitimizing its administration through mobilizing its citizens—to the extent that the other parties now include a diluted version in their programmes.

III

When the idea of holding a Social Forum, in opposition to the Economic Forum in Davos, was first floated, Bernard Cassen of *Le Monde diplomatique* suggested it take place in Porto Alegre—a city on the periphery, whose participatory budgets had become emblematic of an alternative approach. In other words, it was the success of specific political measures, implemented by a left party through a process of democratic state reforms involving a strengthening of the public domain, that initially attracted the moving spirits of the Social Forum to Porto Alegre. In spite of this, the Organizing Committee of both the first and second Social Forums was mainly composed of NGOs, with only minority representation for the country's two main social movements—the CUT trade-union federation, under the central leadership of the PT, and the Sem Terra, identified with the Party's more radical base. It was due to this central role of NGOs that the Forum assumed the function of a meeting place for 'civil society'—a key notion for the new movements—with all the multiple and diverse meanings this concept provides. This is not the place to explore their genealogy, but two features—one inclusive, one exclusive—need to be pointed out. The first relates to the use of NGOs as agents for neoliberalism within civil society—particularly through the World Bank's tactic of using these organizations to implement its social-compensation policies. Mexico has been a test-site for these attempts—increasingly so, under Fox. The NGO practice of entering into 'partnerships' with big business—though never announced as such—is another aspect of the same problem. The ambiguities this overlap has created have not, as yet, had a negative impact on the anti-neoliberal character of the Forum, established under the strong propulsion of another founding element, the anti-WTO demonstrations in Seattle.

The second, exclusive aspect of the emphasis on 'civil society' lies in its rejection of parties and governments, its embrace of the civil society/State opposition. This is more serious, not only because it means rejecting a potential weapon in a radically unequal contest but also, and more importantly, because the movement thus distances itself from the themes of power, the State, public sphere, political leadership and even, in a sense, from ideological struggle—elements that were essential to the choice of Porto Alegre as the Forums' venue. The result of this exclusion of parties and State, if pushed through, would severely limit the formulation of any alternatives to neoliberalism, confining such aspirations to a local or sectoral context—the NGOs' mantra, 'Think global, act local'; proposals for fair trade; 'ecologically sustainable development'—while giving up any attempt to build an alternative hegemony, or any global proposals to counter and defeat world capitalism's current neoliberal project. These limitations were acutely embodied in the structure of the first two Forums, organized, respectively, into twenty-four and twenty-seven round-table discussions on extremely fragmented themes which tended to dissipate still further—giving the whole an academic overtone, with a corresponding intellectual division of labour. The general lectures were more like testimonies from people connected in some way to the movement—and the most successful, at the first Forum, were all made precisely by leaders of parties or social movements—Lula, João Pedro Stedile, José Bové or Eduardo Galeano.

The very act of defining themselves as 'non-governmental' explicitly rejects any ambition on the NGOs' part for an alternative hegemonic project, which would, by its nature, have to include states and governments as the means through which political and economic power is articulated in modern societies. They therefore either insert themselves, explicitly or implicitly, within the liberal critique of the State's actions, or else limit their activity to the sphere of civil society—which, defined in opposition to the State, also ends at the boundaries of liberal politics. In fact, the very concept of 'civil society' masks the class nature of its components—multinational corporations, banks and mafia, set next to social movements, trade unions, civic bodies—while collectively demonizing the State. The leading role of NGOs in the resistance to neoliberalism is a sign of the movement's defensive character, still unable to formulate an alternative hegemonic strategy. A move that brought together the struggle against US imperial dominance with the anti-capitalist elements of the movements would mark the beginning of an offensive, politicized phase in its development.

As the old Left got weaker, lost its mass base or deserted the field, the space of anti-neoliberal resistance was occupied by NGO-type groupings, deliberately distanced from the political arena and thus from any serious reflection on strategy; it was as if this whole area had been abandoned to the enemy. A new class of global citizenship was proposed, transcending national frontiers—the loss of power and political debility of the nation-state were simply taken for granted. Thus the Zapatistas gained international recognition, on the internet and through the global media, which was then projected back into their country of origin. At national level, they are still fighting for an acknowledgement of their right to exist. On the other hand, in a way that differs somewhat from liberalism, the idea of civil society has been used by social movements, NGOs and civil-rights groups that still proclaim their opposition to the State, governments, parliaments and political parties, while searching for 'partnerships' with multinational corporations.

IV

The new is always hard to grasp, especially when it emerges within a landscape transformed from that in which the previous events occurred. The picture presented by the Social Forums would be incomprehensible within the frameworks that have characterized earlier attempts at international coordination—that of the Internationals, for example, or the Third World-dominated Non-Aligned Movement. The world of work intrinsic to the First International, in particular—where solidarity was premised on the universalized exploitation of labour—has been transformed. Not industrial workers but farmers' unions, from peripheral or semi-peripheral countries, have a significant presence at the Forums. They are held in the Third World, and a large fraction of the participants are from the South, but the movement's largest demonstrations since Seattle have been in countries of the core—Genoa, Barcelona—where the young sub-proletariat has played a central role. Comparisons with the Internationals, the Bandung Conference or Woodstock—the media's favourite—can thus fail to capture the historical specificity of the Forums, and the very different set of elements that are combining here to construct a new subjectivity in the fight for a post-neoliberal order.[2]

It was the mass working-class movements of the late nineteenth and twentieth centuries that provided the basis for the Internationals, throwing up Socialist and Communist parties, trade unions, workers' representatives in parliament and manifold forms of cultural expression. Politically, the scenario is now quite different. The long-established parties of the European Left were largely absent from the first Forum, and had only a minimal presence at the second. The reasons for this lie both in the ideological crisis caused by social-democracy's conversion to neoliberalism and in the declining weight, or real implantation, of these currents. Labour-movement concerns were raised instead by the new trade unions of the semi-periphery—South Africa, Korea, Brazil. If common motifs can be traced between the Forum and the First International—the insurgent, pluralist, libertarian, highly ideologized character of the mobilizations; social heterogeneity; internationalism; opposition to a liberal free-trade order—it is impossible to grasp the meaning of the new forms without an examination of the historical rupture that divides them. For what splits the two asunder is the defeat and

---

[2] See Manuel Monereo, 'Porto Alegre II: en transición', *Memoria* 158, April 2002; Michael Hardt, 'Today's Bandung?', above, pp. 230–6.

disappearance of all that once constituted 'actually existing socialism', and the transformation this has wrought upon the Left.

From the moment of the Bolshevik revolution—and especially since the Second World War—the world stage was polarized by the socialist/ capitalist opposition, determining relatively fixed ideological and political reference points. While the Left proclaimed a struggle between the two systems, the Western superpowers called for a battle of 'democracy' against 'totalitarianism'. This was the determining contradiction of the epoch. With the fall of the USSR and the 'socialist bloc', capitalism was once again sole ruler of the world scene. The remaining post-capitalist countries reinvented themselves. China opted for a form of market economy—as in all likelihood will Vietnam. Cuba sought to defend the basic gains of the previous period rather than advance towards socialism. The radical shift in the balance of forces reverberated through the social and political movements. With growing unemployment in Europe, unions were thrown onto the defensive, mounting at best a partial resistance to 'flexibilization' while rapidly losing members. In the increasingly informal and heterogeneous world of labour that was emerging, traditional methods of organizing had ever less effect. Parties had to confront the universalization of neoliberal policies. European social-democracy adapted to this at the very moment when, for the first time, the Centre-Left was in power in nearly every EU state; the Communist parties of the region shrivelled, or vanished altogether. A similar scenario was enacted in Eastern Europe, where former Communist parties took up a radicalized neoliberalism or local versions of the Third Way.

The magnitude of this defeat for the Left—its depth and reach—has not been sufficiently evaluated. Its principal component is the victory of liberalism, on both the economic and political planes. Economically, the expansion of the financial sphere, deregulation and the market-led annulment of social benefits have dissolved the foundations of the welfare state. Commercialization has absorbed and penetrated the field of social relations, daily practice and consciousness, becoming the lodestone of ideological life. The corporation now plays a leading role in determining economic processes, to the detriment of social forces—unions, parties—premised on more associative forms of life and opposed to the unlimited extension of the market. Politically, with the displacement of the 'capitalism/socialism' binary by that of 'democracy/ totalitarianism', liberalism conquered hitherto undreamt-of areas of the Left. Neoliberal economics and representative democracy were embraced as the definitive form of politics by huge swathes of the traditional Left. Parallel to this, 'imperialism' as current historical reality disappeared from the political lexicon, enabling the US to impose its international hegemony, as the model of both 'democracy' and economic success—its deregulated 'Anglo-Saxon' system triumphantly counterposed to the remnants of the European welfare state. Economic progress was identified with free capital flows; levels of deregulation became the measure of potential growth. The process took 'globalization' as its logo, to underline its distinction from 'backward' national models, asserting the international movement of capital as the only possible paradigm.

The combination of these elements has resulted in a deep and wide-ranging hegemony, consolidated at the ideological and cultural level, unlike any that capitalism has previously enjoyed. In the aftermath of the Second World War, Japan—despite its cultural distinctiveness—embraced the basic assumptions of Western capitalism, adapting the system to the national context. In the last two decades, China, undefeated in war, has taken on the same priorities, transforming its social habits, customs and values at a pace previously unseen in Eastern culture. In Western Europe, social-democracy has become the main mouthpiece of neoliberalism. In Latin America, traditional populist tendencies—always characterized by a real or rhetorical nationalism—have played the same role, here opting for extreme variants of neoliberalism, with the PRI in Mexico and Menem in Argentina as the prime examples.

With the disappearance of socialism from the current historical horizon—and with it, all discussion of capitalism as a historically determined social system—the Left was disarmed in face of the conservative counter-offensive launched by Reagan and Thatcher, and continued by

Clinton and Blair. It has abandoned strategic programmes for the construction of a new type of society and turned to defending the rights of
the oppressed, or to creating local and sectoral sites of resistance. The
proliferation of alternative municipal governments and NGOs is the best
example of this.

The project of building an alternative to capitalism was abandoned
in favour of resistance from within—opposition to neoliberalism rather
than to the overall system. 'Anti-totalitarianism' now mutated into
an antagonism towards any overarching analysis—any attempt to see
historical processes as a whole. These would inevitably result in reduc-
tive programmes with the State as their monolithic agent. Pluralist
democracy demanded more 'complex' diagnoses, irreducible to the
'economism' attributed to (actually existing) Marxism, and would therefore renounce 'grand narratives'.

It was in this context that local and sectoral forms of resistance—ecological, feminist, ethnic, human rights, municipal democracy—combined
to form the movement that, together with union organizations and anti-
WTO groups, would surface so explosively in Seattle in November 1999.
If they represent an advance, in creating new spaces in which opposition forces can come together, many of them also implicitly renounce
any attempt to construct an alternative society: as if our indefinite con-
finement within the limits of capitalism and liberal democracy was
accepted as fact.

V

The Social Forum is a unique meeting place for anti-systemic forces
to gather at a world level. It is unprecedented both in its diversity—
bringing together not only parties and political currents but social
movements, NGOs, civil-rights groups, unions—and in its own non-
state, non-partisan character. It proposes to formulate global alternatives
to current capitalist practices, and strategies for their implementation.

In this sense, by its very existence the Forum creates a space in which the anti-neoliberal struggle can escape the narrow limits of the globalization versus nation-state binary, in which its opponents seek to imprison it. Basic to the Forum is the idea that alternatives to neoliberalism need to move beyond it, and therefore have to operate at the international level. The role of the nation-state in these proposals varies, but the common framework is an alternative globalization—not that of capital and the multinational corporations.

Secondly, the Forum recreates the possibility of an alliance between radical forces in the periphery and those in the core—a connexion sundered by the triumph of neoliberalism and the fall of the USSR. During the 1990s, the largely centre-left governments of the core redefined the regions of world power and influence, abandoning the periphery to its fate as privileged victim of capital's new offensive. Thirdly, the Forum allows theoretical, social and political contributions to the project to converge in the same space, without a hierarchy being defined—recovering, in a sense, the legacy of the historical Left, by addressing the themes of an alternative globalization.

The movement reflects both the strengths and weaknesses of the struggle against neoliberalism. Its virtues include the high level of some of the theoretical contributions, whether global or sectoral analyses; the social heterogeneity—trade unions, environmental, gender and ethnic groups alongside political, intellectual and cultural figures; and the moral certainty that the great themes confronting humankind at the beginning of the twenty-first century will be discussed here, not at Davos. Deficiencies include the inability to convert these benefits into political strength—whether at the level of governments and parliaments, or as mass mobilizations—that could effectively exercise a veto on the reigning neoliberal policies, or take other innovative forms of political action. There is also a weakness in the whole field of economics. The movement lacks any strategy for transforming the growing feelings of exasperation and distrust of neoliberal dogma into an alternative policy, or at the very least a project to curb the speculative movement of capital and point towards new forms of international trade. Another shortcoming is the uneven participation in the Forums, with very poor representation from some of the core countries—the US, Germany, Japan, Britain—or emerging superpowers such as China and India.

VI

Important steps were taken to address the Forums' weaknesses at the seminars held by the WSF's International Committee in Barcelona, in April, and Bangkok, in August this year. One of their main decisions was to transfer the political leadership of the Forum from the original organizing committee—consisting of Brazilian organizations, for the most part NGOs—to the International Committee. This is made up of around sixty international networks from all continents, with a fairly representative range. The Committee decided on a more concentrated format for the Forums, with an agenda of five basic themes around which all others would be grouped, in order to move towards a more decisive way to formulate comprehensive political proposals, and strategies to fight for them. It had already been decided that the Forums were not events, but a process of elaborating alternatives, and of struggle for their realization. With this in mind, continental and sectoral Forums will take place before the Forum of 2003, as before, in Porto Alegre.

The Social Forum represents a milestone, marking the shift from a period of fragmented, defensive resistance to a phase of accumulating forces, while looking towards the stage at which an international articulation of political, social and cultural movements can confront neo-liberalism and overcome it. The first decades of the new century are the setting for that challenge, to be taken up in full awareness of its complexity and of the huge discrepancy in relative scale that still exists.

IMMANUEL WALLERSTEIN

NEW REVOLTS AGAINST THE SYSTEM

I coined the term 'antisystemic movement' in the 1970s in order to have a formulation that would group together what had, historically and analytically, been two distinct and in many ways rival kinds of popular movement—those that went under the name 'social', and those that were 'national'. Social movements were conceived primarily as socialist parties and trade unions; they sought to further the class struggle within each state against the bourgeoisie or the employers. National movements were those which fought for the creation of a national state, either by combining separate political units that were considered to be part of one nation—as, for example, in Italy—or by seceding from states considered imperial and oppressive by the nationality in question—colonies in Asia or Africa, for instance.

Both types of movement emerged as significant, bureaucratic structures in the second half of the nineteenth century and grew stronger over time. Both tended to accord their objectives priority over any other kind of political goal—and, specifically, over the goals of their national or social rival. This frequently resulted in severe mutual denunciations. The two types seldom cooperated politically and, if they did so, tended to see such cooperation as a temporary tactic, not a basic alliance. Nonetheless, the history of these movements between 1850 and 1970 reveals a series of shared features.

- Most socialist and nationalist movements repeatedly proclaimed themselves to be 'revolutionary', that is, to stand for fundamental transformations in social relations. It is true that both types usually had a wing, sometimes located in a separate organization, that argued for a more gradualist approach and therefore eschewed revolutionary rhetoric. But generally speaking, initially—and often for many decades—those in power regarded all these movements, even the milder versions, as threats to their stability, or even to the very survival of their political structures.

- Secondly, at the outset, both variants were politically quite weak and had to fight an uphill battle merely to exist. They were repressed or outlawed by their governments, their leaders were arrested and their members often subjected to systematic violence by the State or by private forces. Many early versions of these movements were totally destroyed.

- Thirdly, over the last three decades of the nineteenth century both types of movement went through a parallel series of great debates over strategy that ranged those whose perspectives were 'state-oriented' against those who saw the State as an intrinsic enemy and pushed instead for an emphasis on individual transformation. For the social movement, this was the debate between the Marxists and the anarchists; for the national movement, that between political and cultural nationalists.

- What happened historically in these debates—and this is the fourth similarity—was that those holding the 'state-oriented' position won out. The decisive argument in each case was that the immediate source of real power was located in the state apparatus and that any attempt to ignore its political centrality was doomed to failure, since the State would successfully suppress any thrust towards anarchism or cultural nationalism. In the late nineteenth century, these groups enunciated a so-called two-step strategy: first gain power within the state structure; then transform the world. This was as true for the social as for the national movements.

- The fifth common feature is less obvious, but no less real. Socialist movements often included nationalist rhetoric in their arguments, while nationalist discourse often had a social component. The result was a greater blurring of the two positions than their proponents ever acknowledged. It has frequently been remarked that socialist movements in Europe often functioned more effectively as a force for national integration than either conservatives or the State itself; while the Communist parties that came to power in China, Vietnam and Cuba were clearly serving as movements of national liberation. There were two reasons for this. Firstly, the process of mobilization forced both groups to try to draw increasingly broad sectors of the population into their camps, and widening the scope of their rhetoric was helpful in this regard. But secondly, the leaders of both movements often recognized subconsciously that they had a shared enemy in the existing system—and that they therefore had more in common with each other than their public pronouncements allowed.

- The processes of popular mobilization deployed by the two kinds of movement were basically quite similar. Both types started out, in most countries, as small groups, often composed of a handful of intellectuals plus a few militants drawn from other strata. Those that succeeded did so because they were able, by dint of long campaigns of education and organization, to secure popular bases in concentric circles of militants, sympathizers and passive supporters. When the outer circle of supporters grew large enough for the militants to operate, in Mao Zedong's phrase, like fish swimming in water, the movements became serious contenders for political power. We should, of course, note too that groups calling themselves 'social-democratic' tended to be strong primarily in states located in the core zones of the world-economy, while those that described themselves as movements of national liberation generally flourished in the semi-peripheral and peripheral zones. The latter was largely true of Communist parties as well. The reason seems obvious. Those in weaker zones saw that the struggle for equality hinged on their ability to wrest control of the state structures from imperial powers, whether these exercised direct or indirect rule. Those in the core zones were already in strong states. To make progress in their struggle for equality, they needed to wrest power from their own dominant strata. But precisely because these states were strong and wealthy, insurrection was an implausible tactic, and these parties used the electoral route.

- The seventh common feature is that both these movements struggled with the tension between 'revolution' and 'reform' as prime modes of transformation. Endless discourse has revolved around this debate in both movements—but for both, in the end, it turned out to be based on a misreading of reality. Revolutionaries were not in practice very revolutionary, and reformists not always reformist. Certainly, the difference between the two approaches became more and more unclear as the movements pursued their political trajectories. Revolutionaries had to make many concessions in order to survive. Reformists learned that hypothetical legal paths to change were often firmly blocked in practice and that it required force, or at least the threat of force, to break through the barriers. So-called revolutionary movements usually came to power as a consequence of the wartime destruction of the existing authorities rather than through their own insurrectionary capacities. As the Bolsheviks were reported to have said in Russia, in 1917, 'power was lying about in the streets'. Once installed, the movements sought to stay in power, regardless of how they had got there; this often required sacrificing militancy, as well as solidarity with their counterparts in other countries. The popular support for these movements was initially just as great whether they won by the bullet or by the ballot—the same dancing in the streets greeted their accession to power after a long period of struggle.

- Finally, both movements had the problem of implementing the two-step strategy. Once 'stage one' was completed, and they had come to power, their followers expected them to fulfill the promise of stage two: transforming the world. What they discovered, if they did not know it before, was that state power was more limited than they had thought. Each state was constrained by being part of an interstate system, in which no one nation's sovereignty was absolute. The longer they stayed in office, the more they seemed to postpone the realization of their promises; the cadres of a militant mobilizing movement became the functionaries of a party in power. Their social positions were transformed and so, inevitably, were their individual psychologies. What was known in the Soviet Union as the *Nomenklatura* seemed to emerge, in some form, in every state in which a movement took control—that is, a privileged caste of higher officials, with more power and more real wealth than the rest of the population. At the same time, the ordinary workers were enjoined to toil even harder and sacrifice ever more in the name of national development. The militant, syndicalist tactics that had been the daily bread of the social movement became 'counter-revolutionary', highly discouraged and usually repressed, once it was in office.

Analysis of the world situation in the 1960s reveals these two kinds of movements looking more alike than ever. In most countries, they had completed 'stage one' of the two-step strategy, having come to power practically everywhere. Communist parties ruled over a third of the world, from the Elbe to the Yalu; national liberation movements were in office in Asia and Africa, populist movements in Latin America and social-democratic movements, or their cousins, in most of the pan-European world, at least on an alternating basis. They had not, however, transformed the world.

It was the combination of these factors that underlay a principal feature of the world revolution of 1968. The revolutionaries had different local demands, but shared two fundamental arguments almost everywhere. First of all, they opposed both the hegemony of the United States *and* the collusion in this hegemony by the Soviet Union. Secondly, they condemned the Old Left as being 'not part of the solution but part of the problem'. This second common feature arose out of the massive disillusionment of the popular supporters of the traditional antisystemic movements over their actual performance in power. The countries in which they operated did see a certain number of reforms—usually there was an increase in educational and health facilities and guarantees of employment. But considerable inequalities remained. Alienating wage labour had not disappeared; on the contrary, it had increased as a percentage of work activity. There was little or no expansion of real democratic participation, either at the governmental level or in the work place; often it was the reverse. On the international scale, these countries tended to play a very similar role in the world-system to that which they had played before. Thus, Cuba had been a sugar-exporting economy before the revolution and remained one after it, at least until the demise of the Soviet Union. In short, not enough had changed. The grievances might have altered slightly but they were as real and, generally, as extensive. The populations of these countries were adjured by the movements in power to be patient, for history was on their side. But their patience had worn thin.

The conclusion that the world's populations drew from the performance of the classical antisystemic movements in power was negative. They ceased to believe that these parties would bring about a glorious future or a more egalitarian world and no longer gave them their legitimation; and having lost confidence in the movements, they also withdrew their faith in the State as a mechanism of transformation. This did not mean that large sections of the population would no longer vote for such parties in elections; but it had become a defensive vote, for lesser evils, not an affirmation of ideology or expectations.

Since 1968, there has been a lingering search, nonetheless, for a better kind of antisystemic movement—one that would actually lead to a more democratic, egalitarian world. There have been four different sorts of attempt at this, some of which still continue. The first was the efflorescence of the multiple Maoisms. From the 1960s until around the mid-1970s, there emerged a large number of different, competing movements, usually small but sometimes impressively large, claiming to be Maoist; by which they meant that they were somehow inspired by the example of the Cultural Revolution in China. Essentially, they argued that the Old Left had failed because it was not preaching the pure doctrine of revolution, which they now proposed. But these movements all fizzled out, for two reasons. Firstly, they quarrelled bitterly among themselves as to what the pure doctrine was, and therefore rapidly became tiny, insulated sectarian groups; or if they were very large, as in India, they evolved into newer versions of the Old Left movements. Secondly, and more fundamentally, with the death of Mao Zedong Maoism disintegrated in China, and the fount of their inspiration disappeared. Today, no such movements of any significance exist.

A second, more lasting variety of claimant to antisystemic status was the new social movements—the Greens and other environmentalists, feminists, the campaigns of racial or ethnic 'minorities', such as the Blacks in the United States or the Beurs in France. These movements claimed a long history but, in fact, they either became prominent for the first time in the 1970s or else re-emerged then, in renewed and more militant form. They were also stronger in the pan-European world than in other parts of the world-system. Their common features lay, firstly, in their vigorous rejection of the Old Left's two-step strategy, its internal hierarchies and its priorities—the idea that the needs of women, 'minorities' and the environment were secondary and should be addressed 'after the revolution'. And secondly, they were deeply suspicious of the State and of state-oriented action.

By the 1980s, all these new movements had become divided internally between what the German Greens called the *fundis* and the *realos*. This turned out to be a replay of the 'revolutionary versus reformist' debates of the beginning of the twentieth century. The outcome was that the *fundis* lost out in every case, and more or less disappeared. The victorious *realos* increasingly took on the appearance of a species of social-democratic party, not too different from the classic variety, although with more rhetoric about ecology, sexism, racism, or all three. Today, these movements continue to be significant in certain countries, but they seem little more antisystemic than those of the Old Left—especially since the one lesson the Old Left drew from 1968 was that they, too, needed to incorporate concerns about ecology, gender, sexual choice and racism into their programmatic statements.

The third type of claimant to antisystemic status has been the human-rights organizations. Of course some, like Amnesty International, existed prior to 1968, but in general these became a major political force only in the 1980s, aided by President Carter's adoption of human-rights ter-minology in dealing with Central America, and the signing of the 1975 Helsinki Accord regarding the Communist states of East and Central Europe. Both gave Establishment legitimacy to the numerous organi-zations that were now addressing civil rights. In the 1990s, the media focus on ethnic cleansing, notably in Rwanda and the Balkans, led to considerable public discussion of these issues.

The human-rights organizations claimed to speak in the name of 'civil society'. The term itself indicates the strategy: civil society is by definition *not* the State. The concept draws upon a nineteenth-century distinction between *le pays légal* and *le pays réel*—between those in power and those who represent popular sentiment—posing the question: how can civil society close the gap between itself and the State? How can it come to control the State, or make the State reflect its values? The dist-inction seems to assume that the State is currently controlled by small privileged groups, whereas 'civil society' consists of the enlightened pop-ulation at large.

These organizations have had an impact in getting some states—perhaps all—to inflect their policies in the direction of human-rights concerns; but, in the process, they have come to be more like the adjuncts of states than their opponents and, on the whole, scarcely seem very antisystemic. They have become NGOs, located largely in core zones yet seeking to implement their policies in the periphery, where they have often been regarded as the agents of their home state rather than its critics. In any case, these organizations have seldom mobilized mass support, counting rather on their ability to utilize the power and position of their elite militants in the core.

The fourth and most recent variant has been the so-called anti-globalization movements—a designation applied not so much by these movements themselves as by their opponents. The use of the term by the media scarcely predates its reporting of the protests at the Seattle WTO meetings in 1999. 'Globalization', as the rhetoric of neoliberal advocates of free-trade in goods and capital, had of course become a strong force during the 1990s. Its media focus was the Davos World Economic Forum, and its institutional implementation was brought about via the Washington Consensus, the policies of the IMF and the strengthening of the WTO. Seattle was intended as a key moment in expanding the role of the WTO and the significant protests, which actually disrupted its proceedings, took many by surprise. The demonstrators included a large North American contingent, drawn from the Old Left, trade unions, new movements and anarchist groups. Indeed, the very fact that the AFL–CIO was ready to be on the same side as environmentalist groups in so militant an action was something new, especially for the US.

Following Seattle, the continuing series of demonstrations around the world against intergovernmental meetings inspired by the neoliberal agenda led, in turn, to the construction of the World Social Forum, whose initial meetings have been held in Porto Alegre; the second, in 2002, drew over 50,000 delegates from over a thousand organizations. Since then, there have been a number of regional meetings, preparing for the 2003 WSF.

The characteristics of this new claimant for the role of antisystemic movement are rather different from those of earlier attempts. First of all, the WSF seeks to bring together all the previous types—Old Left, new movements, human-rights bodies, and others not easily falling into these categories—and includes groups organized in a strictly local, regional, national and transnational fashion. The basis of participation is a common objective—struggle against the social ills consequent on neoliberalism—and a common respect for each other's immediate priorities. Importantly, the WSF seeks to bring together movements from the North and the South within a single framework. The only slogan, as yet, is 'Another World is Possible'. Even more strangely, the WSF seeks to do this without creating an overall superstructure. At the moment, it has only an international coordinating committee, some 50-strong, representing a variety of movements and geographic locations.

While there has been some grumbling from Old Left movements that the WSF is a reformist façade, thus far the complaints have been quite minimal. The grumblers question; they do not yet denounce. It is, of course, widely recognized that this degree of success has been based on a negative rejection of neoliberalism, as ideology and as institutional practice. Many have argued that it is essential for the WSF to move towards advocating a clearer, more positive programme. Whether it can do so, and still maintain the level of unity and absence of an overall (inevitably hierarchical) structure, is the big question of the next decade.

If, as I have argued elsewhere, the modern world-system is in structural crisis, and we have entered an 'age of transition'—a period of bifurcation and chaos—then it is clear that the issues confronting antisystemic movements pose themselves in a very different fashion than those of the nineteenth and most of the twentieth centuries. The two-step, state-oriented strategy has become irrelevant, which explains the discomfort of most existing descendants of erstwhile antisystemic organizations in putting forward either long-term or immediate sets of political objectives. Those few who try meet with scepticism from their hoped-for followers; or, worse, with indifference.

Such a period of transition has two characteristics that dominate the very idea of an antisystemic strategy. The first is that those in power will no longer be trying to preserve the existing system (doomed as it is to self-destruction); rather, they will try to ensure that the transition leads to the construction of a new system that will replicate the worst features of the existing one—its hierarchy, privilege and inequalities. They may not yet be using language that reflects the demise of existing structures, but they are implementing a strategy based on such assumptions. Of course, their camp is not united, as is demonstrated by the conflict between the so-called centre-right 'traditionalists' and the ultra-right, militarist hawks. But they are working hard to build backing for changes that will not be changes, a new system as bad as—or worse than—the present one. The second fundamental characteristic is that a period of systemic transition is one of deep uncertainty, in which it is impossible to know what the outcome will be. History is on no one's side. Each of us can affect the future, but we do not and cannot know how others will act to affect it, too. The basic framework of the WSF reflects this dilemma, and underlines it.

A strategy for the period of transition ought therefore to include four components—all of them easier said than done. The first is a process of constant, open debate about the transition and the outcome we hope for. This has never been easy, and the historic antisystemic movements were never very good at it. But the atmosphere is more favourable today than it has ever been, and the task remains urgent and indispensable—underlining the role of intellectuals in this conjuncture. The structure of the WSF has lent itself to encouraging this debate; we shall see if it is able to maintain this openness.

The second component should be self-evident: an antisystemic movement cannot neglect short-term defensive action, including electoral action. The world's populations live in the present, and their immediate needs have to be addressed. Any movement that neglects them is bound to lose the widespread passive support that is essential for its long-term success. But the motive and justification for defensive action should not be that of remedying a failing system but rather of preventing its negative effects from getting worse in the short run. This is quite different psychologically and politically.

The third component has to be the establishment of interim, middle-range goals that seem to move in the right direction. I would suggest that one of the most useful—substantively, politically, psychologically—is the attempt to move towards selective, but ever-widening, decommod-ification. We are subject today to a barrage of neoliberal attempts to commodify what was previously seldom or never appropriated for priv-ate sale—the human body, water, hospitals. We must not only oppose this but move in the other direction. Industries, especially failing indus-tries, should be decommodified. This does not mean they should be 'nationalized'—for the most part, simply another version of commodifi-cation. It means we should create structures, operating in the market, whose objective is performance and survival rather than profit. This can be done, as we know, from the history of universities or hospitals—not all, but the best. Why is such a logic impossible for steel factories threa-tened with delocalization?

Finally, we need to develop the substantive meaning of our long-term emphases, which I take to be a world that is relatively democratic and relatively egalitarian. I say 'relatively' because that is realistic. There will always be gaps—but there is no reason why they should be wide, encrusted or hereditary. Is this what used to be called socialism, or even communism? Perhaps, but perhaps not. That brings us back to the issue of debate. We need to stop assuming what the better (not the perfect) society will be like. We need to discuss it, outline it, experiment with alternative structures to realize it; and we need to do this at the same time as we carry out the first three parts of our programme for a chaotic world in systemic transition. And if this programme is insufficient, and it probably is, then this very insufficiency ought to be part of the debate which is Point One of the programme.

NOTES ON CONTRIBUTORS

Walden Bello: co-director of Focus on the Global South; national chairman of the Citizens' Action Party, Akbayan; most recent book: *Deglobalization: Ideas for a New World Economy* (2002); the interview in this volume was first published as 'Pacific Panopticon' in NLR 16, July–August 2002

José Bové: author of *The World is Not For Sale: Farmers Against Junk Food* (2001); 'A Farmers' International' was first published in NLR 12, November–December 2001

Bernard Cassen: member of the editorial collective of *Le Monde diplomatique*; honorary president of ATTAC; the interview in this volume was first published as 'On the Attack' in NLR 19, January–February 2003

David Graeber: teaches anthropology at Yale University; author of *Toward an Anthropological Theory of Value* (2001); 'The New Anarchists' was first published in NLR 13, January–February 2002

Michael Hardt: teaches literature at Duke University; co-author of *Empire* (2000); 'Today's Bandung?' was first published in NLR 14, March–April 2002

Naomi Klein: author of *No Logo* (2000) and *Fences and Windows* (2002); 'Reclaiming the Commons' was first published in NLR 9, May–June 2001

Subcomandante Marcos: sometimes thought to be Rafael Guillén of Tampico; author of *Our Word is Our Weapon* (2001); the interview in this volume first appeared in *Revista Cambio*, Bogotá, 26 March 2001; first published in English as 'The Punch-Card and the Hourglass' in NLR 9, May–June 2001

Tom Mertes: administrator of the Center for Social Theory and Comparative History at UCLA and a member of the NLR Editorial Committee; 'Grass-Roots Globalization' was first published in NLR 17, September–October 2002

Bhumika Muchhala: former member of the national office of Students against Sweatshops; interviewed in June 2002

Trevor Ngwane: leading member of the Soweto Electricity Crisis Committee and the South African Anti-Privatization Forum; 'Sparks in the Township' was first published in NLR 22, July–August 2003

Njoki Njehu: director of 50 Years is Enough Network; interviewed in May 2003

Chittaroopa Palit: activist in the Narmada Bachao Andolan; 'Monsoon Rising' was first published in NLR 21, May–June 2003

Emir Sader: most recent book: *A Vingança da História* (2003); 'Beyond Civil Society' was first published in NLR 17, September–October 2002

John Sellers: director of the Ruckus Society; 'Raising a Ruckus' was first published in NLR 10, July–August 2001

João Pedro Stedile: on the national committee of the MST; co-author of *A luta pela terra no Brasil* (1993); the interview in this volume was first published as 'Landless Battalions' in NLR 15, May–June 2002

Immanuel Wallerstein: research scholar at Yale University and director of the Fernand Braudel Centre at Binghamton; most recent book: *The Decline of American Power* (2003); 'New Revolts Against the System' was first published in NLR 18, November–December 2002

ACKNOWLEDGEMENTS

An extensive network of activists and intellectuals worked with the *New Left Review* editorial committee in the production of this volume; between them, they provided the energy and optimism that ensured this collection would see the light of day. We would particularly like to thank Francisco de Oliveira, who discussed the Sem Terra's history with João Pedro Stedile, and Achin Vanaik, who interviewed Chittaroopa Palit; thanks, too, to Arundhati Roy and Sanjay Kak. The interview with Subcomandante Marcos by Gabriel García Márquez and Roberto Pombo first appeared in *Revista Cambio*. Soren Ambrose, Patrick Bond, Lucy Braham, Jason Mark and Emir Sader played vital roles in enlarging our understanding of the movements and helping connect with the activists in these pages. Charles Peyton expertly transcribed many of the interviews: his perseverance, in the face of poorly recorded conversations conducted in a wide range of dialects, was invaluable. At *New Left Review*, Tony Wood, Jacob Stevens, Susan Watkins and Perry Anderson played major roles, as did Robert Brenner at the Center for Social Theory and Comparative History. Gavin Everall and Tim Clark at Verso worked diligently to see the NLR series become a book.

Tom Mertes would like to thank all of his comrades and friends for their support and understanding, but especially Lissa Wadewitz for her guidance, patience and good humor.

INDEX